The Common Reader

Virginia Woolf was born in London in 1882, the daughter of the editor and critic Sir Leslie Stephen, and a granddaughter of Thackeray. In 1912 she married Leonard Woolf, and together they founded the Hogarth Press. Her first novel, *The Voyage Out*, was published in 1915, and was followed by *Jacob's Room* (1922), *Mrs. Dalloway* (1925), *To the Lighthouse* (1927), *Orlando* (1928), *The Waves* (1931), *The Years* (1937), and *Between the Acts* (1941). Her books of essays include *The Common Reader* (1925), *The Common Reader: Second Series* (1932), *The Death of the Moth* (1942), *The Moment and Other Essays* (1948), and *The Captain's Deathbed and Other Essays* (1950). She died in 1941. A portion of her journal was published in 1954 as *A Writer's Diary*.

Virginia Woolf

THE COMMON READER

FIRST SERIES

I rejoice to concur with the common reader;
for by the common sense of readers, uncorrupted by literary prejudices, after all
the refinements of subtilty and the dogmatism of learning, must be generally decided
all claim to poetical honours.

DR. JOHNSON, *Life of Gray*

A Harvest Book

HARCOURT, BRACE AND COMPANY
NEW YORK

TO LYTTON STRACHEY

AUTHOR'S NOTE

Some of these papers appeared originally in the *Times Literary Supplement* and the *Dial*. I have to thank the Editors for allowing me to reprint them here; some are based upon articles written for various newspapers, while others appear now for the first time.

CONTENTS

*

The Common Reader

*

There is a sentence in Dr. Johnson's Life of Gray which might well be written up in all those rooms, too humble to be called libraries, yet full of books, where the pursuit of reading is carried on by private people. ". . . I rejoice to concur with the common reader; for by the common sense of readers, uncorrupted by literary prejudices, after all the refinements of subtilty and the dogmatism of learning, must be finally decided all claim to poetical honours." It defines their qualities; it dignifies their aims; it bestows upon a pursuit which devours a great deal of time, and is yet apt to leave behind it nothing very substantial, the sanction of the great man's approval.

The common reader, as Dr. Johnson implies, differs from the critic and the scholar. He is worse educated, and nature has not gifted him so generously. He reads for his own pleasure rather than to impart knowledge or correct the opinions of others. Above all, he is guided by an instinct to create for himself, out of whatever odds and ends he can come by, some kind of whole—a portrait of a man, a sketch of an age, a theory of the art of writing. He never ceases, as he reads, to run up some rickety and ramshackle fabric which shall give him the temporary satisfaction of looking sufficiently like the real object to allow of affection, laughter, and argument. Hasty, inaccurate, and superficial, snatching now

this poem, now that scrap of old furniture without caring where he finds it or of what nature it may be so long
as it serves his purpose and rounds his structure, his de-
ficiencies as a critic are too obvious to be pointed out;
but if he has, as Dr. Johnson maintained, some say in the
final distribution of poetical honours, then, perhaps, it
may be worth while to write down a few of the ideas
and opinions which, insignificant in themselves, yet contribute to so mighty a result.

*

The Pastons and Chaucer†

*

The tower of Caister Castle still rises ninety feet into the air, and the arch still stands from which Sir John Fastolf's barges sailed out to fetch stone for the building of the great castle. But now jackdaws nest on the tower, and of the castle, which once covered six acres of ground, only ruined walls remain, pierced by loopholes and surmounted by battlements, though there are neither archers within nor cannon without. As for the "seven religious men" and the "seven poor folk" who should, at this very moment, be praying for the souls of Sir John and his parents, there is no sign of them nor sound of their prayers. The place is a ruin. Antiquaries speculate and differ.

Not so very far off lie more ruins—the ruins of Bromholm Priory, where John Paston was buried, naturally enough, since his house was only a mile or so away, lying on low ground by the sea, twenty miles north of Norwich. The coast is dangerous, and the land, even in our time, inaccessible. Nevertheless the little bit of wood at Bromholm, the fragment of the true Cross, brought pilgrims incessantly to the Priory, and sent them away with eyes opened and limbs straightened. But some of them with their newly-opened eyes saw a sight which shocked them—the grave of John Paston in

† *The Paston Letters*, edited by Dr. James Gairdner (1904), 4 vols.

Bromholm Priory without a tombstone. The news spread over the country-side. The Pastons had fallen; they that had been so powerful could no longer afford a stone to put above John Paston's head. Margaret, his widow, could not pay her debts; the eldest son, Sir John, wasted his property upon women and tournaments, while the younger, John also, though a man of greater parts, thought more of his hawks than of his harvests.

The pilgrims of course were liars, as people whose eyes have just been opened by a piece of the true Cross have every right to be; but their news, none the less, was welcome. The Pastons had risen in the world. People said even that they had been bondmen not so very long ago. At any rate, men still living could remember John's grandfather Clement tilling his own land, a hard-working peasant; and William, Clement's son, becoming a judge and buying land; and John, William's son, marrying well and buying more land and quite lately inheriting the vast new castle at Caister, and all Sir John's lands in Norfolk and Suffolk. People said that he had forged the old knight's will. What wonder, then, that he lacked a tombstone? But, if we consider the character of Sir John Paston, John's eldest son, and his upbringing and his surroundings, and the relations between himself and his father as the family letters reveal them, we shall see how difficult it was, and how likely to be neglected— this business of making his father's tombstone.

For let us imagine, in the most desolate part of England known to us at the present moment, a raw, new-built house, without telephone, bathroom, or drains, arm-chairs or newspapers, and one shelf perhaps of books, unwieldy to hold, expensive to come by. The windows look out upon a few cultivated fields and a dozen hovels, and beyond them there is the sea on one side, on the other a vast fen. A single road crosses the fen, but there is a hole in it, which, one of the farm hands reports, is big enough to swallow a carriage. And, the man adds, Tom Topcroft, the mad bricklayer, has broken loose again and ranges the country half-naked, threatening to kill any one who approaches him. That is what they talk about at dinner in the desolate house, while the chimney smokes horribly, and the draught lifts the carpets on the floor. Orders are given to lock all gates at sunset, and, when the long dismal evening has worn itself away, simply and solemnly, girt about with dangers as they are, these isolated men and women fall upon their knees in prayer.

In the fifteenth century, however, the wild landscape was broken suddenly and very strangely by vast piles of brand-new masonry. There rose out of the sandhills and heaths of the Norfolk coast a huge bulk of stone, like a modern hotel in a watering-place; but there was no parade, no lodging houses, and no pier at Yarmouth then, and this gigantic building on the outskirts of the town was built to house one solitary old gentleman without any children—Sir John Fastolf, who had fought at Agincourt and acquired great wealth. He had fought at Agincourt and got but little reward. No one took his advice. Men spoke ill of him behind his back. He was well aware of it; his temper was none the sweeter for it. He was a hot-tempered old man, powerful, embittered by a sense of grievance. But whether on the battlefield or at court he thought perpetually of Caister, and how, when his duties allowed, he would settle down on his father's land and live in a great house of his own building.

The gigantic structure of Caister Castle was in progress not so many miles away when the little Pastons were children. John Paston, the father, had charge of some part of the business, and the children listened, as soon as they could listen at all, to talk of stone and building, of barges gone to London and not yet returned, of the twenty-six private chambers, of the hall and chapel; of foundations, measurements, and rascally work-people. Later, in 1454, when the work was finished and Sir John had come to spend his last years at Caister, they may have seen for themselves the mass of treasure that was stored there; the tables laden with gold and silver plate; the wardrobes stuffed with gowns of velvet and satin and cloth of gold, with hoods and tippets and beaver hats and leather jackets and velvet doublets; and how the very pillow-cases on the beds were of green and purple silk. There were tapestries everywhere. The beds were laid and the bedrooms hung with tapestries representing sieges, hunting and hawking, men fishing, archers shooting, ladies playing on their harps, dallying with ducks, or a giant "bearing the leg of a bear in his hand." Such were the fruits of a well-spent life. To buy land, to build great houses, to stuff these houses full of gold and silver plate (though the privy might well be in the bedroom), was the proper aim of mankind. Mr. and Mrs. Paston spent the greater part of their energies in the same exhausting occupation. For since the passion to acquire was universal, one could never rest secure in one's possessions for long. The outlying parts of one's property were in perpetual jeopardy. The Duke of Norfolk might covet this manor, the Duke of Suffolk that. Some trumped-up excuse, as for instance that the Pastons were bondmen, gave them the right to seize the house and batter down the lodges in the owner's absence. And how could the owner of Paston and Mauteby and Drayton and Gresham be in five or six places at once, especially now that Caister Castle was his, and he must be in London trying to get his rights recognised by the King? The King was mad too, they said; did not know his own child, they said; or the King was in flight; or there was civil war in the land. Norfolk was always the most distressed of counties and its country gentlemen the most quarrelsome of mankind. Indeed, had Mrs. Paston chosen, she could have told her children how when she was a young woman a thousand men with bows and arrows and pans of burning fire had marched upon Gresham and broken the gates and mined the walls of the room where she sat alone. But much worse things than that had happened to

women. She neither bewailed her lot nor thought herself
a heroine. The long, long letters which she wrote so
laboriously in her clear cramped hand to her husband,
who was (as usual) away, make no mention of herself.
The sheep had wasted the hay. Heyden's and Tudden-
ham's men were out. A dyke had been broken and a bul-
lock stolen. They needed treacle badly, and really she
must have stuff for a dress.

But Mrs. Paston did not talk about herself.

Thus the little Pastons would see their mother writing
or dictating page after page, hour after hour, long, long
letters, but to interrupt a parent who writes so laboriously of such important matters would have been a
sin. The prattle of children, the lore of the nursery or
schoolroom, did not find its way into these elaborate
communications. For the most part her letters are the
letters of an honest bailiff to his master, explaining, ask-
ing advice, giving news, rendering accounts. There was
robbery and manslaughter; it was difficult to get in the
rents; Richard Calle had gathered but little money; and
what with one thing and another Margaret had not had
time to make out, as she should have done, the inventory
of the goods which her husband desired. Well might old
Agnes, surveying her son's affairs rather grimly from a
distance, counsel him to contrive it so that "ye may have
less to do in the world; your father said, In little business lieth much rest. This world is but a thoroughfare,
and full of woe; and when we depart therefrom, right
nought bear with us but our good deeds and ill."

The thought of death would thus come upon them in
a clap. Old Fastolf, cumbered with wealth and property,
had his vision at the end of Hell fire, and shrieked aloud
to his executors to distribute alms, and see that prayers
were said "in perpetuum," so that his soul might escape
the agonies of purgatory. William Paston, the judge, was
urgent too that the monks of Norwich should be re-
tained to pray for his soul "for ever." The soul was no
wisp of air, but a solid body capable of eternal suffering,

and the fire that destroyed it was as fierce as any that burnt on mortal grates. For ever there would be monks and the town of Norwich, and for ever the Chapel of Our Lady in the town of Norwich. There was something matter-of-fact, positive, and enduring in their conception both of life and of death.

With the plan of existence so vigorously marked out, children of course were well beaten, and boys and girls taught to know their places. They must acquire land; but they must obey their parents. A mother would clout her daughter's head three times a week and break the skin if she did not conform to the laws of behaviour. Agnes Paston, a lady of birth and breeding, beat her daughter Elizabeth. Margaret Paston, a softer-hearted woman, turned her daughter out of the house for loving the honest bailiff Richard Calle. Brothers would not suffer their sisters to marry beneath them, and "sell candle and mustard in Framlingham." The fathers quarrelled with the sons, and the mothers, fonder of their boys than of their girls, yet bound by all law and custom to obey their husbands, were torn asunder in their efforts to keep the peace. With all her pains, Margaret failed to prevent rash acts on the part of her eldest son John, or the bitter words with which his father denounced him. He was a "drone among bees," the father burst out, "which labour for gathering honey in the fields, and the drone doth naught but taketh his part of it." He treated his parents with insolence, and yet was fit for no charge of responsibility abroad.

But the quarrel was ended, very shortly, by the death (22nd May 1466) of John Paston, the father, in London. The body was brought down to Bromholm to be buried. Twelve poor men trudged all the way bearing torches beside it. Alms were distributed; masses and dirges were said. Bells were rung. Great quantities of fowls, sheep, pigs, eggs, bread, and cream were devoured, ale and wine drunk, and candles burnt. Two panes were taken from the church windows to let out the reek of the torches. Black cloth was distributed, and a light set burning on the grave. But John Paston, the heir, delayed to make his father's tombstone.

He was a young man, something over twenty-four years of age. The discipline and the drudgery of a country life bored him. When he ran away from home, it was, apparently, to attempt to enter the King's household. Whatever doubts, indeed, might be cast by their enemies on the blood of the Pastons, Sir John was unmistakably a gentleman. He had inherited his lands; the honey was his that the bees had gathered with so much labour. He had the instincts of enjoyment rather than of acquisition, and with his mother's parsimony was strangely mixed something of his father's ambition. Yet his own indolent and luxurious temperament took the edge from both. He was attractive to women, liked society and tournaments, and court life and making bets, and sometimes, even, reading books. And so life, now that John Paston was buried, started afresh upon rather a different foundation. There could be little outward change indeed. Margaret still ruled the house. She still ordered the lives of the younger children as she had ordered the lives of the elder. The boys still needed to be beaten into booklearning by their tutors, the girls still loved the wrong men and must be married to the right. Rents had to be collected; the interminable lawsuit for the Fastolf property dragged on. Battles were fought; the roses of York and Lancaster alternately faded and flourished. Norfolk was full of poor people seeking redress for their grievances, and Margaret worked for her son as she had worked for her husband, with this significant change only, that now, instead of confiding in her husband, she took the advice of her priest.

But inwardly there was a change. It seems at last as if the hard outer shell had served its purpose and something sensitive, appreciative, and pleasure-loving had formed within. At any rate Sir John, writing to his brother John at home, strayed sometimes from the busi-

ness on hand to crack a joke, to send a piece of gossip,
or to instruct him, knowingly and even subtly, upon the
conduct of a love affair. Be "as lowly to the mother as
ye list, but to the maid not too lowly, nor that ye be too
glad to speed, nor too sorry to fail. And I shall always
be your herald both here, if she come hither, and at
home, when I come home, which I hope hastily within
XI. days at the furthest." And then a hawk was to be
bought, a hat, or new silk laces sent down to John in
Norfolk, prosecuting his suit flying his hawks, and
attending with considerable energy and not too nice a
'sense of honesty to the affairs of the Paston estates.

The lights had long since burnt out on John Paston's
grave. But still Sir John delayed; no tomb replaced them.
He had his excuses; what with the business of the lawsuit, and his duties at Court, and the disturbance of the
civil wars, his time was occupied and his money spent.
But perhaps something strange had happened to Sir
John himself, and not only to Sir John dallying in London, but to his sister Margery falling in love with the
bailiff, and to Walter making Latin verses at Eton, and
to John flying his hawks at Paston. Life was a little more
various in its pleasures. They were not quite so sure as
the elder generation had been of the rights of man and
of the dues of God, of the horrors of death, and of the
importance of tombstones. Poor Margaret Paston scented
the change and sought uneasily, with the pen which had
marched so stiffly through so many pages, to lay bare
the root of her troubles. It was not that the lawsuit sad-
dened her; she was ready to defend Caister with her own
hands if need be, "though I cannot well guide nor rule
soldiers"; but there was something wrong with the family since the death of her husband and master. Perhaps
her son had failed in his service to God; he had been too
proud or too lavish in his expenditure; or perhaps he had
shown too little mercy to the poor. Whatever the fault
might be, she only knew that Sir John spent twice as
much money as his father for less result; that they could

scarcely pay their debts without selling land, wood, or
household stuff ("It is a death to me to think of it");
while every day people spoke ill of them in the country
because they left John Paston to lie without a tombstone. The money that might have bought it, or more
land, and more goblets and more tapestry, was spent by
Sir John on clocks and trinkets, and upon paying a clerk
to copy out Treatises upon Knighthood and other such
stuff. There they stood at Paston—eleven volumes, with
the poems of Lydgate and Chaucer among them, diffus-
ing a strange air into the gaunt, comfortless house, inviting men to indolence and vanity, distracting their
thoughts from business, and leading them not only to
neglect their own profit but to think lightly of the sa-
cred dues of the dead.

For sometimes, instead of riding off on his horse to
inspect his crops or bargain with his tenants, Sir John
would sit, in broad daylight, reading. There, on the hard
chair in the comfortless room with the wind lifting the
carpet and the smoke stinging his eyes, he would sit
reading Chaucer, wasting his time, dreaming—or what
strange intoxication was it that he drew from books?
Life was rough, cheerless, and disappointing. A whole
year of days would pass fruitlessly in dreary business,
like dashes of rain on the window pane. There was no
reason in it as there had been for his father; no impera-
tive need to establish a family and acquire an important
position for children who were not born, or if born,
had no right to bear their father's name. But Lydgate's
poems or Chaucer's, like a mirror in which figures move
brightly, silently, and compactly, showed him the very
skies, fields, and people whom he knew, but rounded and
complete. Instead of waiting listlessly for news from
London or piecing out from his mother's gossip some
country tragedy of love and jealousy, here, in a few
pages, the whole story was laid before him. And then as
he rode or sat at table he would remember some description or saying which bore upon the present moment

and fixed it, or some string of words would charm him, and putting aside the pressure of the moment, he would hasten home to sit in his chair and learn the end of the story.

To learn the end of the story—Chaucer can still make us wish to do that. He has pre-eminently that story-teller's gift, which is almost the rarest gift among writers at the present day. Nothing happens to us as it did to our ancestors; events are seldom important; if we recount them, we do not really believe in them; we have perhaps things of greater interest to say, and for these reasons natural story-tellers like Mr. Garnett, whom we must distinguish from self-conscious story-tellers like Mr. Masefield, have become rare. For the story-teller, besides his indescribable zest for facts, must tell his story craft-ily, without undue stress or excitement, or we shall swal-low it whole and jumble the parts together; he must let us stop, give us time to think and look about us, yet always be persuading us to move on. Chaucer was helped to this to some extent by the time of his birth; and in addition he had another advantage over the moderns which will never come the way of English poets again. England was an unspoilt country. His eyes rested on a virgin land, all unbroken grass and wood except for the small towns and an occasional castle in the building. No villa roofs peered through Kentish tree-tops; no factory chimney smoked on the hillside. The state of the coun-try, considering how poets go to Nature, how they use her for their images and their contrasts even when they do not describe her directly, is a matter of some im-portance. Her cultivation or her savagery influences the poet far more profoundly than the prose writer. To the modern poet, with Birmingham, Manchester, and London the size they are, the country is the sanctuary of moral excellence in contrast with the town which is the sink of vice. It is a retreat, the haunt of modesty and virtue, where men go to hide and moralise. There is something morbid, as if shrinking from human contact, in the nature worship of Wordsworth, still more in the microscopic devotion which Tennyson lavished upon the petals of roses and the buds of lime trees. But these were great poets. In their hands, the country was no mere jeweller's shop, or museum of curious objects to be described, even more curiously, in words. Poets of smaller gift, since the view is so much spoilt, and the garden or the meadow must replace the barren heath and the precipitous mountain-side, are now confined to little landscapes, to birds' nests, to acorns with every wrinkle drawn to the life. The wider landscape is lost.

But to Chaucer the country was too large and too wild to be altogether agreeable. He turned instinctively, as if he had painful experience of their nature, from tempests and rocks to the bright May day and the jocund landscape, from the harsh and mysterious to the gay and definite. Without possessing a tithe of the virtuosity in word-painting which is the modern inheritance, he could give, in a few words, or even, when we come to look, without a single word of direct description, the sense of the open air.

And se the fresshe floures how they sprynge

—that is enough.

Nature, uncompromising, untamed, was no looking-glass for happy faces, or confessor of unhappy souls. She was herself; sometimes, therefore, disagreeable enough and plain, but always in Chaucer's pages with the hardness and the freshness of an actual presence. Soon, however, we notice something of greater importance than the gay and picturesque appearance of the mediaeval world—the solidity which plumps it out, the conviction which animates the characters. There is immense variety in the *Canterbury Tales*, and yet, persisting underneath, one consistent type. Chaucer has his world; he has his young men; he has his young women. If one met them straying in Shakespeare's world one

would know them to be Chaucer's, not Shakespeare's.
He wants to describe a girl, and this is what she looks
like:

> Ful semely hir wimpel pinched was,
> Hir nose tretys; hir eyen greye as glas;
> Hir mouth ful smal, and ther-to soft and reed;
> But sikerly she hadde a fair foreheed;
> It was almost a spanne brood, I trowe;
> For, hardily, she was nat undergrowe.

Then he goes on to develop her; she was a girl, a virgin,
cold in her virginity:

> I am, thou woost, yet of thy companye,
> A mayde, and love hunting and venerye,
> And for to walken in the wodes wilde,
> And noght to been a wyf and be with childe.

Next he bethinks him how

> Discreet she was in answering alway;
> And though she had been as wise as Pallas
> No countrefeted termes hadde she
> To seme wys; but after hir degree
> She spak, and alle hir wordes more and lesse
> Souninge in vertu and in gentillesse.

Each of these quotations, in fact, comes from a different Tale, but they are parts, one feels, of the same per-
sonage, whom he had in mind, perhaps unconsciously,
when he thought of a young girl, and for this reason,
as she goes in and out of the *Canterbury Tales* bearing
different names, she has a stability which is only to be
found where the poet has made up his mind about young
women, of course, but also about the world they live in,
its end, its nature, and his own craft and technique, so
that his mind is free to apply its force fully to its object.
It does not occur to him that his Griselda might be improved or altered. There is no blur about her, no hesi-
tation; she proves nothing; she is content to be herself.
Upon her, therefore, the mind can rest with that uncon-

scious ease which allows it, from hints and suggestions, to endow her with many more qualities than are actually referred to. Such is the power of conviction, a rare gift, a gift shared in our day by Joseph Conrad in his earlier novels, and a gift of supreme importance, for upon it the whole weight of the building depends. Once believe in Chaucer's young men and women and we have no need of preaching or protest. We know what he finds good, what evil; the less said the better. Let him get on with his story, paint knights and squires, good women and bad, cooks, shipmen, priests, and we will supply the landscape, give his society its belief, its standing towards life and death, and make of the journey to Canterbury a spiritual pilgrimage.

This simple faithfulness to his own conceptions was easier then than now in one respect at least, for Chaucer could write frankly where we must either say nothing or say it slyly. He could sound every note in the language instead of finding a great many of the best gone dumb from disuse, and thus, when struck by daring fingers, giving off a loud discordant jangle out of keeping with the rest. Much of Chaucer—a few lines perhaps in each of the Tales—is improper and gives us as we read it the strange sensation of being naked to the air after being muffled in old clothing. And, as a certain kind of humour depends upon being able to speak without self-consciousness of the parts and functions of the body, so with the advent of decency literature lost the use of one of its limbs. It lost its power to create the Wife of Bath, Juliet's nurse, and their recognisable though already colourless relation, Moll Flanders. Sterne, from fear of coarseness, is forced into indecency. He must be witty, not humorous. He must hint instead of speaking outright. Nor can we believe, with Mr. Joyce's *Ulysses* before us, that laughter of the old kind will ever be heard again.

> But, lord Christ! When that it remembreth me
> Up-on my yowthe, and on my Iolitee,

It tikleth me aboute myn herte rote.
Unto this day it doth myn herte bote
That I have had my world as in my tyme.

The sound of that old woman's voice is still.

But there is another and more important reason for the surprising brightness, the still effective merriment of the *Canterbury Tales*. Chaucer was a poet; but he never flinched from the life that was being lived at the moment before his eyes. A farmyard, with its straw, its dung, its cocks and its hens is not (we have come to think) a poetic subject; poets seem either to rule out the farmyard entirely or to require that it shall be a farmyard in Thessaly and its pigs of mythological origin. But Chaucer says outright:

> Three large sowes hadde she, and namo,
> Three kyn, and eek a sheep that highte Malle;

or again,

> A yard she hadde, enclosed al aboute
> With stikkes, and a drye ditch with-oute.

He is unabashed and unafraid. He will always get close up to his object—an old man's chin—

> With thikke bristles of his berde unsofte,
> Lyk to the skin of houndfish, sharp as brere;

or an old man's neck—

> The slakke skin aboute his nekke shaketh
> Whyl that he sang;

and he will tell you what his characters wore, how they looked, what they ate and drank, as if poetry could handle the common facts of this very moment of Tuesday, the sixteenth day of April, 1387, without dirtying her hands. If he withdraws to the time of the Greeks or the Romans, it is only that his story leads him there. He has no desire to wrap himself round in antiquity, to take refuge in age, or to shirk the associations of common grocer's English.

Therefore when we say that we know the end of the journey, it is hard to quote the particular lines from which we take our knowledge. He fixed his eyes upon the road before him, not upon the world to come. He was little given to abstract contemplation. He deprecated, with peculiar archness, any competition with the scholars and divines:

> The answere of this I lete to divynis,
> But wel I woot, that in this world grey pyne is.

> What is this world? What asketh men to have?
> Now with his love, now in the colde grave
> Allone, withouten any companye,

he asks, or ponders

>   O cruel goddes, that governe
> This world with binding of your worde eterne,
> And wryten in the table of athamaunt
> Your parlement, and your eterne graunt,
> What is mankinde more un-to yow holde
> Than is the sheepe, that rouketh in the folde?

Questions press upon him; he asks questions, but he is too true a poet to answer them; he leaves them unsolved, uncramped by the solution of the moment, thus fresh for the generations that come after him. In his life, too, it would be impossible to write him down a man of this party or of that, a democrat or an aristocrat. He was a staunch churchman, but he laughed at priests. He was an able public servant and a courtier, but his views upon sexual morality were extremely lax. He sympathised with poverty, but did nothing to improve the lot of the poor. It is safe to say that not a single law has been framed or one stone set upon another because of anything that Chaucer said or wrote; and yet, as we read him, we are of course absorbing morality at every pore. For among writers there are two kinds: there are the priests who

take you by the hand and lead you straight up to the
mystery; there are the laymen who imbed their doctrines in flesh and blood and make a complete model
of the world without excluding the bad or laying stress
upon the good. Wordsworth, Coleridge, and Shelley are
among the priests; they give us text after text to be
hung upon the wall, saying after saying to be laid upon
the heart like an amulet against disaster—

> Farewell, farewell, the heart that lives alone
>
> > He prayeth best that loveth best
> > All things both great and small

—such lines of exhortation and command spring to memory instantly. But Chaucer lets us go our ways doing the
ordinary things with the ordinary people. His morality
lies in the way men and women behave to each other.
We see them eating, drinking, laughing, and making
love, and come to feel without a word being said
what their standards are and so are steeped through and
through with their morality. There can be no more
forcible preaching than this where all actions and passions are represented, and instead of being solemnly exhorted we are left to stray and stare and make out a
meaning for ourselves. It is the morality of ordinary intercourse, the morality of the novel, which parents and
librarians rightly judge to be far more persuasive than
the morality of poetry.

And so, when we shut Chaucer, we feel that without
a word being said the criticism is complete; what we are
saying, thinking, reading, doing has been commented
upon. Nor are we left merely with the sense, powerful
though that is, of having been in good company and got
used to the ways of good society. For as we have jogged
through the real, the unadorned country-side, with first
one good fellow cracking his joke or singing his song
and then another, we know that though this world resembles, it is not in fact our daily world. It is the world

of poetry. Everything happens here more quickly and
more intensely, and with better order than in life or in
prose; there is a formal elevated dullness which is part
of the incantation of poetry; there are lines speaking half
a second in advance what we were about to say, as if we
read our thoughts before words cumbered them; and
lines which we go back to read again with that heightened quality, that enchantment which keeps them glitter-
ing in the mind long afterwards. And the whole is held
in its place, and its variety and divagations ordered by
the power which is among the most impressive of all—
the shaping power, the architect's power. It is the peculiarity of Chaucer, however, that though we feel at once
this quickening, this enchantment, we cannot prove it by
quotation. From most poets quotation is easy and obvious; some metaphor suddenly flowers; some passage
breaks off from the rest. But Chaucer is very equal, very
even-paced, very unmetaphorical. If we take six or seven
lines in the hope that the quality will be contained in
them it has escaped.

> My lord, ye woot that in my fadres place,
> Ye dede me strepe out of my povre wede,
> And richely me cladden, o your grace
> To yow broghte I noght elles, out of drede,
> But feyth and nakedness and maydenhede.

In its place that seemed not only memorable and moving but fit to set beside striking beauties. Cut out and
taken separately it appears ordinary and quiet. Chaucer,
it seems, has some art by which the most ordinary words
and the simplest feelings when laid side by side make
each other shine; when separated lose their lustre. Thus
the pleasure he gives us is different from the pleasure
that other poets give us, because it is more closely connected with what we have ourselves felt or observed.
Eating, drinking and fine weather, the May, cocks and
hens, millers, old peasant women, flowers—there is a spe-
cial stimulus in seeing all these common things so ar-

ranged that they affect us as poetry affects us, and are
yet bright, sober, precise as we see them out of doors.
There is a pungency in this unfigurative language; a
stately and memorable beauty in the undraped sentences
which follow each other like women so slightly veiled
that you see the lines of their bodies as they go—

> And she set down hir water pot anon
> Biside the threshold in an oxe's stall.

And then, as the procession takes its way, tranquilly,
beautifully, out from behind peeps the face of Chaucer,
grinning, malicious, in league with all foxes, donkeys,
and hens, to mock the pomp and ceremonies of life—
witty, intellectual, French, at the same time based upon
a broad bottom of English humour.

So Sir John read his Chaucer in the comfortless room
with the wind blowing and the smoke stinging, and left
his father's tombstone unmade. But no book, no tomb,
had power to hold him long. He was one of those am-
biguous characters who haunt the boundary line where
one age merges in another and are not able to inhabit
either. At one moment he was all for buying books
cheap; next he was off to France and told his mother,
"My mind is now not most upon books." In his own
house, where his mother Margaret was perpetually making out inventories or confiding in Gloys the priest, he
had no peace or comfort. There was always reason on
her side; she was a brave woman, for whose sake one
must put up with the priest's insolence and choke down
one's rage when the grumbling broke into open abuse,
and "Thou proud priest" and "Thou proud Squire" were
bandied angrily about the room. All this, with the dis-
comforts of life and the weakness of his own character,
drove him to loiter in pleasanter places, to put off coming, to put off writing, to put off, year after year, the
making of his father's tombstone.

Yet John Paston had now lain for twelve years under

the bare ground. The Prior of Bromholm sent word that
the grave cloth was in tatters, and he had tried to patch
it himself. Worse still, for a proud woman like Margaret
Paston, the country people murmured at the Pastons'
lack of piety, and other families she heard, of no greater
standing than theirs, spent money in pious restoration
in the very church where her husband lay unremem-
bered. At last, turning from tournaments and Chaucer
and Mistress Anne Hault, Sir John bethought him of a
piece of cloth of gold which had been used to cover his
father's hearse and might now be sold to defray the ex-
penses of his tomb. Margaret had it in safe keeping; she
had hoarded it and cared for it, and spent twenty marks
on its repair. She grudged it; but there was no help for
it. She sent it him, still distrusting his intentions or his
power to put them into effect. "If you sell it to any
other use," she wrote, "by my troth I shall never trust
you while I live."

But this final act, like so many that Sir John had un-
dertaken in the course of his life, was left undone. A
dispute with the Duke of Suffolk in the year 1479 made
it necessary for him to visit London in spite of the epi-
demic of sickness that was abroad; and there, in dirty
lodgings, alone, busy to the end with quarrels, clamor-
ous to the end for money, Sir John died and was buried
at Whitefriars in London. He left a natural daughter;
he left a considerable number of books; but his father's
tomb was still unmade.

The four thick volumes of the Paston letters, however, swallow up this frustrated man as the sea absorbs
a raindrop. For, like all collections of letters, they seem
to hint that we need not care overmuch for the fortunes of individuals. The family will go on whether Sir
John lives or dies. It is their method to heap up in
mounds of insignificant and often dismal dust the innumerable trivialities of daily life, as it grinds itself out,
year after year. And then suddenly they blaze up; the
day shines out, complete, alive, before our eyes. It is

early morning and strange men have been whispering
among the women as they milk. It is evening, and there
in the churchyard Warne's wife bursts out against old
Agnes Paston: "All the devils of Hell draw her soul
to Hell." Now it is the autumn in Norfolk and Cecily
Dawne comes whining to Sir John for clothing. "Moreover, Sir, liketh it your mastership to understand that
winter and cold weather draweth nigh and I have
few clothes but of your gift." There is the ancient day,
spread out before us, hour by hour.

But in all this there is no writing for writing's sake;
no use of the pen to convey pleasure or amusement or
any of the million shades of endearment and intimacy
which have filled so many English letters since. Only occasionally, under stress of anger for the most part, does
Margaret Paston quicken into some shrewd saw or solemn curse. "Men cut large thongs here out of other
men's leather. . . . We beat the brushes and other men
have the birds. . . . Haste reweth . . . which is to my
heart a very spear." That is her eloquence and that her
anguish. Her sons, it is true, bend their pens more easily
to their will. They jest rather stiffly; they hint rather
clumsily; they make a little scene like a rough puppet
show of the old priest's anger and give a phrase or two
directly as they were spoken in person. But when Chaucer lived he must have heard this very language, matter
of fact, unmetaphorical, far better fitted for narrative
than for analysis, capable of religious solemnity or of
broad humour, but very stiff material to put on the lips
of men and women accosting each other face to face. In
short it is easy to see, from the Paston letters, why Chaucer wrote not *Lear* or *Romeo and Juliet*, but the *Canterbury Tales*.

Sir John was buried; and John the younger brother
succeeded in his turn. The Paston letters go on; life
at Paston continues much the same as before. Over it
all broods a sense of discomfort and nakedness; of un-
washed limbs thrust into splendid clothing; of tapestry

blowing on the draughty walls; of the bedroom with
its privy; of winds sweeping straight over land unmitigated by hedge or town; of Caister Castle covering with
solid stone six acres of ground, and of the plain-faced
Pastons indefatigably accumulating wealth, treading out
the roads of Norfolk, and persisting with an obstinate
courage which does them infinite credit in furnishing
the bareness of England.

*

On Not Knowing Greek

*

For it is vain and foolish to talk of Knowing Greek, since in our ignorance we should be at the bottom of any class of schoolboys, since we do not know how the words sounded, or where precisely we ought to laugh, or how the actors acted, and between this foreign people and ourselves there is not only difference of race and tongue but a tremendous breach of tradition. All the more strange, then, is it that we should wish to know Greek, try to know Greek, feel for ever drawn back to Greek, and be for ever making up some notion of the meaning of Greek, though from what incongruous odds and ends, with what slight resemblance to the real meaning of Greek, who shall say?

It is obvious in the first place that Greek literature is the impersonal literature. Those few hundred years that separate John Paston from Plato, Norwich from Athens, make a chasm which the vast tide of European chatter can never succeed in crossing. When we read Chaucer, we are floated up to him insensibly on the current of our ancestors' lives, and later, as records increase and memories lengthen, there is scarcely a figure which has not its nimbus of association, its life and letters, its wife and family, its house, its character, its happy or dismal catastrophe. But the Greeks remain in a fastness of their own. Fate has been kind there too. She has preserved them from vulgarity. Euripides was eaten by dogs; Aeschylus killed by a stone; Sappho leapt from a cliff. We know no more of them than that. We have their poetry, and that is all.

But that is not, and perhaps never can be, wholly true. Pick up any play by Sophocles, read—

Son of him who led our hosts at Troy of old, son of Agamemnon,

and at once the mind begins to fashion itself surroundings. It makes some background, even of the most provisional sort, for Sophocles; it imagines some village, in a remote part of the country, near the sea. Even nowadays such villages are to be found in the wilder parts of England, and as we enter them we can scarcely help feeling that here, in this cluster of cottages, cut off from rail or city, are all the elements of a perfect existence. Here is the Rectory; here the Manor house, the farm and the cottages; the church for worship, the club for meeting, the cricket field for play. Here life is simply sorted out into its main elements. Each man and woman has his work; each works for the health or happiness of others. And here, in this little community, characters become part of the common stock; the eccentricities of the clergyman are known; the great ladies' defects of temper; the blacksmith's feud with the milkman, and the loves and matings of the boys and girls. Here life has cut the same grooves for centuries; customs have arisen; legends have attached themselves to hilltops and solitary trees, and the village has its history, its festivals, and its rivalries.

It is the climate that is impossible. If we try to think of Sophocles here, we must annihilate the smoke and the damp and the thick wet mists. We must sharpen the lines of the hills. We must imagine a beauty of stone and earth rather than of woods and greenery. With warmth and sunshine and months of brilliant, fine weather, life of course is instantly changed; it is transacted out of

doors, with the result, known to all who visit Italy, that
small incidents are debated in the street, not in the sit-
ting-room, and become dramatic; make people voluble;
inspire in them that sneering, laughing, nimbleness of wit
and tongue peculiar to the Southern races, which has
nothing in common with the slow reserve, the low half-
tones, the brooding introspective melancholy of people
accustomed to live more than half the year indoors.

That is the quality that first strikes us in Greek literature, the lightning-quick, sneering, out-of-doors manner. It is apparent in the most august as well as in the
most trivial places. Queens and Princesses in this very
tragedy by Sophocles stand at the door bandying words
like village women, with a tendency, as one might expect,
to rejoice in language, to split phrases into slices, to be
intent on verbal victory. The humour of the people was
not good natured like that of our postmen and cab-
drivers. The taunts of men lounging at the street corners
had something cruel in them as well as witty. There is
a cruelty in Greek tragedy which is quite unlike our
English brutality. Is not Pentheus, for example, that
highly respectable man, made ridiculous in the *Bacchae*
before he is destroyed? In fact, of course, these Queens
and Princesses were out of doors, with the bees buzzing
past them, shadows crossing them, and the wind taking
their draperies. They were speaking to an enormous audience rayed round them on one of those brilliant southern days when the sun is so hot and yet the air so
exciting. The poet, therefore, had to bethink him, not
of some theme which could be read for hours by people
in privacy, but of something emphatic, familiar, brief,
that would carry, instantly and directly, to an audience
of seventeen thousand people, perhaps, with ears and
eyes eager and attentive, with bodies whose muscles
would grow stiff if they sat too long without diversion.
Music and dancing he would need, and naturally would
choose one of those legends, like our Tristram and
Iseult, which are known to every one in outline, so that

a great fund of emotion is ready prepared, but can be stressed in a new place by each new poet.

Sophocles would take the old story of Electra, for instance, but would at once impose his stamp upon it. Of that, in spite of our weakness and distortion, what remains visible to us? That his genius was of the extreme kind in the first place; that he chose a design which, if it failed, would show its failure in gashes and ruin, not in the gentle blurring of some insignificant detail; which, if it succeeded, would cut each stroke to the bone, would stamp each finger-print in marble. His Electra stands before us like a figure so tightly bound that she can only move an inch this way, an inch that. But each movement must tell to the utmost, or, bound as she is, denied the relief of all hints, repetitions, suggestions, she will be nothing but a dummy, tightly bound. Her words in crisis are, as a matter of fact, bare; mere cries of despair, joy, hate

> οἲ 'γὼ τάλαιν', ὄλωλα τῇδ' ἐν ἡμέρᾳ.
> παῖσον, εἰ σθένεις, διπλῆν·

But these cries give angle and outline to the play. It is thus, with a thousand differences of degree, that in English literature Jane Austen shapes a novel. There comes a moment—"I will dance with you," says Emma—which rises higher than the rest, which, though not eloquent in itself, or violent, or made striking by beauty of language, has the whole weight of the book behind it. In Jane Austen, too, we have the same sense, though the ligatures are much less tight, that her figures are bound, and restricted to a few definite movements. She, too, in her modest, everyday prose, chose the dangerous art where one slip means death.

But it is not so easy to decide what it is that gives these cries of Electra in her anguish their power to cut and wound and excite. It is partly that we know her, that we have picked up from little turns and twists of the dialogue hints of her character, of her appearance, which, characteristically, she neglected; of something suffering in her, outraged and stimulated to its utmost stretch of capacity, yet, as she herself knows ("my behaviour is unseemly and becomes me ill"), blunted and debased by the horror of her position, an unwed girl made to witness her mother's vileness and denounce it in loud, almost vulgar, clamour to the world at large. It is partly, too, that we know in the same way that Clytemnestra is no unmitigated villainess. "δεινὸν τὸ τίκτειν ἐστίν," she says—"there is a strange power in motherhood." It is no murderess, violent and unredeemed, whom Orestes kills within the house, and Electra bids him utterly destroy —"strike again." No; the men and women standing out in the sunlight before the audience on the hillside were alive enough, subtle enough, not mere figures, or plaster casts of human beings.

Yet it is not because we can analyse them into feelings that they impress us. In six pages of Proust we can find more complicated and varied emotions than in the whole of the *Electra*. But in the *Electra* or in the *Antigone* we are impressed by something different, by something perhaps more impressive—by heroism itself, by fidelity itself. In spite of the labour and the difficulty it is this that draws us back and back to the Greeks; the stable, the permanent, the original human being is to be found there. Violent emotions are needed to rouse him into action, but when thus stirred by death, by betrayal, by some other primitive calamity, Antigone and Ajax and Electra behave in the way in which we should behave thus struck down; the way in which everybody has always behaved; and thus we understand them more easily and more directly than we understand the characters in the *Canterbury Tales*. These are the originals, Chaucer's the varieties of the human species.

It is true, of course, that these types of the original man or woman, these heroic Kings, these faithful daughters, these tragic Queens who stalk through the ages always planting their feet in the same places, twitching their robes with the same gestures, from habit not from impulse, are among the greatest bores and the most demoralising companions in the world. The plays of Addison, Voltaire, and a host of others are there to prove it. But encounter them in Greek. Even in Sophocles, whose reputation for restraint and mastery has filtered down to us from the scholars, they are decided, ruthless, direct. A fragment of their speech broken off would, we feel, colour oceans and oceans of the respectable drama. Here we meet them before their emotions have been worn into uniformity. Here we listen to the nightingale whose song echoes through English literature singing in her own Greek tongue. For the first time Orpheus with his lute makes men and beasts follow him. Their voices ring out clear and sharp; we see the hairy tawny bodies at play in the sunlight among the olive trees, not posed gracefully on granite plinths in the pale corridors of the British Museum. And then suddenly, in the midst of all this sharpness and compression, Electra, as if she swept her veil over her face and forbade us to think of her any more, speaks of that very nightingale: "that bird distraught with grief, the messenger of Zeus. Ah, queen of sorrow, Niobe, thee I deem divine—thee; who evermore weepest in thy rocky tomb."

And as she silences her own complaint, she perplexes us again with the insoluble question of poetry and its nature, and why, as she speaks thus, her words put on the assurance of immortality. For they are Greek; we cannot tell how they sounded; they ignore the obvious sources of excitement; they owe nothing of their effect to any extravagance of expression, and certainly they throw no light upon the speaker's character or the writer's. But they remain, something that has been stated and must eternally endure.

Yet in a play how dangerous this poetry, this lapse from the particular to the general must of necessity be, with the actors standing there in person, with their bodies and their faces passively waiting to be made use of! For

this reason the later plays of Shakespeare, where there is
more of poetry than of action, are better read than seen,
better understood by leaving out the actual body than by
having the body, with all its associations and movements,
visible to the eye. The intolerable restrictions of the
drama could be loosened, however, if a means could be
found by which what was general and poetic, comment,
not action, could be freed without interrupting the
movement of the whole. It is this that the choruses supply; the old men or women who take no active part in
the drama, the undifferentiated voices who sing like birds
in the pauses of the wind; who can comment, or sum up,
or allow the poet to speak himself or supply, by contrast,
another side to his conception. Always in imaginative literature, where characters speak for themselves and the
author has no part, the need of that voice is making itself
felt. For though Shakespeare (unless we consider that his
fools and madmen supply the part) dispensed with the
chorus, novelists are always devising some substitute—
Thackeray speaking in his own person, Fielding coming
out and addressing the world before his curtain rises. So
to grasp the meaning of the play the chorus is of the utmost importance. One must be able to pass easily into
those ecstasies, those wild and apparently irrelevant ut-
terances, those sometimes obvious and commonplace
statements, to decide their relevance or irrelevance, and
give them their relation to the play as a whole.

We must "be able to pass easily"; but that of course is
exactly what we cannot do. For the most part the
choruses, with all their obscurities, must be spelt out and
their symmetry mauled. But we can guess that Sophocles
used them not to express something outside the action of
the play, but to sing the praises of some virtue, or the
beauties of some place mentioned in it. He selects what
he wishes to emphasise and sings of white Colonus and
its nightingale, or of love unconquered in fight. Lovely,
lofty, and serene his choruses grow naturally out of his
situations, and change, not the point of view, but the

mood. In Euripides, however, the situations are not contained within themselves; they give off an atmosphere of doubt, of suggestion, of questioning; but if we look to the choruses to make this plain we are often baffled rather than instructed. At once in the *Bacchae* we are in the world of psychology and doubt; the world where the mind twists facts and changes them and makes the familiar aspects of life appear new and questionable. What is Bacchus, and who are the Gods, and what is man's duty to them, and what the rights of his subtle brain? To these questions the chorus makes no reply, or replies mockingly, or speaks darkly as if the straitness of the dramatic form had tempted Euripides to violate it in order to relieve his mind of its weight. Time is so short and I have so much to say, that unless you will allow me to place together two apparently unrelated statements and trust to you to pull them together, you must be content with a mere skeleton of the play I might have given you. Such is the argument. Euripides therefore suffers less than Sophocles and less than Aeschylus from being read privately in a room, and not seen on a hillside in the sunshine. He can be acted in the mind; he can comment upon the questions of the moment; more than the others he will vary in popularity from age to age.

If then in Sophocles the play is concentrated in the figures themselves, and in Euripides is to be retrieved from flashes of poetry and questions far flung and unanswered, Aeschylus makes these little dramas (the *Agamemnon* has 1663 lines; *Lear* about 2600), tremendous by stretching every phrase to the utmost, by sending them floating forth in metaphors, by bidding them rise and stalk eyeless and majestic through the scene. To understand him it is not so necessary to understand Greek as to understand poetry. It is necessary to take that dangerous leap through the air without the support of words which Shakespeare also asks of us. For words, when opposed to such a blast of meaning, must give out, must be blown astray, and only by collecting in com-

panies convey the meaning which each one separately is
too weak to express. Connecting them in a rapid flight
of the mind we know instantly and instinctively what
they mean, but could not decant that meaning afresh into
any other words. There is an ambiguity which is the mark
of the highest poetry; we cannot know exactly what it
means. Take this from the *Agamemnon* for instance—

ὀμμάτων δ' ἐν ἀχηνίαις ἔρρει πᾶσ' 'Αφροδίτα.

The meaning is just on the far side of language. It is the
meaning which in moments of astonishing excitement
and stress we perceive in our minds without words; it is
the meaning that Dostoevsky (hampered as he was by
prose and as we are by translation) leads us to by some
astonishing run up the scale of emotions and points at but
cannot indicate; the meaning that Shakespeare succeeds
in snaring.

Aeschylus thus will not give, as Sophocles gives, the
very words that people might have spoken, only so arranged that they have in some mysterious way a general
force, a symbolic power, nor like Euripides will he com-
bine incongruities and thus enlarge his little space, as a
small room is enlarged by mirrors in odd corners. By the
bold and running use of metaphor he will amplify and
give us, not the thing itself, but the reverberation and reflection which, taken into his mind, the thing has made;
close enough to the original to illustrate it, remote
enough to heighten, enlarge, and make splendid.

For none of these dramatists had the license which belongs to the novelist, and, in some degree, to all writers
of printed books, of modelling their meaning with an in-
finity of slight touches which can only be properly
applied by reading quietly, carefully, and sometimes two
or three times over. Every sentence had to explode on
striking the ear, however slowly and beautifully the
words might then descend, and however enigmatic might
their final purport be. No splendour or richness of metaphor could have saved the *Agamemnon* if either images

or allusions of the subtlest or most decorative had got
between us and the naked cry

$$\mathit{ὀτοτοτοῖ\ πόποι\ δᾶ.\ ὦ\ 'πολλον,\ ὦ\ 'πολλον.}$$

Dramatic they had to be at whatever cost.

But winter fell on these villages, darkness and extreme
cold descended on the hill-side. There must have been
some place indoors where men could retire, both in the
depths of winter and in the summer heats, where they
could sit and drink, where they could lie stretched at
their ease, where they could talk. It is Plato, of course,
who reveals the life indoors, and describes how, when a
party of friends met and had eaten not at all luxuriously
and drunk a little wine, some handsome boy ventured a
question, or quoted an opinion, and Socrates took it up,
fingered it, turned it round, looked at it this way and
that, swiftly stripped it of its inconsistencies and falsities
and brought the whole company by degrees to gaze with
him at the truth. It is an exhausting process; to contract
painfully upon the exact meaning of words; to judge
what each admission involves; to follow intently, yet
critically, the dwindling and changing of opinion as it
hardens and intensifies into truth. Are pleasure and good
the same? Can virtue be taught? Is virtue knowledge?
The tired or feeble mind may easily lapse as the remorse-
less questioning proceeds; but no one, however weak, can
fail, even if he does not learn more from Plato, to love
knowledge better. For as the argument mounts from step
to step, Protagoras yielding, Socrates pushing on, what
matters is not so much the end we reach as our manner
of reaching it. That all can feel—the indomitable honesty, the courage, the love of truth which draw Socrates
and us in his wake to the summit where, if we too may
stand for a moment, it is to enjoy the greatest felicity of
which we are capable.

Yet such an expression seems ill fitted to describe the
state of mind of a student to whom, after painful argument, the truth has been revealed. But truth is various;

truth comes to us in different disguises; it is not with the
intellect alone that we perceive it. It is a winter's night;
the tables are spread at Agathon's house; the girl is playing the flute; Socrates has washed himself and put on
sandals; he has stopped in the hall; he refuses to move
when they send for him. Now Socrates has done; he is
bantering Alcibiades; Alcibiades takes a fillet and binds
it round "this wonderful fellow's head." He praises Socrates. "For he cares not for mere beauty, but despises
more than any one can imagine all external possessions,
whether it be beauty or wealth or glory, or any other
thing for which the multitude felicitates the possessor.
He esteems these things and us who honour them, as
nothing, and lives among men, making all the objects of
their admiration the playthings of his irony. But I know
not if any one of you has ever seen the divine images
which are within, when he has been opened and is serious. I have seen them, and they are so supremely beautiful, so golden, divine, and wonderful, that everything
which Socrates commands surely ought to be obeyed
even like the voice of a God." All this flows over the
arguments of Plato—laughter and movement; people
getting up and going out; the hour changing; tempers
being lost; jokes cracked; the dawn rising. Truth, it
seems, is various; truth is to be pursued with all our faculties. Are we to rule out the amusements, the tender-
nesses, the frivolities of friendship because we love
truth? Will truth be quicker found because we stop our
ears to music and drink no wine, and sleep instead of
talking through the long winter's night? It is not to the
cloistered disciplinarian mortifying himself in solitude
that we are to turn, but to the well-sunned nature, the
man who practises the art of living to the best advantage, so that nothing is stunted but some things are
permanently more valuable than others.

So in these dialogues we are made to seek truth with
every part of us. For Plato, of course, had the dramatic
genius. It is by means of that, by an art which conveys

in a sentence or two the setting and the atmosphere, and then with perfect adroitness insinuates itself into the coils of the argument without losing its liveliness and grace, and then contracts to bare statement, and then, mounting, expands and soars in that higher air which is generally reached only by the more extreme measures of poetry—it is this art which plays upon us in so many ways at once and brings us to an exultation of mind which can only be reached when all the powers are called upon to contribute their energy to the whole.

But we must beware. Socrates did not care for "mere beauty," by which he meant, perhaps, beauty as ornament. A people who judged as much as the Athenians did by ear, sitting out-of-doors at the play or listening to argument in the market-place, were far less apt than we are to break off sentences and appreciate them apart from the context. For them there were no Beauties of Hardy, Beauties of Meredith, Sayings from George Eliot. The writer had to think more of the whole and less of the detail. Naturally, living in the open, it was not the lip or the eye that struck them, but the carriage of the body and the proportions of its parts. Thus when we quote and extract we do the Greeks more damage than we do the English. There is a bareness and abruptness in their literature which grates upon a taste accustomed to the intricacy and finish of printed books. We have to stretch our minds to grasp a whole devoid of the prettiness of detail or the emphasis of eloquence. Accustomed to look directly and largely rather than minutely and aslant, it was safe for them to step into the thick of emotions which blind and bewilder an age like our own. In the vast catastrophe of the European war our emotions had to be broken up for us, and put at an angle from us, before we could allow ourselves to feel them in poetry or fiction. The only poets who spoke to the purpose spoke in the sidelong, satiric manner of Wilfrid Owen and Siegfried Sassoon. It was not possible for them to be direct without being clumsy; or to speak

simply of emotion without being sentimental. But the
Greeks could say, as if for the first time, "Yet being dead
they have not died." They could say, "If to die nobly is
the chief part of excellence, to us out of all men Fortune
gave this lot; for hastening to set a crown of freedom on
Greece we lie possessed of praise that grows not old."
They could march straight up, with their eyes open; and
thus fearlessly approached, emotions stand still and suffer
themselves to be looked at.

But again (the question comes back and back), Are
we reading Greek as it was written when we say this?
When we read these few words cut on a tombstone, a
stanza in a chorus, the end or the opening of a dialogue
of Plato's, a fragment of Sappho, when we bruise our
minds upon some tremendous metaphor in the *Agamemnon* instead of stripping the branch of its flowers instantly as we do in reading *Lear*—are we not reading
wrongly? losing our sharp sight in the haze of associations? reading into Greek poetry not what they have but
what we lack? Does not the whole of Greece heap itself
behind every line of its literature? They admit us to a
vision of the earth unravaged, the sea unpolluted, the
maturity, tried but unbroken, of mankind. Every word is
reinforced by a vigour which pours out of olive-tree and
temple and the bodies of the young. The nightingale has
only to be named by Sophocles and she sings; the grove
has only to be called ἄβατον, "untrodden," and we imagine the twisted branches and the purple violets. Back
and back we are drawn to steep ourselves in what, perhaps, is only an image of the reality, not the reality
itself, a summer's day imagined in the heart of a northern winter. Chief among these sources of glamour and
perhaps misunderstanding is the language. We can never
hope to get the whole fling of a sentence in Greek as
we do in English. We cannot hear it, now dissonant,
now harmonious, tossing sound from line to line across a
page. We cannot pick up infallibly one by one all those
minute signals by which a phrase is made to hint, to turn,

to live. Nevertheless it is the language that has us most in bondage; the desire for that which perpetually lures us back. First there is the compactness of the expression. Shelley takes twenty-one words in English to translate thirteen words of Greek.

πᾶς γοῦν ποιητής γίγνεται, χἂν ἄμουσος ᾖ τὸ πρίν ὂν ἂν Ἔρως ἄψηται.

. . . For every one, even if before he were ever so undisciplined, becomes a poet as soon as he is touched by love.

Every ounce of fat has been pared off, leaving the flesh firm. Then, spare and bare as it is, no language can move more quickly, dancing, shaking, all alive, but controlled. Then there are the words themselves which, in so many instances, we have made expressive to us of our own emotions, *thalassa, thanatos, anthos, aster*—to take the first that come to hand; so clear, so hard, so intense, that to speak plainly yet fittingly without blurring the outline or clouding the depths Greek is the only expression. It is useless, then, to read Greek in translations. Translators can but offer us a vague equivalent; their language is necessarily full of echoes and associations. Professor Mackail says "wan," and the age of Burne-Jones and Morris is at once evoked. Nor can the subtler stress, the flight and the fall of the words, be kept even by the most skilful of scholars—

. . . thee, who evermore weepest in thy rocky tomb

is not

ἅτ' ἐν τάφῳ πετραίῳ,
αἱ, δακρύεις.

Further, in reckoning the doubts and difficulties there is this important problem—Where are we to laugh in reading Greek? There is a passage in the *Odyssey* where laughter begins to steal upon us, but if Homer were looking we should probably think it better to control our merriment. To laugh instantly it is almost necessary (though Aristophanes may supply us with an exception) to laugh in English. Humour, after all, is closely bound up with a sense of the body. When we laugh at the humour of Wycherley, we are laughing with the body of that burly rustic who was our common ancestor on the village green. The French, the Italians, the Americans, who derive physically from so different a stock, pause, as we pause in reading Homer, to make sure that they are laughing in the right place, and the pause is fatal. Thus humour is the first of the gifts to perish in a foreign tongue, and when we turn from Greek to Elizabethan literature it seems, after a long silence, as if our great age were ushered in by a burst of laughter.

These are all difficulties, sources of misunderstanding, of distorted and romantic, of servile and snobbish passion. Yet even for the unlearned some certainties remain. Greek is the impersonal literature; it is also the literature of masterpieces. There are no schools; no forerunners; no heirs. We cannot trace a gradual process working in many men imperfectly until it expresses itself adequately at last in one. Again, there is always about Greek literature that air of vigour which permeates an "age," whether it is the age of Aeschylus, or Racine, or Shakespeare. One generation at least in that fortunate time is blown on to be writers to the extreme; to attain that unconsciousness which means that the consciousness is stimulated to the highest extent; to surpass the limits of small triumphs and tentative experiments. Thus we have Sappho with her constellations of adjectives, Plato daring extravagant flights of poetry in the midst of prose; Thucydides, constricted and contracted; Sophocles gliding like a shoal of trout smoothly and quietly, apparently motionless, and then with a flicker of fins off and away; while in the *Odyssey* we have what remains the triumph of narrative, the clearest and at the same time the most romantic story of the fortunes of men and women.

The *Odyssey* is merely a story of adventure, the instinctive story-telling of a sea-faring race. So we may begin it, reading quickly in the spirit of children wanting amusement to find out what happens next. But here is nothing immature; here are full-grown people, crafty, subtle, and passionate. Nor is the world itself a small one, since the sea which separates island from island has to be crossed by little hand-made boats and is measured by the flight of the sea-gulls. It is true that the islands are not thickly populated, and the people, though everything is made by hand, are not closely kept at work. They have had time to develop a very dignified, a very stately society, with an ancient tradition of manners behind it, which makes every relation at once orderly, natural, and full of reserve. Penelope crosses the room; Telemachus goes to bed; Nausicaa washes her linen; and their actions seem laden with beauty because they do not know that they are beautiful, have been born to their possessions, are no more self-conscious than children, and yet, all those thousands of years ago, in their little islands, know all that is to be known. With the sound of the sea in their ears, vines, meadows, rivulets about them, they are even more aware than we are of a ruthless fate. There is a sadness at the back of life which they do not attempt to mitigate. Entirely aware of their own standing in the shadow, and yet alive to every tremor and gleam of existence, there they endure, and it is to the Greeks that we turn when we are sick of the vagueness, of the confusion, of the Christianity and its consolations, of our own age.

*

The Elizabethan Lumber Room

*

These magnificent volumes* are not often, perhaps,
read through. Part of their charm consists in the fact
that Hakluyt is not so much a book as a great bundle of
commodities loosely tied together, an emporium, a lumber room strewn with ancient sacks, obsolete nautical
instruments, huge bales of wool, and little bags of rubies
and emeralds. One is for ever untying this packet here,
sampling that heap over there, wiping the dust off some
vast map of the world, and sitting down in semi-darkness
to snuff the strange smells of silks and leathers and ambergris, while outside tumble the huge waves of the
uncharted Elizabethan sea.

For this jumble of seeds, silks, unicorns' horns, elephants' teeth, wool, common stones, turbans, and bars
of gold, these odds and ends of priceless value and complete worthlessness, were the fruit of innumerable voyages, traffics, and discoveries to unknown lands in the
reign of Queen Elizabeth. The expeditions were manned
by "apt young men" from the West country, and financed
in part by the great Queen herself. The ships, says
Froude, were no bigger than modern yachts. There in
the river by Greenwich the fleet lay gathered, close to
the Palace. "The Privy council looked out of the windows of the court . . . the ships thereupon discharge
their ordnance . . . and the mariners they shouted in

* Hakluyt's Collection of the Early Voyages, Travels, and
Discoveries of the English Nation, five volumes, 4to, 1810.

such sort that the sky rang again with the noise thereof."
Then, as the ships swung down the tide, one sailor after
another walked the hatches, climbed the shrouds, stood
upon the mainyards to wave his friends a last farewell.
Many would come back no more. For directly England
and the coast of France were beneath the horizon, the
ships sailed into the unfamiliar; the air had its voices,
the sea its lions and serpents, its evaporations of fire and
tumultuous whirlpools. But God too was very close; the
clouds but sparely hid the divinity Himself; the limbs of
Satan were almost visible. Familiarly the English sailors
pitted their God against the God of the Turks, who "can
speake never a word for dulnes, much lesse can he helpe
them in such an extremitie. . . . But howsoever their
God behaved himself, our God showed himself a God indeed. . . ." God was as near by sea as by land, said Sir
Humphrey Gilbert, riding through the storm. Suddenly
one light disappeared; Sir Humphrey Gilbert had gone beneath the waves; when morning came, they sought his
ship in vain. Sir Hugh Willoughby sailed to discover the
North-West Passage and made no return. The Earl of
Cumberland's men, hung up by adverse winds off the
coast of Cornwall for a fortnight, licked the muddy
water off the deck in agony. And sometimes a ragged
and wornout man came knocking at the door of an English country house and claimed to be the boy who had
left it years ago to sail the seas. "Sir William his father,
and my lady his mother knew him not to be their son,
until they found a secret mark, which was a wart upon
one of his knees." But he had with him a black stone,
veined with gold, or an ivory tusk, or a silver ingot, and
urged on the village youth with talk of gold strewn over
the land as stones are strewn in the fields of England. One
expedition might fail, but what if the passage to the
fabled land of uncounted riches lay only a little further
up the coast? What if the known world was only the
prelude to some more splendid panorama? When, after
the long voyage, the ships dropped anchor in the great

river of the Plate and the men went exploring through
the undulating lands, startling grazing herds of deer,
seeing the limbs of savages between the trees, they filled
their pockets with pebbles that might be emeralds or sand
that might be gold; or sometimes, rounding a headland,
they saw, far off, a string of savages slowly descending
to the beach bearing on their heads and linking their
shoulders together with heavy burdens for the Spanish
King.

These are the fine stories used effectively all through
the West country to decoy "the apt young men" lounging by the harbour-side to leave their nets and fish for
gold. But the voyagers were sober merchants into the
bargain, citizens with the good of English trade and the
welfare of English work-people at heart. The captains
are reminded how necessary it is to find a market abroad
for English wool; to discover the herb from which blue
dyes are made; above all to make inquiry as to the
methods of producing oil, since all attempts to make it
from radish seed have failed. They are reminded of the
misery of the English poor, whose crimes, brought about
by poverty, make them "daily consumed by the gallows."
They are reminded how the soil of England had been
enriched by the discoveries of travellers in the past; how
Dr. Linaker brought seeds of the damask rose and tulipas,
and how beasts and plants and herbs, "without which our
life were to be said barbarous," have all come to England gradually from abroad. In search of markets and of
goods, of the immortal fame success would bring them,
the apt young men set sail for the North, and were left,
a little company of isolated Englishmen surrounded by
snow and the huts of savages, to make what bargains
they could and pick up what knowledge they might before the ships returned in the summer to fetch them home
again. There they endured, an isolated company, burning
on the rim of the dark. One of them, carrying a charter
from his company in London, went inland as far as Moscow, and there saw the Emperor "sitting in his chair of

estate with his crown on his head, and a staff of gold-
smiths' work in his left hand." All the ceremony that he
saw is carefully written out, and the sight upon which
the English merchant first set eyes has the brilliancy of a
Roman vase dug up and stood for a moment in the sun,
until, exposed to the air, seen by millions of eyes, it dulls
and crumbles away. There, all these centuries, on the outskirts of the world, the glories of Moscow, the glories of
Constantinople have flowered unseen. The Englishman
was bravely dressed for the occasion, led "three fair mas-
tiffs in coats of red cloth," and carried a letter from
Elizabeth "the paper whereof did smell most fragrantly
of camphor and ambergris, and the ink of perfect musk."
And sometimes, since trophies from the amazing new
world were eagerly awaited at home, together with unicorns' horns and lumps of ambergris and the fine stories
of the engendering of whales and "debates" of elephants
and dragons whose blood, mixed, congealed into ver-
milion, a living sample would be sent, a live savage
caught somewhere off the coast of Labrador, taken to
England, and shown about like a wild beast. Next year
they brought him back, and took a woman savage on
board to keep him company. When they saw each other
they blushed; they blushed profoundly, but the sailors,
though they noted it, knew not why. Later the two
savages set up house together on board ship, she attending to his wants, he nursing her in sickness. But, as the
sailors noted again, the savages lived together in perfect chastity.

All this, the new words, the new ideas, the waves, the
savages, the adventures, found their way naturally into
the plays which were being acted on the banks of the
Thames. There was an audience quick to seize upon the
coloured and the high-sounding; to associate those

> frigates bottom'd with rich Sethin planks,
> Topt with the lofty firs of Lebanon

with the adventures of their own sons and brothers

abroad. The Verneys, for example, had a wild boy who had gone as pirate, turned Turk, and died out there, sending back to Claydon to be kept as relics of him some silk, a turban, and a pilgrim's staff. A gulf lay between the spartan domestic housecraft of the Paston women and the refined tastes of the Elizabethan Court ladies, who, grown old, says Harrison, spent their time reading histories, or "writing volumes of their own, or translating of other men's into our English and Latin tongue," while the younger ladies played the lute and the citharne and spent their leisure in the enjoyment of music. Thus, with singing and with music, springs into existence the characteristic Elizabethan extravagance; the dolphins and lavoltas of Greene; the hyperbole, more surprising in a writer so terse and muscular, of Ben Jonson. Thus we find the whole of Elizabethan literature strewn with gold and silver; with talk of Guiana's rarities, and references to that America—"O my America! my new-found-land"—which was not merely a land on the map, but symbolised the unknown territories of the soul. So, over the water, the imagination of Montaigne brooded in fascination upon savages, cannibals, society, and government.

But the mention of Montaigne suggests that though the influence of the sea and the voyages, of the lumber-room crammed with sea beasts and horns and ivory and old maps and nautical instruments, helped to inspire the greatest age of English poetry, its effects were by no means so beneficial upon English prose. Rhyme and metre helped the poets to keep the tumult of their perceptions in order. But the prose writer, without these restrictions, accumulated clauses, petered out in interminable catalogues, tripped and stumbled over the convolutions of his own rich draperies. How little Elizabethan prose was fit for its office, how exquisitely French prose was already adapted, can be seen by comparing a passage from Sidney's *Defense of Poesie* with one from Montaigne's *Essays*.

He beginneth not with obscure definitions, which must blur the margent with interpretations, and load the memory with doubtfulness: but he cometh to you with words set in delightful proportion, either accompanied with, or prepared for the well enchanting Skill of Music, and with a tale (forsooth) he cometh unto you, with a tale which holdeth children from play, and old men from the Chimney corner; and pretending no more, doth intend the winning of the mind from wickedness to virtue; even as the child is often brought to take most wholesome things by hiding them in such other as have a pleasant taste: which if one should begin to tell them the nature of the *Aloës* or *Rhubarbarum* they should receive, would sooner take their physic at their ears than at their mouth, so is it in men (most of which are childish in the best things, till they be cradled in their graves) glad they will be to hear the tales of Hercules. . . .

And so it runs on for seventy-six words more. Sidney's prose is an uninterrupted monologue, with sudden flashes of felicity and splendid phrases, which lends itself to lamentations and moralities, to long accumulations and catalogues, but is never quick, never colloquial, unable to grasp a thought closely and firmly, or to adapt itself flexibly and exactly to the chops and changes of the mind. Compared with this, Montaigne is master of an instrument which knows its own powers and limitations, and is capable of insinuating itself into crannies and crevices which poetry can never reach; of cadences different but no less beautiful; capable of subtleties and intensities which Elizabethan prose entirely ignores. He is considering the way in which certain of the ancients met death:

   . . . *ils l'ont faicte couler et glisser parmy la lascheté de leurs occupations accoustumées entre des garses et bons compaignons; nul propos de consolation, nulle mention de testament, nulle affectation ambitieuse de constance, nul discours de leur condition future; mais entre les jeux, les festins, facecies, entretiens communs et populaires, et la musique, et des vers amoureux.*

An age seems to separate Sidney from Montaigne. The English compared with the French are as boys compared with men.

But the Elizabethan prose writers, if they have the formlessness of youth have, too, its freshness and audacity. In the same essay Sidney shapes language, masterfully and easily, to his liking; freely and naturally reaches his hand for a metaphor. To bring this prose to perfection (and Dryden's prose is very near perfection) only the discipline of the stage was necessary and the growth of self-consciousness. It is in the plays, and especially in the comic passages of the plays, that the finest Elizabethan prose is to be found. The stage was the nursery where prose learnt to find its feet. For on the stage people had to meet, to quip and crank, to suffer interruptions, to talk of ordinary things.

Cler. A box of her autumnal face, her pieced beauty! there's no man can be admitted till she be ready now-a-days, till she has painted, and perfumed, and washed, and scoured, but the boy here; and him she wipes her oiled lips upon, like a sponge. I have made a song (I pray thee hear it) on the subject. [Page sings

Still to be neat, still to be drest &c.

True. And I am clearly on the other side: I love a good dressing before any beauty o' the world. O, a woman is then like a delicate garden; nor is there one kind of it; she may vary every hour; take often counsel of her glass, and choose the best. If she have good ears, show them; good hair, lay it out; good legs, wear short clothes; a good hand, discover it often: practise any art to mend breath, cleanse teeth, repair eyebrows; paint and profess it.

So the talk runs in Ben Jonson's *Silent Woman*, knocked into shape by interruptions, sharpened by collisions, and never allowed to settle into stagnancy or swell into turbidity. But the publicity of the stage and the perpetual presence of a second person were hostile to that growing consciousness of one's self, that brooding in solitude over the mysteries of the soul, which, as the years went by, sought expression and found a champion in the sublime genius of Sir Thomas Browne. His immense egotism has paved the way for all psychological novelists, autobiographers, confession-mongers, and dealers in the curious shades of our private life. He it was who first turned from the contacts of men with men to their lonely life within. "The world that I regard is myself; it is the microcosm of my own frame that I cast mine eye on; for the other I use it but like my globe, and turn it round sometimes for my recreation." All was mystery and darkness as the first explorer walked the catacombs swinging his lanthorn. "I feel sometimes a hell within myself; Lucifer keeps his court in my breast; Legion is revived in me." In these solitudes there were no guides and no companions. "I am in the dark to all the world, and my nearest friends behold me but in a cloud." The strangest thoughts and imaginings have play with him as he goes about his work, outwardly the most sober of mankind and esteemed the greatest physician in Norwich. He has wished for death. He has doubted all things. What if we are asleep in this world and the conceits of life are as mere dreams? The tavern music, the Ave Mary bell, the broken pot that the workman has dug out of the field—at the sight and sound of them he stops dead, as if transfixed by the astonishing vista that opens before his imagination. "We carry with us the wonders we seek without us; there is all Africa and her prodigies in us." A halo of wonder encircles everything that he sees; he turns his light gradually upon the flowers and insects and grasses at his feet so as to disturb nothing in the mysterious processes of their existence. With the same awe, mixed with a sublime complacency, he records the discovery of his own qualities and attainments. He was charitable and brave and averse from nothing. He was full of feeling for others and merciless upon himself. "For my conversation, it is like the sun's, with all men, and with a friendly aspect to good and bad." He knows six languages, the laws, the customs and policies of several states, the names of all the constellations and most of the plants of his country, and yet, so sweeping is his imagination, so large the horizon in which he sees this little figure walking that "methinks I do not know so many as when I did but know a hundred, and had scarcely ever simpled further than Cheapside."

He is the first of the autobiographers. Swooping and soaring at the highest altitudes he stoops suddenly with loving particularity upon the details of his own body. His height was moderate, he tells us, his eyes large and luminous; his skin dark but constantly suffused with blushes. He dressed very plainly. He seldom laughed. He collected coins, kept maggots in boxes, dissected the lungs of frogs, braved the stench of the spermaceti whale, tolerated Jews, had a good word for the deformity of the toad, and combined a scientific and sceptical attitude towards most things with an unfortunate belief in witches. In short, as we say when we cannot help laughing at the oddities of people we admire most, he was a character, and the first to make us feel that the most sublime speculations of the human imagination are issued from a particular man, whom we can love. In the midst of the solemnities of the Urn Burial we smile when he remarks that afflictions induce callosities. The smile broadens to laughter as we mouth out the splendid pomposities, the astonishing conjectures of the *Religio Medici*. Whatever he writes is stamped with his own idiosyncrasy, and we first became conscious of impurities which hereafter stain literature with so many freakish colours that, however hard we try, make it difficult to be certain whether we are looking at a man or his writing. Now we are in the presence of sublime imagination; now rambling through one of the finest lumber rooms in the world—a chamber stuffed from floor to ceiling with ivory, old iron, broken pots, urns, unicorns' horns, and magic glasses full of emerald lights and blue mystery.

*

Notes on an Elizabethan Play

*

There are, it must be admitted, some highly formidable tracts in English literature, and chief among them that jungle, forest, and wilderness which is the Elizabethan drama. For many reasons, not here to be examined, Shakespeare stands out, Shakespeare who has had the light on him from his day to ours, Shakespeare who towers highest when looked at from the level of his own contemporaries. But the plays of the lesser Elizabethans —Greene, Dekker, Peele, Chapman, Beaumont and Fletcher—to adventure into that wilderness is for the ordinary reader an ordeal, an upsetting experience which plies him with questions, harries him with doubts, alternately delights and vexes him with pleasures and pains. For we are apt to forget, reading, as we tend to do, only the masterpieces of a bygone age how great a power the body of a literature possesses to impose itself: how it will not suffer itself to be read passively, but takes us and reads us; flouts our preconceptions; questions principles which we had got into the habit of taking for granted, and, in fact, splits us into two parts as we read, making us, even as we enjoy, yield our ground or stick to our guns.

At the outset in reading an Elizabethan play we are overcome by the extraordinary discrepancy between the Elizabethan view of reality and our own. The reality to which we have grown accustomed, is, speaking roughly, based upon the life and death of some knight called Smith, who succeeded his father in the family business of pitwood importers, timber merchants and coal exporters, was well known in political, temperance, and church circles, did much for the poor of Liverpool, and died last Wednesday of pneumonia while on a visit to his son at Muswell Hill. That is the world we know. That is the reality which our poets and novelists have to expound and illuminate. Then we open the first Elizabethan play that comes to hand and read how

> I once did see
> In my young travels through Armenia
> An angry unicorn in his full career
> Charge with too swift a foot a jeweller
> That watch'd him for the treasure of his brow
> And ere he could get shelter of a tree
> Nail him with his rich antlers to the earth.

Where is Smith, we ask, where is Liverpool? And the groves of Elizabethan drama echo "Where?" Exquisite is the delight, sublime the relief of being set free to wander in the land of the unicorn and the jeweller among dukes and grandees, Gonzaloes and Bellimperias, who spend their lives in murder and intrigue, dress up as men if they are women, as women if they are men, see ghosts, run mad, and die in the greatest profusion on the slightest provocation, uttering as they fall imprecations of superb vigour or elegies of the wildest despair. But soon the low, the relentless voice, which if we wish to identify it we must suppose typical of a reader fed on modern English literature, and French and Russian, asks why, then, with all this to stimulate and enchant these old plays are for long stretches of time so intolerably dull? Is it not that literature, if it is to keep us on the alert through five acts or thirty-two chapters must somehow be based on Smith, have one toe touching Liverpool, take off into whatever heights it pleases from reality? We are not so purblind as to suppose that a man because his name is Smith and he lives at Liverpool is therefore "real." We know indeed that this reality is a chameleon quality, the fantastic becoming as we grow used to it often the closest to the truth, the sober the furthest from it, and nothing proving a writer's greatness more than his capacity to consolidate his scene by the use of what, until he touched them, seemed wisps of cloud and threads of gossamer. Our contention merely is that there is a station, somewhere in mid-air, whence Smith and Liverpool can be seen to the best advantage; that the great artist is the man who knows where to place himself above the shifting scenery; that while he never loses sight of Liverpool he never sees it in the wrong perspective. The Elizabethans bore us, then, because their Smiths are all changed to dukes, their Liverpools to fabulous islands and palaces in Genoa. Instead of keeping a proper poise above life they soar miles into the empyrean, where nothing is visible for long hours at a time but clouds at their revelry, and a cloud landscape is not ultimately satisfactory to human eyes. The Elizabethans bore us because they suffocate our imaginations rather than set them to work.

Still, though potent enough, the boredom of an Elizabethan play is of a different quality altogether from the boredom which a nineteenth-century play, a Tennyson or a Henry Taylor play, inflicts. The riot of images, the violent volubility of language, all that cloys and satiates in the Elizabethans yet appears to be drawn up with a roar as a feeble fire is sucked up by a newspaper. There is, even in the worst, an intermittent bawling vigour which gives us the sense in our quiet arm-chairs of ostlers and orange-girls catching up the lines, flinging them back, hissing or stamping applause. But the deliberate drama of the Victorian age is evidently written in a study. It has for audience ticking clocks and rows of classics bound in half morocco. There is no stamping, no applause. It does not, as, with all its faults, the Elizabethan audience did, leaven the mass with fire. Rhe-

torical and bombastic, the lines are flung and hurried
into existence and reach the same impromptu felicities,
have the same lip-moulded profusion and unexpected-
ness, which speech sometimes achieves, but seldom in
our day the deliberate, solitary pen. Indeed half the
work of the dramatists one feels was done in the Elizabethan age by the public.

Against that, however, is to be set the fact that the
influence of the public was in many respects detestable.
To its door we must lay the greatest infliction that Elizabethan drama puts upon us—the plot; the incessant,
improbable, almost unintelligible convolutions which
presumably gratified the spirit of an excitable and unlet-
tered public actually in the playhouse, but only confuse
and fatigue a reader with the book before him. Undoubtedly something must happen; undoubtedly a play
where nothing happens is an impossibility. But we have
a right to demand (since the Greeks have proved that it
is perfectly possible) that what happens shall have an
end in view. It shall agitate great emotions; bring into
existence memorable scenes; stir the actors to say what
could not be said without this stimulus. Nobody can
fail to remember the plot of the *Antigone*, because what
happens is so closely bound up with the emotions of the
actors that we remember the people and the plot at one
and the same time. But who can tell us what happens in
the *White Devil*, or the *Maid's Tragedy*, except by remembering the story apart from the emotions which it
has aroused? As for the lesser Elizabethans, like Greene
and Kyd, the complexities of their plots are so great,
and the violence which those plots demand so terrific,
that the actors themselves are obliterated and emotions
which, according to our convention at least, deserve the
most careful investigation, the most delicate analysis, are
clean sponged off the slate. And the result is inevitable.
Outside Shakespeare and perhaps Ben Jonson, there
are no characters in Elizabethan drama, only violences
whom we know so little that we can scarcely care what

becomes of them. Take any hero or heroine in those early plays—Bellimperia in the *Spanish Tragedy* will serve as well as another—and can we honestly say that we care a jot for the unfortunate lady who runs the whole gamut of human misery to kill herself in the end? No more than for an animated broomstick, we must reply, and in a work dealing with men and women the prevalence of broomsticks is a drawback. But the *Spanish Tragedy* is admittedly a crude forerunner, chiefly valuable because such primitive efforts lay bare the formidable framework which greater dramatists could modify, but had to use. Ford, it is claimed, is of the school of Stendhal and of Flaubert; Ford is a psychologist. Ford is an analyst. "This man," says Mr. Havelock Ellis, "writes of women not as a dramatist nor as a lover, but as one who has searched intimately and felt with instinctive sympathy the fibres of their hearts."

The play—*'Tis Pity She's a Whore*—upon which this judgement is chiefly based shows us the whole nature of Annabella spun from pole to pole in a series of tremendous vicissitudes. First, her brother tells her that he loves her; next she confesses her love for him; next finds herself with child by him; next forces herself to marry Soranzo; next is discovered; next repents; finally is killed, and it is her lover and brother who kills her. To trace the trail of feelings which such crises and calamities might be expected to breed in a woman of ordinary sensibility might have filled volumes. A dramatist of course has no volumes to fill. He is forced to contract. Even so, he can illumine; he can reveal enough for us to guess the rest. But what is it that we know without using microscopes and splitting hairs about the character of Annabella? Gropingly we make out that she is a spirited girl, with her defiance of her husband when he abuses her, her snatches of Italian song, her ready wit, her simple glad love-making. But of character as we understand the word there is no trace. We do not know how she reaches her conclusions, only that she has reached them.

Nobody describes her. She is always at the height of her passion, never at its approach. Compare her with Anna Karenina. The Russian woman is flesh and blood, nerves and temperament, has heart, brain, body and mind where the English girl is flat and crude as a face painted on a playing card; she is without depth, without range, without intricacy. But as we say this we know that we have missed something. We have let the meaning of the play slip through our hands. We have ignored the emotion which has been accumulating because it has accumulated in places where we have not expected to find it. We have been comparing the play with prose, and the play, after all, is poetry.

The play is poetry, we say, and the novel prose. Let us attempt to obliterate detail, and place the two before us side by side, feeling, so far as we can, the angles and edges of each, recalling each, so far as we are able, as a whole. Then, at once, the prime differences emerge; the long leisurely accumulated novel; the little contracted play; the emotion all split up, dissipated and then woven together, slowly and gradually massed into a whole, in the novel; the emotion concentrated, generalised, heightened in the play. What moments of intensity, what phrases of astonishing beauty the play shot at us!

> O, my lords,
> I but deceived your eyes with antic gesture,
> When one news straight came huddling on another
> Of death! and death! and death! still I danced forward.

or

> You have oft for these two lips
> Neglected cassia or the natural sweets
> Of the spring-violet: they are not yet much wither'd.

With all her reality, Anna Karenina could never say

> "You have oft, for these two lips
> Neglected cassia."

Some of the most profound of human emotions are
therefore beyond her reach. The extremes of passion
are not for the novelist; the perfect marriages of sense
and sound are not for him; he must tame his swiftness
to sluggardry; keep his eyes on the ground not on the
sky: suggest by description, not reveal by illumination.
Instead of singing

> Lay a garland on my hearse
>   Of the dismal yew;
> Maidens, willow branches bear;
>   Say I died true,

he must enumerate the chrysanthemums fading on the
grave and the undertakers' men snuffling past in their
four-wheelers. How then can we compare this lumber-
ing and lagging art with poetry? Granted all the little
dexterities by which the novelist makes us know the
individual and recognise the real, the dramatist goes beyond the single and the separate, shows us not Annabella
in love, but love itself; not Anna Karenina throwing herself under the train, but ruin and death and the

> . . . soul, like a ship in a black storm,
> . . . driven, I know not whither.

So with pardonable impatience we might exclaim as
we shut our Elizabethan play. But what then is the ex-
clamation with which we close *War and Peace?* Not one
of disappointment; we are not left lamenting the super-
ficiality, upbraiding the triviality of the novelist's art.
Rather we are made more than ever aware of the inex-
haustible richness of human sensibility. Here, in the play,
we recognise the general; here, in the novel, the particular. Here we gather all our energies into a bunch and
spring. Here we extend and expand and let come slowly
in from all quarters deliberate impressions, accumulated
messages. The mind is so saturated with sensibility, language so inadequate to its experience, that far from rul-
ing off one form of literature or decreeing its inferiority

to others we complain that they are still unable to keep pace with the wealth of material, and wait impatiently the creation of what may yet be devised to liberate us of the enormous burden of the unexpressed.

Thus, in spite of dullness, bombast, rhetoric, and confusion we still read the lesser Elizabethans, still find ourselves adventuring in the land of the jeweller and the unicorn. The familiar factories of Liverpool fade into thin air and we scarcely recognise any likeness between the knight who imported timber and died of pneumonia at Muswell Hill and the Armenian Duke who fell like a Roman on his sword while the owl shrieked in the ivy and the Duchess gave birth to a still-born babe 'mongst women howling. To join those territories and recognise the same man in different disguises we have to adjust and revise. But make the necessary alterations in perspective, draw in those filaments of sensibility which the moderns have so marvellously developed, use instead the ear and the eye which the moderns have so basely starved, hear words as they are laughed and shouted, not as they are printed in black letters on the page, see before your eyes the changing faces and living bodies of men and women, put yourself, in short, into a different, but not more elementary stage of your reading development and then the true merits of Elizabethan drama will assert themselves. The power of the whole is undeniable. Theirs, too, is the word-coining genius, as if thought plunged into a sea of words and came up dripping. Theirs is that broad humour based upon the nakedness of the body, which, however arduously the public spirited may try, is impossible, since the body is draped. Then at the back of this, imposing not unity but some sort of stability, is what we may briefly call a sense of the presence of the Gods. He would be a bold critic who should attempt to impose any creed upon the swarm and variety of the Elizabethan dramatists, and yet it implies some timidity if we take it for granted that a whole literature with common characteristics is a mere evaporation of high spirits, a

money-making enterprise, a fluke of the mind which,
owing to favourable circumstances, came off successfully. Even in the jungle and the wilderness the compass
still points.

> "Lord, Lord, that I were dead!"

they are for ever crying.

> O thou soft natural death that art joint-twin
> To sweetest slumber——

The pageant of the world is marvellous, but the pageant
of the world is vanity.

> glories
> Of human greatness are but pleasing dreams
> And shadows soon decaying: on the stage
> Of my mortality my youth hath acted
> Some scenes of vanity——

To die and be quit of it all is their desire; the bell that
tolls throughout the drama is death and disenchantment.

> All life is but a wandering to find home,
> When we're gone, we're there.

Ruin, weariness, death, perpetually death, stand grimly
to confront the other presence of Elizabethan drama
which is life: life compact of frigates, fir trees and ivory,
of dolphins and the juice of July flowers, of the milk of
unicorns and panthers' breath, of ropes of pearl, brains
of peacocks and Cretan wine. To this, life at its most
reckless and abundant, they reply

> Man is a tree that hath no top in cares,
> No root in comforts; all his power to live
> Is given to no end but t' have power to grieve.

It is this echo flung back and back from the other side
of the play which, if it has not the name, still has the
effect of the presence of the Gods.

So we ramble through the jungle, forest, and wilderness of Elizabethan drama. So we consort with Emperors and clowns, jewellers and unicorns, and laugh and exult and marvel at the splendour and humour and fantasy of it all. A noble rage consumes us when the curtain falls; we are bored too, and nauseated by the wearisome old tricks and florid bombast. A dozen deaths of full-grown men and women move us less than the suffering of one of Tolstoi's flies. Wandering in the maze of the impossible and tedious story suddenly some passionate intensity seizes us; some sublimity exalts, or some melodious snatch of song enchants. It is a world full of tedium and delight; pleasure and curiosity, of extravagant laughter, poetry, and splendour. But gradually it comes over us, what then are we being denied? What is it that we are coming to want so persistently that unless we get it instantly we must seek elsewhere? It is solitude. There is no privacy here. Always the door opens and some one comes in. All is shared, made visible, audible, dramatic. Meanwhile, as if tired with company, the mind steals off to muse in solitude; to think, not to act; to comment, not to share; to explore its own darkness, not the bright-lit-up surfaces of others. It turns to Donne, to Montaigne, to Sir Thomas Browne—the keepers of the keys of solitude.

Montaigne

Once at Bar-le-Duc Montaigne saw a portrait which
René, King of Sicily, had painted of himself, and asked,
"Why is it not, in like manner, lawful for every one to
draw himself with a pen, as he did with a crayon?" Offhand one might reply, Not only is it lawful, but nothing could be easier. Other people may evade us, but our
own features are almost too familiar. Let us begin. And
then, when we attempt the task, the pen falls from our
fingers; it is a matter of profound, mysterious, and overwhelming difficulty.

After all, in the whole of literature, how many people
have succeeded in drawing themselves with a pen? Only
Montaigne and Pepys and Rousseau perhaps. The *Religio
Medici* is a coloured glass through which darkly one sees
racing stars and a strange and turbulent soul. A bright
polished mirror reflects the face of Boswell peeping between other people's shoulders in the famous biography.
But this talking of oneself, following one's own vagaries,
giving the whole map, weight, colour, and circumfer-
ence of the soul in its confusion, its variety, its imperfection—this art belonged to one man only: to Montaigne.
As the centuries go by, there is always a crowd before
that picture, gazing into its depths, seeing their own
faces reflected in it, seeing more the longer they look,
never being able to say quite what it is that they see.
New editions testify to the perennial fascination. Here

is the Navarre Society in England reprinting in five fine
volumes* Cotton's translation; while in France the firm
of Louis Conard is issuing the complete works of Montaigne with the various readings in an edition to which
Dr. Armaingaud has devoted a long lifetime of research.

To tell the truth about oneself, to discover oneself
near at hand, is not easy.

We hear of but two or three of the ancients who have beaten
this road [said Montaigne]. No one since has followed the
track; 'tis a rugged road, more so than it seems, to follow a
pace so rambling and uncertain, as that of the soul; to penetrate the dark profundities of its intricate internal windings;
to choose and lay hold of so many little nimble motions; 'tis
a new and extraordinary undertaking, and that withdraws us
from the common and most recommended employments of the
world.

There is, in the first place, the difficulty of expression.
We all indulge in the strange, pleasant process called
thinking, but when it comes to saying, even to some one
opposite, what we think, then how little we are able to
convey! The phantom is through the mind and out of
the window before we can lay salt on its tail, or slowly
sinking and returning to the profound darkness which
it has lit up momentarily with a wandering light. Face,
voice, and accent eke out our words and impress their
feebleness with character in speech. But the pen is a rigid
instrument; it can say very little; it has all kinds of habits
and ceremonies of its own. It is dictatorial too: it is always making ordinary men into prophets, and changing
the natural stumbling trip of human speech into the solemn and stately march of pens. It is for this reason that
Montaigne stands out from the legions of the dead with
such irrepressible vivacity. We can never doubt for an
instant that his book was himself. He refused to teach;
he refused to preach; he kept on saying that he was

* *Essays of Montaigne*, translated by Charles Cotton, five
volumes.

just like other people. All his effort was to write himself
down, to communicate, to tell the truth, and that is a
"rugged road, more than it seems."

For beyond the difficulty of communicating oneself,
there is the supreme difficulty of being oneself. This
soul, or life within us, by no means agrees with the life
outside us. If one has the courage to ask her what she
thinks, she is always saying the very opposite to what
other people say. Other people, for instance, long ago
made up their minds that old invalidish gentlemen ought
to stay at home and edify the rest of us by the spectacle
of their connubial fidelity. The soul of Montaigne said,
on the contrary, that it is in old age that one ought
to travel, and marriage, which, rightly, is very seldom
founded on love, is apt to become, towards the end of
life, a formal tie better broken up. Again with politics,
statesmen are always praising the greatness of Empire,
and preaching the moral duty of civilising the savage.
But look at the Spanish in Mexico, cried Montaigne in
a burst of rage. "So many cities levelled with the ground,
so many nations exterminated . . . and the richest and
most beautiful part of the world turned upside down
for the traffic of pearl and pepper! Mechanic victories!"
And then when the peasants came and told him that they
had found a man dying of wounds and deserted him
for fear lest justice might incriminate them, Montaigne
asked:

What could I have said to these people? 'Tis certain that
this office of humanity would have brought them into trouble.
. . . There is nothing so much, nor so grossly, nor so ordi-
narily faulty as the laws.

Here the soul, getting restive, is lashing out at the
more palpable forms of Montaigne's great bugbears,
convention and ceremony. But watch her as she broods
over the fire in the inner room of that tower which,
though detached from the main building, has so wide a
view over the estate. Really she is the strangest creature

in the world, far from heroic, variable as a weathercock,
"bashful, insolent; chaste, lustful; prating, silent; laborious, delicate; ingenious, heavy; melancholic, pleasant;
lying, true; knowing, ignorant; liberal, covetous, and
prodigal"—in short, so complex, so indefinite, corresponding so little to the version which does duty for her
in public, that a man might spend his life merely in trying to run her to earth. The pleasure of the pursuit more
than rewards one for any damage that it may inflict upon
one's worldly prospects. The man who is aware of himself is henceforward independent; and he is never bored,
and life is only too short, and he is steeped through and
through with a profound yet temperate happiness. He
alone lives, while other people, slaves of ceremony, let
life slip past them in a kind of dream. Once conform,
once do what other people do because they do it, and a
lethargy steals over all the finer nerves and faculties of
the soul. She becomes all outer show and inward empti-
ness; dull, callous, and indifferent.

Surely then, if we ask this great master of the art of
life to tell us his secret, he will advise us to withdraw to
the inner room of our tower and there turn the pages
of books, pursue fancy after fancy as they chase each
other up the chimney, and leave the government of the
world to others. Retirement and contemplation—these
must be the main elements of his prescription. But no;
Montaigne is by no means explicit. It is impossible to
extract a plain answer from that subtle, half smiling, half
melancholy man, with the heavy-lidded eyes and the
dreamy, quizzical expression. The truth is that life in the
country, with one's books and vegetables and flowers, is
often extremely dull. He could never see that his own
green peas were so much better than other people's.
Paris was the place he loved best in the whole world—
"*jusques à ses verrues et à ses taches.*" As for reading,
he could seldom read any book for more than an hour
at a time, and his memory was so bad that he forgot
what was in his mind as he walked from one room to

another. Book learning is nothing to be proud of, and as for the achievements of science, what do they amount to? He had always mixed with clever men, and his father had a positive veneration for them, but he had observed that, though they have their fine moments, their rhapsodies, their visions, the cleverest tremble on the verge of folly. Observe yourself: one moment you are exalted; the next a broken glass puts your nerves on edge. All extremes are dangerous. It is best to keep in the middle of the road, in the common ruts, however muddy. In writing choose the common words; avoid rhapsody and eloquence—yet, it is true, poetry is delicious; the best prose is that which is most full of poetry.

It appears, then, that we are to aim at a democratic simplicity. We may enjoy our room in the tower, with the painted walls and the commodious bookcases, but down in the garden there is a man digging who buried his father this morning, and it is he and his like who live the real life and speak the real language. There is certainly an element of truth in that. Things are said very finely at the lower end of the table. There are perhaps more of the qualities that matter among the ignorant than among the learned. But again, what a vile thing the rabble is! "the mother of ignorance, injustice, and inconstancy. Is it reasonable that the life of a wise man should depend upon the judgment of fools?" Their minds are weak, soft and without power of resistance. They must be told what it is expedient for them to know. It is not for them to face facts as they are. The truth can only be known by the well-born soul—"*l'âme bien née.*" Who, then, are these well-born souls, whom we would imitate, if only Montaigne would enlighten us more precisely?

But no. "*Je n'enseigne poinct; je raconte.*" After all, how could he explain other people's souls when he could say nothing "entirely simply and solidly, without confusion or mixture, in one word," about his own, when indeed it became daily more and more in the dark to him? One quality or principle there is perhaps—that one must not lay down rules. The souls whom one would wish to resemble, like Etienne de La Boétie, for example, are always the supplest. "*C'est estre, mais ce n'est pas vivre, que de se tenir attaché et obligé par necessité a un seul train.*" The laws are mere conventions, utterly unable to keep touch with the vast variety and turmoil of human impulses; habits and customs are a convenience devised for the support of timid natures who dare not allow their souls free play. But we, who have a private life and hold it infinitely the dearest of our possessions, suspect nothing so much as an attitude. Directly we begin to protest, to attitudinise, to lay down laws, we perish. We are living for others, not for ourselves. We must respect those who sacrifice themselves in the public service, load them with honours, and pity them for allowing, as they must, the inevitable compromise; but for ourselves let us fly fame, honour, and all offices that put us under an obligation to others. Let us simmer over our incalculable cauldron, our enthralling confusion, our hotch-potch of impulses, our perpetual miracle—for the soul throws up wonders every second. Movement and change are the essence of our being; rigidity is death; conformity is death: let us say what comes into our heads, repeat ourselves, contradict ourselves, fling out the wildest nonsense, and follow the most fantastic fancies without caring what the world does or thinks or says. For nothing matters except life; and, of course, order.

This freedom, then, which is the essence of our being, has to be controlled. But it is difficult to see what power we are to invoke to help us, since every restraint of private opinion or public law has been derided, and Montaigne never ceases to pour scorn upon the misery, the weakness, the vanity of human nature. Perhaps, then, it will be well to turn to religion to guide us? "Perhaps" is one of his favourite expressions; "perhaps" and "I think" and all those words which qualify the rash assumptions of human ignorance. Such words help one to muffle up opinions which it would be highly impolitic to speak outright. For one does not say everything; there are some things which at present it is advisable only to hint. One writes for a very few people, who understand. Certainly, seek the Divine guidance by all means, but meanwhile there is, for those who live a private life, another monitor, an invisible censor within, *"un patron au dedans,"* whose blame is much more to be dreaded than any other because he knows the truth; nor is there anything sweeter than the chime of his approval. This is the judge to whom we must submit; this is the censor who will help us to achieve that order which is the grace of a well-born soul. For *"C'est une vie exquise, celle qui se maintient en ordre jusques en son prive."* But he will act by his own light; by some internal balance will achieve that precarious and ever changing poise which, while it controls, in nò way impedes the soul's freedom to explore and experiment. Without other guide, and without precedent, undoubtedly it is far more difficult to live well the private life than the public. It is an art which each must learn separately, though there are, perhaps, two or three men, like Homer, Alexander the Great, and Epaminondas among the ancients, and Etienne de La Boétie among the moderns, whose example may help us. But it is an art; and the very material in which it works is variable and complex and infinitely mysterious— human nature. To human nature we must keep close. ". . . *il faut vivre entre les vivants."* We must dread any eccentricity or refinement which cuts us off from our fellow-beings. Blessed are those who chat easily with their neighbours about their sport or their buildings or their quarrels, and honestly enjoy the talk of carpenters and gardeners. To communicate is our chief business; society and friendship our chief delights; and reading, not to acquire knowledge, not to earn a living, but to extend our intercourse beyond our own time and province. Such wonders there are in the world; halcyons and undiscovered lands, men with dogs' heads and eyes in their chests, and laws and customs, it may well be, far superior

to our own. Possibly we are asleep in this world; possibly
there is some other which is apparent to beings with a
sense which we now lack.

Here then, in spite of all contradictions and of all
qualifications, is something definite. These essays are an
attempt to communicate a soul. On this point at least
he is explicit. It is not fame that he wants; it is not that
men shall quote him in years to come; he is setting up
no statue in the market-place; he wishes only to communicate his soul. Communication is health; communication is truth; communication is happiness. To share is our
duty; to go down boldly and bring to light those hidden
thoughts which are the most diseased; to conceal nothing; to pretend nothing; if we are ignorant to say so; if
we love our friends to let them know it.

> . . . *car, comme je scay par une trop certaine expérience,
> il n'est aucune si douce consolation en la perte de nos amis que
> celle que nous aporte la science de n'avoir rien oublié a leur
> dire et d'avoir eu avec eux une parfaite et entière communica-
> tion.*

There are people who, when they travel, wrap themselves up "*se défendans de la contagion d'un air incogn-
eu*" in silence and suspicion. When they dine they must
have the same food they get at home. Every sight and
custom is bad unless it resembles those of their own village. They travel only to return. That is entirely the
wrong way to set about it. We should start without any
fixed idea where we are going to spend the night, or
when we propose to come back; the journey is everything. Most necessary of all, but rarest good fortune, we
should try to find before we start some man of our own
sort who will go with us and to whom we can say the
first thing that comes into our heads. For pleasure has no
relish unless we share it. As for the risks—that we may
catch cold or get a headache—it is always worth while
to risk a little illness for the sake of pleasure. "*Le plaisir
est des principales espèces du profit.*" Besides if we do

what we like, we always do what is good for us. Doctors and wise men may object, but let us leave doctors and wise men to their own dismal philosophy. For ourselves, who are ordinary men and women, let us return thanks to Nature for her bounty by using every one of the senses she has given us; vary our state as much as possible; turn now this side, now that, to the warmth, and relish to the full before the sun goes down the kisses of youth and the echoes of a beautiful voice singing Catullus. Every season is likeable, and wet days and fine, red wine and white, company and solitude. Even sleep, that deplorable curtailment of the joy of life, can be full of dreams; and the most common actions—a walk, a talk, solitude in one's own orchard—can be enhanced and lit up by the association of the mind. Beauty is everywhere, and beauty is only two fingers' breadth from goodness. So, in the name of health and sanity, let us not dwell on the end of the journey. Let death come upon us planting our cabbages, or on horseback, or let us steal away to some cottage and there let strangers close our eyes, for a servant sobbing or the touch of a hand would break us down. Best of all, let death find us at our usual occupations, among girls and good fellows who make no protests, no lamentations; let him find us "*parmy les jeux, les festins, faceties, entretiens communs et populaires, et la musique, et des vers amoureux.*" But enough of death; it is life that matters.

It is life that emerges more and more clearly as these essays reach not their end, but their suspension in full career. It is life that becomes more and more absorbing as death draws near, one's self, one's soul, every fact of existence: that one wears silk stockings summer and winter; puts water in one's wine; has one's hair cut after dinner; must have glass to drink from; has never worn spectacles; has a loud voice; carries a switch in one's hand; bites one's tongue; fidgets with one's feet; is apt to scratch one's ears; likes meat to be high; rubs one's teeth with a napkin (thank God, they are good!); must have curtains to one's bed; and, what is rather curious, began by liking radishes, then disliked them, and now likes them again. No fact is too little to let it slip through one's fingers and besides the interest of facts themselves, there is the strange power we have of changing facts by the force of the imagination. Observe how the soul is always casting her own lights and shadows; makes the substantial hollow and the frail substantial; fills broad daylight with dreams; is as much excited by phantoms as by reality; and in the moment of death sports with a trifle. Observe, too, her duplicity, her complexity. She hears of a friend's loss and sympathises, and yet has a bitter-sweet malicious pleasure in the sorrows of others. She believes; at the same time she does not believe. Observe her extraordinary susceptibility to impressions, especially in youth. A rich man steals because his father kept him short of money as a boy. This wall one builds not for oneself, but because one's father loved building. In short the soul is all laced about with nerves and sympathies which affect her every action, and yet, even now in 1580, no one has any clear knowledge—such cowards we are, such lovers of the smooth conventional ways— how she works or what she is except that of all things she is the most mysterious, and one's self the greatest monster and miracle in the world. ". . . *plus je me hante et connois, plus ma difformité m'estonne, moins je m'entens en moy*." Observe, observe perpetually, and, so long as ink and paper exist, "*sans cesse et sans travail*" Montaigne will write.

But there remains one final question which, if we could make him look up from his enthralling occupation, we should like to put to this great master of the art of life. In these extraordinary volumes of short and broken, long and learned, logical and contradictory statements, we have heard the very pulse and rhythm of the soul, beating day after day, year after year through a veil which, as time goes on, fines itself almost to transparency. Here is some one who succeeded in the hazardous enterprise of living; who served his country and lived retired; was landlord, husband, father; entertained kings, loved women, and mused for hours alone over old books. By means of perpetual experiment and observation of the subtlest he achieved at last a miraculous adjustment of all these wayward parts that constitute the human soul. He laid hold of the beauty of the world with all his fingers. He achieved happiness. If he had had to live again, he said, he would have lived the same life over. But, as we watch with absorbed interest the enthralling spectacle of a soul living openly beneath our eyes, the question frames itself, Is pleasure the end of all? Whence this overwhelming interest in the nature of the soul? Why this overmastering desire to communicate with others? Is the beauty of this world enough, or is there, elsewhere, some explanation of the mystery? To this what answer can there be? There is none. There is only one more question: *"Que scais-je?"*

The Duchess of Newcastle†

"... All I desire is fame," wrote Margaret Cavendish, Duchess of Newcastle. And while she lived her wish was granted. Garish in her dress, eccentric in her habits, chaste in her conduct, coarse in her speech, she succeeded during her lifetime in drawing upon herself the ridicule of the great and the applause of the learned. But the last echoes of that clamour have now all died away; she lives only in the few splendid phrases that Lamb scattered upon her tomb; her poems, her plays, her philosophies, her orations, her discourses—all those folios and quartos in which, she protested, her real life was shrined—moulder in the gloom of public libraries, or are decanted into tiny thimbles which hold six drops of their profusion. Even the curious student, inspired by the words of Lamb, quails before the mass of her mausoleum, peers in, looks about him, and hurries out again, shutting the door.

But that hasty glance has shown him the outlines of a memorable figure. Born (it is conjectured) in 1624, Margaret was the youngest child of a Thomas Lucas, who died when she was an infant, and her upbringing was due

† *The Life of William Cavendish, Duke of Newcastle, Etc.*, edited by C. H. Firth; *Poems and Fancies*, by the Duchess of Newcastle; *The World's Olio*; *Orations of divers Sorts Accommodated to Divers Places*; *Female Orations*; *Plays*; *Philosophical Letters*, etc., etc.

to her mother, a lady of remarkable character, of majestic grandeur and beauty "beyond the ruin of time." "She was very skilful in leases, and setting of lands and court keeping, ordering of stewards, and the like affairs." The wealth which thus accrued she spent, not on marriage portions, but on generous and delightful pleasures, "out of an opinion that if she bred us with needy necessity it might chance to create in us sharking qualities." Her eight sons and daughters were never beaten, but reasoned with, finely and gayly dressed, and allowed no conversation with servants, not because they are servants but because servants "are for the most part ill-bred as well as meanly born." The daughters were taught the usual accomplishments "rather for formality than for benefit," it being their mother's opinion that character, happiness, and honesty were of greater value to a woman than fiddling and singing, or "the prating of several languages."

Already Margaret was eager to take advantage of such indulgence to gratify certain tastes. Already she liked reading better than needlework, dressing and "inventing fashions" better than reading, and writing best of all. Sixteen paper books of no title, written in straggling letters, for the impetuosity of her thought always outdid the pace of her fingers, testify to the use she made of her mother's liberality. The happiness of their home life had other results as well. They were a devoted family. Long after they were married, Margaret noted, these handsome brothers and sisters, with their well-proportioned bodies, their clear complexions, brown hair, sound teeth, "tunable voices," and plain way of speaking, kept themselves "in a flock together." The presence of strangers silenced them. But when they were alone, whether they walked in Spring Gardens or Hyde Park, or had music, or supped in barges upon the water, their tongues were loosed and they made "very merry amongst themselves, . . . judging, condemning, approving, commending, as they thought good."

The happy family life had its effect upon Margaret's character. As a child, she would walk for hours alone, musing and contemplating and reasoning with herself of "everything her senses did present." She took no pleasure in activity of any kind. Toys did not amuse her, and she could neither learn foreign languages nor dress as other people did. Her great pleasure was to invent dresses for herself, which nobody else was to copy, "for," she remarks, "I always took delight in a singularity, even in accoutrements of habits."

Such a training, at once so cloistered and so free, should have bred a lettered old maid, glad of her seclusion, and the writer perhaps of some volume of letters or translations from the classics, which we should still quote as proof of the cultivation of our ancestresses. But there was a wild streak in Margaret, a love of finery and extravagance and fame, which was for ever upsetting the orderly arrangements of nature. When she heard that the Queen, since the outbreak of the Civil War, had fewer maids-of-honour than usual, she had "a great desire" to become one of them. Her mother let her go against the judgement of the rest of the family, who, knowing that she had never left home and had scarcely been beyond their sight, justly thought that she might behave at Court to her disadvantage. "Which indeed I did," Margaret confessed; "for I was so bashful when I was out of my mother's, brothers', and sisters' sight that . . . I durst neither look up with my eyes, nor speak, nor be any way sociable, insomuch as I was thought a natural fool." The courtiers laughed at her; and she retaliated in the obvious way. People were censorious; men were jealous of brains in a woman; women suspected intellect in their own sex; and what other lady, she might justly ask, pondered as she walked on the nature of matter and whether snails have teeth? But the laughter galled her, and she begged her mother to let her come home. This being refused, wisely as the event turned out, she stayed on for two years (1643-45), finally going with the Queen

to Paris, and there, among the exiles who came to pay
their respects to the Court, was the Marquis of Newcastle. To the general amazement, the princely nobleman, who had led the King's forces to disaster with
indomitable courage but little skill, fell in love with the
shy, silent, strangely dressed maid-of-honour. It was not
"amorous love, but honest, honourable love," according
to Margaret. She was no brilliant match; she had gained
a reputation for prudery and eccentricity. What, then,
could have made so great a nobleman fall at her feet?
The onlookers were full of derision, disparagement, and
slander. "I fear," Margaret wrote to the Marquis, "others
foresee we shall be unfortunate, though we see it not
ourselves, or else there would not be such pains to untie
the knot of our affections." Again, "Saint Germains is a
place of much slander, and thinks I send too often to
you." "Pray consider," she warned him, "that I have enemies." But the match was evidently perfect. The Duke,
with his love of poetry and music and play-writing, his
interest in philosophy, his belief "that nobody knew or
could know the cause of anything," his romantic and
generous temperament, was naturally drawn to a woman
who wrote poetry herself, was also a philosopher of the
same way of thinking, and lavished upon him not only
the admiration of a fellow-artist, but the gratitude of a
sensitive creature who had been shielded and succoured
by his extraordinary magnanimity. "He did approve,"
she wrote, "of those bashful fears which many condemned, . . . and though I did dread marriage and
shunned men's company as much as I could, yet I . . .
had not the power to refuse him." She kept him company during the long years of exile; she entered with
sympathy, if not with understanding, into the conduct
and acquirements of those horses which he trained to
such perfection that the Spaniards crossed themselves
and cried "Miraculo!" as they witnessed their corvets,
voltoes, and pirouettes; she believed that the horses even
made a "trampling action" for joy when he came into

the stables; she pleaded his cause in England during the
Protectorate; and, when the Restoration made it possible for them to return to England, they lived together
in the depths of the country in the greatest seclusion
and perfect contentment, scribbling plays, poems, philosophies, greeting each other's works with raptures of
delight, and confabulating doubtless upon such marvels
of the natural world as chance threw their way. They
were laughed at by their contemporaries; Horace Walpole sneered at them. But there can be no doubt that
they were perfectly happy.

For now Margaret could apply herself uninterruptedly
to her writing. She could devise fashions for herself
and her servants. She could scribble more and more furi-
ously with fingers that became less and less able to form
legible letters. She could even achieve the miracle of
getting her plays acted in London and her philosophies
humbly perused by men of learning. There they stand,
in the British Museum, volume after volume, swarming
with a diffused, uneasy, contorted vitality. Order, continuity, the logical development of her argument are all
unknown to her. No fears impede her. She has the irresponsibility of a child and the arrogance of a Duchess.
The wildest fancies come to her, and she canters away
on their backs. We seem to hear her, as the thoughts boil
and bubble, calling to John, who sat with a pen in his
hand next door, to come quick, "John, John, I conceive!"
And down it goes—whatever it may be; sense or nonsense; some thought on women's education—"Women
live like Bats or Owls, labour like Beasts, and die like
Worms, . . . the best bred women are those whose
minds are civilest"; some speculation that had struck her
perhaps walking that afternoon alone—why "hogs have
the measles," why "dogs that rejoice swing their tails,"
or what the stars are made of, or what this chrysalis is
that her maid has brought her, and she keeps warm in
a corner of her room. On and on, from subject to subject she flies, never stopping to correct, "for there is

more pleasure in making than in mending," talking aloud to herself of all those matters that filled her brain to her perpetual diversion—of wars, and boarding-schools, and cutting down trees, of grammar and morals, of monsters and the British, whether opium in small quantities is good for lunatics, why it is that musicians are mad. Looking upwards, she speculates still more ambitiously upon the nature of the moon, and if the stars are blazing jellies; looking downwards she wonders if the fishes know that the sea is salt; opines that our heads are full of fairies, "dear to God as we are"; muses whether there are not other worlds than ours, and reflects that the next ship may bring us word of a new one. In short, "we are in utter darkness." Meanwhile, what a rapture is thought!

As the vast books appeared from the stately retreat at Welbeck the usual censors made the usual objections, and had to be answered, despised, or argued with, as her mood varied, in the preface to every work. They said, among other things, that her books were not her own, because she used learned terms, and "wrote of many matters outside her ken." She flew to her husband for help, and he answered, characteristically, that the Duchess "had never conversed with any professed scholar in learning except her brother and myself." The Duke's scholarship, moreover, was of a peculiar nature. "I have lived in the great world a great while, and have thought of what has been brought to me by the senses, more than was put into me by learned discourse; for I do not love to be led by the nose, by authority, and old authors; *ipse dixit* will not serve my turn." And then she takes up the pen and proceeds, with the importunity and indiscretion of a child, to assure the world that her ignorance is of the finest quality imaginable. She has only seen Des Cartes and Hobbes, not questioned them; she did indeed ask Mr. Hobbes to dinner, but he could not come; she often does not listen to a word that is said to her; she does not know any French, though she lived abroad for five years; she has only read the old philosophers in Mr.

Stanley's account of them; of Des Cartes she has read but half of his work on Passion; and of Hobbes only "the little book called *De Cive*," all of which is infinitely to the credit of her native wit, so abundant that outside succour pained it, so honest that it would not accept help from others. It was from the plain of complete ignorance, the untilled field of her own consciousness, that she proposed to erect a philosophic system that was to oust all others. The results were not altogether happy. Under the pressure of such vast structures, her natural gift, the fresh and delicate fancy which had led her in her first volume to write charmingly of Queen Mab and fairyland, was crushed out of existence.

> The palace of the Queen wherein she dwells,
> Its fabric's built all of hodmandod shells;
> The hangings of a Rainbow made that's thin,
> Shew wondrous fine, when one first enters in;
> The chambers made of Amber that is clear,
> Do give a fine sweet smell, if fire be near;
> Her bed a cherry stone, is carved throughout,
> And with a butterfly's wing hung about;
> Her sheets are of the skin of Dove's eyes made
> Where on a violet bud her pillow's laid.

So she could write when she was young. But her fairies, if they survived at all, grew up into hippopotami. Too generously her prayer was granted:

> Give me the free and noble style,
> Which seems uncurb'd, though it be wild.

She became capable of involutions, and contortions and conceits of which the following is among the shortest, but not the most terrific:

> The human head may be likened to a town:
> The mouth when full, begun
> Is market day, when empty, market's done;
> The city conduct, where the water flows,
> Is with two spouts, the nostrils and the nose.

She similised, energetically, incongruously, eternally; the sea became a meadow, the sailors shepherds, the mast a maypole. The fly was the bird of summer, trees were senators, houses ships, and even the fairies, whom she loved better than any earthly thing, except the Duke, are changed into blunt atoms and sharp atoms, and take part in some of those horrible manoeuvres in which she delighted to marshal the universe. Truly, "my Lady Sanspareille hath a strange spreading wit." Worse still, without an atom of dramatic power, she turned to playwriting. It was a simple process. The unwieldy thoughts which turned and tumbled within her were christened Sir Golden Riches, Moll Meanbred, Sir Puppy Dogman, and the rest, and sent revolving in tedious debate upon the parts of the soul, or whether virtue is better than riches, round a wise and learned lady who answered their questions and corrected their fallacies at considerable length in tones which we seem to have heard before.

Sometimes, however, the Duchess walked abroad. She would issue out in her own proper person, dressed in a thousand gems and furbelows, to visit the houses of the neighbouring gentry. Her pen made instant report of these excursions. She recorded how Lady C. R. "did beat her husband in a public assembly"; Sir F. O. "I am sorry to hear hath undervalued himself so much below his birth and wealth as to marry his kitchen-maid"; "Miss P. I. has become a sanctified soul, a spiritual sister, she has left curling her hair, black patches are become abominable to her, laced shoes and Galoshoes are steps to pride—she asked me what posture I thought was the best to be used in prayer." Her answer was probably unacceptable. "I shall not rashly go there again," she says of one such "gossip-making." She was not, we may hazard, a welcome guest or an altogether hospitable hostess. She had a way of "bragging of myself" which frightened visitors so that they left, nor was she sorry to see them go. Indeed, Welbeck was the best place for her, and her

own company the most congenial, with the amiable Duke
wandering in and out, with his plays and his speculations,
always ready to answer a question or refute a slander.
Perhaps it was this solitude that led her, chaste as she was
in conduct, to use language which in time to come much
perturbed Sir Egerton Brydges. She used, he complained,
"expressions and images of extraordinary coarseness as
flowing from a female of high rank brought up in
courts." He forgot that this particular female had long
ceased to frequent the Court; she consorted chiefly with
fairies; and her friends were among the dead. Naturally,
then, her language was coarse. Nevertheless, though her
philosophies are futile, and her plays intolerable, and her
verses mainly dull, the vast bulk of the Duchess is leav-
ened by a vein of authentic fire. One cannot help following the lure of her erratic and lovable personality as it
meanders and twinkles through page after page. There
is something noble and Quixotic and high-spirited, as
well as crack-brained and bird-witted, about her. Her
simplicity is so open; her intelligence so active; her sympathy with fairies and animals so true and tender. She
has the freakishness of an elf, the irresponsibility of some
non-human creature, its heartlessness, and its charm. And
although "they," those terrible critics who had sneered
and jeered at her ever since, as a shy girl, she had not
dared look her tormentors in the face at Court, continued to mock, few of her critics, after all, had the wit to
trouble about the nature of the universe, or cared a
straw for the sufferings of the hunted hare, or longed,
as she did, to talk to some one "of Shakespeare's fools."
Now, at any rate, the laugh is not all on their side.

But laugh they did. When the rumour spread that the
crazy Duchess was coming up from Welbeck to pay her
respects at Court, people crowded the streets to look at
her, and the curiosity of Mr. Pepys twice brought him
to wait in the Park to see her pass. But the pressure of
the crowd about her coach was too great. He could only
catch a glimpse of her in her silver coach with her foot-

men all in velvet, a velvet cap on her head, and her hair about her ears. He could only see for a moment between the white curtains the face of "a very comely woman," and on she drove through the crowd of staring Cockneys, all pressing to catch a glimpse of that romantic lady, who stands in the picture at Welbeck, with large melancholy eyes, and something fastidious and fantastic in her bearing, touching a table with the tips of long pointed fingers in the calm assurance of immortal fame.

*

Rambling Round Evelyn

*

Should you wish to make sure that your birthday will be celebrated three hundred years hence, your best course is undoubtedly to keep a diary. Only first be certain that you have the courage to lock your genius in a private book and the humour to gloat over a fame that will be yours only in the grave. For the good diarist writes either for himself alone or for a posterity so distant that it can safely hear every secret and justly weigh every motive. For such an audience there is need neither of affectation nor of restraint. Sincerity is what they ask, detail, volume; skill with the pen comes in conveniently, but brilliance is not necessary; genius is a hindrance even; and should you know your business and do it manfully, posterity will let you off mixing with great men, reporting famous affairs, or having lain with the first ladies in the land.

The diary, for whose sake we are remembering the three hundredth anniversary of the birth of John Evelyn,* is a case in point. It is sometimes composed like a memoir, sometimes jotted down like a calendar; but he never used its pages to reveal the secrets of his heart, and all that he wrote might have been read aloud in the evening with a calm conscience to his children. If we wonder, then, why we still trouble to read what we must

* Written in 1920.

consider the uninspired work of a good man we have to
confess, first that diaries are always diaries, books, that
is, that we read in convalescence, on horseback, in the
grip of death; second, that this reading, about which so
many fine things have been said, is for the most part mere
dreaming and idling; lying in a chair with a book; watching the butterflies on the dahlias; a profitless occupation
which no critic has taken the trouble to investigate, and
on whose behalf only the moralist can find a good word
to say. For he will allow it to be an innocent employ-
ment; and happiness, he will add, though derived from
trivial sources, has probably done more to prevent
human beings from changing their religions and killing
their kings than either philosophy or the pulpit.

It may be well, indeed, before reading much further
in Evelyn's book, to decide where it is that our modern
view of happiness differs from his. Ignorance, surely, ignorance is at the bottom of it; his ignorance, and our
comparative erudition. No one can read the story of
Evelyn's foreign travels without envying in the first
place his simplicity of mind, in the second his activity.
To take a simple example of the difference between us
—that butterfly will sit motionless on the dahlia while the
gardener trundles his barrow past it, but let him flick the
wings with the shadow of a rake, and off it flies, up it
goes, instantly on the alert. So, we may reflect, a butterfly sees but does not hear; and here no doubt we are
much on a par with Evelyn. But as for going into the
house to fetch a knife and with that knife dissecting a
Red Admiral's head, as Evelyn would have done, no sane
person in the twentieth century would entertain such a
project for a second. Individually we may know as little
as Evelyn, but collectively we know so much that there
is little incentive to venture on private discoveries. We
seek the encyclopaedia, not the scissors; and know in
two minutes not only more than was known to Evelyn
in his lifetime, but that the mass of knowledge is so vast
that it is scarcely worth while to possess a single crumb.

Ignorant, yet justly confident that with his own hands
he might advance not merely his private knowledge but
the knowledge of mankind, Evelyn dabbled in all the arts
and sciences, ran about the Continent for ten years,
gazed with unflagging gusto upon hairy women and ra-
tional dogs, and drew inferences and framed speculations
which are now only to be matched by listening to the
talk of old women round the village pump. The moon,
they say, is so much larger than usual this autumn that
no mushrooms will grow, and the carpenter's wife will
be brought to bed of twins. So Evelyn, Fellow of the
Royal Society, a gentleman of the highest culture and
intelligence, carefully noted all comets and portents, and
thought it a sinister omen when a whale came up the
Thames. In 1658, too, a whale had been seen. "That year
died Cromwell." Nature, it seems, was determined to
stimulate the devotion of her seventeenth-century ad-
mirers by displays of violence and eccentricity from
which she now refrains. There were storms, floods, and
droughts; the Thames frozen hard; comets flaring in the
sky. If a cat so much as kittened in Evelyn's bed the kit-
ten was inevitably gifted with eight legs, six ears, two
bodies, and two tails.

But to return to happiness. It sometimes appears that
if there is an insoluble difference between our ancestors
and ourselves it is that we draw our happiness from different sources. We rate the same things at different values. Something of this we may ascribe to their ignorance
and our knowledge. But are we to suppose that ignorance alters the nerves and the affections? Are we to
believe that it would have been an intolerable penance
for us to live familiarly with the Elizabethans? Should
we have found it necessary to leave the room because of
Shakespeare's habits, and to have refused Queen Elizabeth's invitation to dinner? Perhaps so. For Evelyn was a
sober man of unusual refinement, and yet he pressed into
a torture chamber as we crowd to see the lions fed.

. . . they first bound his wrists with a strong rope or small cable, and one end of it to an iron ring made fast to the wall about four feet from the floor, and then his feet with another cable, fastened about five feet farther than his utmost length to another ring on the floor of the room. Thus suspended, and yet lying but aslant, they slid a horse of wood under the rope which bound his feet, which so exceedingly stiffened it, as severed the fellow's joints in miserable sort, drawing him out at length in an extraordinary manner, he having only a pair of linen drawers upon his naked body . . .

And so on. Evelyn watched this to the end, and then remarked that "the spectacle was so uncomfortable that I was not able to stay the sight of another," as we might say that the lions growl so loud and the sight of raw meat is so unpleasant that we will now visit the penguins. Allowing for his discomfort, there is enough discrepancy between his view of pain and ours to make us wonder whether we see any fact with the same eyes, marry any woman from the same motives, or judge any conduct by the same standards. To sit passive when muscles tore and bones cracked, not to flinch when the wooden horse was raised higher and the executioner fetched a horn and poured two buckets of water down the man's throat, to suffer this iniquity on a suspicion of robbery which the man denied—all this seems to put Evelyn in one of those cages where we still mentally seclude the riff-raff of Whitechapel. Only it is obvious that we have somehow got it wrong. If we could maintain that our susceptibility to suffering and love of justice were proof that all our humane instincts were as highly developed as these, then we could say that the world improves, and we with it. But let us get on with the diary.

In 1652, when it seemed that things had settled down unhappily enough, "all being entirely in the rebels' hands," Evelyn returned to England with his wife, his Tables of Veins and Arteries, his Venetian glass and the rest of his curiosities, to lead the life of a country gentleman of strong Royalist sympathies at Deptford. What with going to church and going to town, settling his accounts and planting his garden—"I planted the orchard at Sayes Court; new moon, wind west"—his time was spent much as ours is. But there was one difference which it is difficult to illustrate by a single quotation, because the evidence is scattered all about in little insignificant phrases. The general effect of them is that he used his eyes. The visible world was always close to him. The visible world has receded so far from us that to hear all this talk of buildings and gardens, statues and carving, as if the look of things assailed one out of doors as well as in, and were not confined to a few small canvases hung upon the wall, seems strange. No doubt there are a thousand excuses for us; but hitherto we have been finding excuses for him. Wherever there was a picture to be seen by Julio Romano, Polydore, Guido, Raphael, or Tintoretto, a finely-built house, a prospect, or a garden nobly designed, Evelyn stopped his coach to look at it, and opened his diary to record his opinion. On August 27 Evelyn, with Dr. Wren and others, was in St. Paul's surveying "the general decay of that ancient and venerable church"; held with Dr. Wren another judgement from the rest; and had a mind to build it with "a noble cupola, a form of church building not as yet known in England but of wonderful grace," in which Dr. Wren concurred. Six days later the Fire of London altered their plans. It was Evelyn again who, walking by himself, chanced to look in at the window of "a poor solitary thatched house in a field in our parish," there saw a young man carving at a crucifix, was overcome with an enthusiasm which does him the utmost credit, and carried Grinling Gibbons and his carving to Court.

Indeed, it is all very well to be scrupulous about the sufferings of worms and sensitive to the dues of servant girls, but how pleasant also if, with shut eyes, one could call up street after street of beautiful houses. A flower is red; the apples rosy-gilt in the afternoon sun; a picture

has charm, especially as it displays the character of a
grandfather and dignifies a family descended from such
a scowl; but these are scattered fragments—little relics
of beauty in a world that has grown indescribably drab.
To our charge of cruelty Evelyn might well reply by
pointing to Bayswater and the purlieus of Clapham; and
if he should assert that nothing now has character or
conviction, that no farmer in England sleeps with an
open coffin at his bedside to remind him of death, we
could not retort effectually offhand. True, we like the
country. Evelyn never looked at the sky.

But to return. After the Restoration Evelyn emerged
in full possession of a variety of accomplishments which
in our time of specialists seems remarkable enough. He
was employed on public business; he was Secretary to
the Royal Society; he wrote plays and poems; he was
the first authority upon trees and gardens in England;
he submitted a design for the rebuilding of London; he
went into the question of smoke and its abatement—the
lime trees in St. James's Park being, it is said, the result
of his cogitations; he was commissioned to write a history of the Dutch war—in short, he completely outdid
the Squire of "The Princess," whom in many respects he
anticipated—

> A lord of fat prize oxen and of sheep,
> A raiser of huge melons and of pine,
> A patron of some thirty charities,
> A pamphleteer on guano and on grain,
> A quarter sessions chairman abler none.

All that he was, and shared with Sir Walter another
characteristic which Tennyson does not mention. He
was, we cannot help suspecting, something of a bore, a
little censorious, a little patronising, a little too sure of
his own merits, and a little obtuse to those of other people. Or what is the quality, or absence of quality, that
checks our sympathies partly, perhaps, it is due to some
inconsistency which it would be harsh to call by so

strong a name as hypocrisy. Though he deplored the vices of his age he could never keep away from the centre of them. "The luxurious dallying and profaneness" of the Court, the sight of "Mrs. Nelly" looking over her garden wall and holding "very familiar discourse" with King Charles on the green walk below, caused him acute disgust; yet he could never decide to break with the Court and retire to "my poor but quiet villa," which was of course the apple of his eye and one of the show-places in England. Then, though he loved his daughter Mary, his grief at her death did not prevent him from counting the number of empty coaches drawn by six horses apiece that attended her funeral. His women friends combined virtue with beauty to such an extent that we can hardly credit them with wit into the bargain. Poor Mrs. Godolphin at least, whom he celebrated in a sincere and touching biography, "loved to be at funerals" and chose habitually "the dryest and leanest morsels of meat," which may be the habits of an angel but do not present her friendship with Evelyn in an alluring light. But it is Pepys who sums up our case against Evelyn; Pepys who said of him after a long morning's entertainment: "In fine a most excellent person he is and must be allowed a little for a little conceitedness; but he may well be so, being a man so much above others." The words exactly hit the mark, "A most excellent person he was"; but a little conceited.

Pepys it is who prompts us to another reflection, inevitable, unnecessary, perhaps unkind. Evelyn was no genius. His writing is opaque rather than transparent; we see no depths through it, nor any very secret movements of mind or heart. He can neither make us hate a regicide nor love Mrs. Godolphin beyond reason. But he writes a diary; and he writes it supremely well. Even as we drowse, somehow or other the bygone gentleman sets up, through three centuries, a perceptible tingle of communication, so that without laying stress on anything in particular, stopping to dream, stopping to laugh, stopping merely to look, we are yet taking notice all the time. His garden for example—how delightful is his disparagement of it, and how acid his criticism of the gardens of others! Then, we may be sure, the hens at Sayes Court laid the very best eggs in England, and when the Tsar drove a wheelbarrow through his hedge what a catastrophe it was, and we can guess how Mrs. Evelyn dusted and polished, and how Evelyn himself grumbled, and how punctilious and efficient and trustworthy he was, how prone to give advice, how ready to read his own works aloud, and how affectionate, withal, lamenting bitterly but not effusively, for the man with the long-drawn sensitive face was never that, the death of the little prodigy Richard, and recording how "after evening prayers was my child buried near the rest of his brothers—my very dear children." He was not an artist; no phrases linger in the mind; no paragraphs build themselves up in memory; but as an artistic method this of going on with the day's story circumstantially, bringing in people who will never be mentioned again, leading up to crises which never take place, introducing Sir Thomas Browne but never letting him speak, has its fascination. All through his pages good men, bad men, celebrities, nonentities are coming into the room and going out again. The greater number we scarcely notice; the door shuts upon them and they disappear. But now and again the sight of a vanishing coat-tail suggests more than a whole figure sitting still in a full light. They have struck no attitude, arranged no mantle. Little they think that for three hundred years and more they will be looked at in the act of jumping a gate, or observing, like the old Marquis of Argyle, that the turtle doves in the aviary are owls. Our eyes wander from one to the other; our affections settle here or there—on hot-tempered Captain Wray, for instance, who was choleric, had a dog that killed a goat, was for shooting the goat's owner, was for shooting his horse when it fell down a precipice; on Mr. Saladine; on Mr. Saladine's beautiful daughter;

on Captain Wray lingering at Geneva to make love to Mr. Saladine's daughter; on Evelyn himself most of all, grown old, walking in his garden at Wooton, his sorrows smoothed out, his grandson doing him credit, the Latin quotations falling pat from his lips, his trees flourishing, and the butterflies flying and flaunting on his dahlias too

*

Defoe†

*

The fear which attacks the recorder of centenaries lest
he should find himself measuring a diminishing spectre
and forced to foretell its approaching dissolution is not
only absent in the case of *Robinson Crusoe* but the mere
thought of it is ridiculous. It may be true that *Robinson
Crusoe* is two hundred years of age upon the twenty-
fifth of April 1919, but far from raising the familiar
speculations as to whether people now read it and will
continue to read it, the effect of the bicentenary is to
make us marvel that *Robinson Crusoe*, the perennial and
immortal, should have been in existence so short a time
as that. The book resembles one of the anonymous pro-
ductions of the race itself rather than the effort of a
single mind; and as for celebrating its centenary we
should as soon think of celebrating the centenaries of
Stonehenge itself. Something of this we may attribute
to the fact that we have all had *Robinson Crusoe* read
aloud to us as children, and were thus much in the same
state of mind towards Defoe and his story that the Greeks
were in towards Homer. It never occurred to us that
there was such a person as Defoe, and to have been told
that *Robinson Crusoe* was the work of a man with a pen
in his hand would either have disturbed us unpleasantly
or meant nothing at all. The impressions of childhood are
those that last longest and cut deepest. It still seems that

† Written in 1919.

the name of Daniel Defoe has no right to appear upon
the title-page of *Robinson Crusoe*, and if we celebrate the
bi-centenary of the book we are making a slightly unnecessary allusion to the fact that, like Stonehenge, it
is still in existence.

The great fame of the book has done its author some
injustice; for while it has given him a kind of anonymous
glory it has obscured the fact that he was a writer of
other works which, it is safe to assert, were not read
aloud to us as children. Thus when the Editor of the
Christian World in the year 1870 appealed to "the boys
and girls of England" to erect a monument upon the
grave of Defoe, which a stroke of lightning had mutilated, the marble was inscribed to the memory of the
author of *Robinson Crusoe*. No mention was made of
Moll Flanders. Considering the topics which are dealt
with in that book, and in *Roxana, Captain Singleton,
Colonel Jack* and the rest, we need not be surprised,
though we may be indignant, at the omission. We may
agree with Mr. Wright, the biographer of Defoe, that
these "are not works for the drawing-room table." But
unless we consent to make that useful piece of furniture
the final arbiter of taste, we must deplore the fact that
their superficial coarseness, or the universal celebrity of
Robinson Crusoe, has led them to be far less widely
famed than they deserve. On any monument worthy of
the name of monument the names of *Moll Flanders* and
Roxana, at least, should be carved as deeply as the name
of Defoe. They stand among the few English novels
which we can call indisputably great. The occasion of
the bi-centenary of their more famous companion may
well lead us to consider in what their greatness, which
has so much in common with his, may be found to consist.

Defoe was an elderly man when he turned novelist,
many years the predecessor of Richardson and Fielding, and one of the first indeed to shape the novel and
launch it on its way. But it is unnecessary to labour the

fact of his precedence, except that he came to his novel-writing with certain conceptions about the art which he derived partly from being himself one of the first to practise it. The novel had to justify its existence by telling a true story and preaching a sound moral. "This supplying a story by invention is certainly a most scandalous crime," he wrote. "It is a sort of lying that makes a great hole in the heart, in which by degrees a habit of lying enters in." Either in the preface or in the text of each of his works, therefore, he takes pains to insist that he has not used his invention at all but has depended upon facts, and that his purpose has been the highly moral desire to convert the vicious or to warn the innocent. Happily these were principles that tallied very well with his natural disposition and endowments. Facts had been drilled into him by sixty years of varying fortunes before he turned his experience to account in fiction. "I have some time ago summed up the Scenes of my life in this distich," he wrote:

> No man has tasted differing fortunes more,
> And thirteen times I have been rich and poor.

He had spent eighteen months in Newgate and talked with thieves, pirates, highwaymen, and coiners before he wrote the history of Moll Flanders. But to have facts thrust upon you by dint of living and accident is one thing; to swallow them voraciously and retain the imprint of them indelibly, is another. It is not merely that Defoe knew the stress of poverty and had talked with the victims of it, but that the unsheltered life, exposed to circumstances and forced to shift for itself, appealed to him imaginatively as the right matter for his art. In the first pages of each of his great novels he reduces his hero or heroine to such a state of unfriended misery that their existence must be a continued struggle, and their survival at all the result of luck and their own exertions. Moll Flanders was born in Newgate of a criminal mother; Captain Singleton was stolen as a child and sold to the gipsies; Colonel Jack, though "born a gentleman, was put 'prentice to a pickpocket"; Roxana starts under better auspices, but, having married at fifteen, she sees her husband go bankrupt and is left with five children in "a condition the most deplorable that words can express."

Thus each of these boys and girls has the world to begin and the battle to fight for himself. The situation thus created was entirely to Defoe's liking. From her very birth or with half a year's respite at most, Moll Flanders, the most notable of them, is goaded by "that worst of devils, poverty," forced to earn her living as soon as she can sew, driven from place to place, making no demands upon her creator for the subtle domestic atmosphere which he was unable to supply, but drawing upon him for all he knew of strange people and customs. From the outset the burden of proving her right to exist is laid upon her. She has to depend entirely upon her own wits and judgement, and to deal with each emergency as it arises by a rule-of-thumb morality which she has forged in her own head. The briskness of the story is due partly to the fact that having transgressed the accepted laws at a very early age she has henceforth the freedom of the outcast. The one impossible event is that she should settle down in comfort and security. But from the first the peculiar genius of the author asserts itself, and avoids the obvious danger of the novel of adventure. He makes us understand that Moll Flanders was a woman on her own account and not only material for a succession of adventures. In proof of this she begins, as Roxana also begins, by falling passionately, if unfortunately, in love. That she must rouse herself and marry some one else and look very closely to her settlements and prospects is no slight upon her passion, but to be laid to the charge of her birth; and, like all Defoe's women, she is a person of robust understanding. Since she makes no scruple of telling lies when they serve her purpose, there is something undeniable about her truth when she speaks it. She has no time to waste upon the refinements of personal affection, one tear is dropped, one moment of despair allowed, and then "on with the story." She has a spirit that loves to breast the storm. She delights in the exercise of her own powers. When she discovers that the man she has married in Virginia is her own brother she is violently disgusted; she insists upon leaving him; but as soon as she sets foot in Bristol, "I took the diversion of going to Bath, for as I was still far from being old so my humour, which was always gay, continued so to an extreme." Heartless she is not, nor can any one charge her with levity; but life delights her, and a heroine who lives has us all in tow. Moreover, her ambition has that slight strain of imagination in it which puts it in the category of the noble passions. Shrewd and practical of necessity, she is yet haunted by a desire for romance and for the quality which to her perception makes a man a gentleman. "It was really a true gallant spirit he was of, and it was the more grievous to me. 'Tis something of relief even to be undone by a man of honour rather than by a scoundrel," she writes when she had misled a highwayman as to the extent of her fortune. It is in keeping with this temper that she should be proud of her final partner because he refuses to work when they reach the plantations but prefers hunting, and that she should take pleasure in buying him wigs and silver-hilted swords "to make him appear, as he really was, a very fine gentleman." Her very love of hot weather is in keeping, and the passion with which she kissed the ground that her son had trod on, and her noble tolerance of every kind of fault so long as it is not "complete baseness of spirit, imperious, cruel, and relentless when uppermost, abject and low-spirited when down." For the rest of the world she has nothing but good-will.

Since the list of the qualities and graces of this seasoned old sinner is by no means exhausted we can well understand how it was that Borrow's apple-woman on London Bridge called her "blessed Mary" and valued her book above all the apples on her stall; and that Borrow, taking the book deep into the booth, read till his eyes ached. But we dwell upon such signs of character only by way of proof that the creator of Moll Flanders was not, as he has been accused of being, a mere journalist and literal recorder of facts with no conception of the nature of psychology. It is true that his characters take shape and substance of their own accord, as if in despite of the author and not altogether to his liking. He never lingers or stresses any point of subtlety or pathos, but presses on imperturbably as if they came there without his knowledge. A touch of imagination, such as that when the Prince sits by his son's cradle and Roxana observes how "he loved to look at it when it was asleep," seems to mean much more to us than to him. After the curiously modern dissertation upon the need of communicating matters of importance to a second person lest, like the thief in Newgate, we should talk of it in our sleep, he apologises for his digression. He seems to have taken his characters so deeply into his mind that he lived them without exactly knowing how; and, like all unconscious artists, he leaves more gold in his work than his own generation was able to bring to the surface.

The interpretation that we put on his characters might therefore well have puzzled him. We find for ourselves meanings which he was careful to disguise even from himself. Thus it comes about that we admire Moll Flanders far more than we blame her. Nor can we believe that Defoe had made up his mind as to the precise degree of her guilt, or was unaware that in considering the lives of the abandoned he raised many deep questions and hinted, if he did not state, answers quite at variance with his professions of belief. From the evidence supplied by his essay upon the "Education of Women" we know that he had thought deeply and much in advance of his age upon the capacities of women, which he rated very high, and the injustice done to them, which he rated very harsh.

I have often thought of it as one of the most barbarous customs in the world, considering us as a civilised and a Christian country, that we deny the advantages of learning to women. We reproach the sex every day with folly and impertinence; which I am confident, had they the advantages of education equal to us, they would be guilty of less than ourselves.

The advocates of women's rights would hardly care, perhaps, to claim Moll Flanders and Roxana among their patron saints; and yet it is clear that Defoe not only intended them to speak some very modern doctrines upon the subject, but placed them in circumstances where their peculiar hardships are displayed in such a way as to elicit our sympathy. Courage, said Moll Flanders, was what women needed, and the power to "stand their ground"; and at once gave practical demonstration of the benefits that would result. Roxana, a lady of the same profession, argues more subtly against the slavery of marriage. She "had started a new thing in the world" the merchant told her; "it was a way of arguing contrary to the general practise." But Defoe is the last writer to be guilty of bald preaching. Roxana keeps our attention because she is blessedly unconscious that she is in any good sense an example to her sex and is thus at liberty to own that part of her argument is "of an elevated strain which was really not in my thoughts at first, at all." The knowledge of her own frailties and the honest questioning of her own motives, which that knowledge begets, have the happy result of keeping her fresh and human when the martyrs and pioneers of so many problem novels have shrunken and shrivelled to the pegs and props of their respective creeds.

But the claim of Defoe upon our admiration does not rest upon the fact that he can be shown to have anticipated some of the views of Meredith, or to have written scenes which (the odd suggestion occurs) might have been turned into plays by Ibsen. Whatever his ideas upon the position of women, they are an incidental result of his chief virtue, which is that he deals with the important and lasting side of things and not with the passing and trivial. He is often dull. He can imitate the matter-of-fact precision of a scientific traveller until we wonder that his pen could trace or his brain conceive what has not even the excuse of truth to soften its dryness. He leaves out the whole of vegetable nature, and a large part of human nature. All this we may admit, though we have to admit defects as grave in many writers whom we call great. But that does not impair the peculiar merit of what remains. Having at the outset limited his scope and confined his ambitions he achieves a truth of insight which is far rarer and more enduring than the truth of fact which he professed to make his aim. Moll Flanders and her friends recommended themselves to him not because they were, as we should say, "picturesque"; nor, as he affirmed, because they were examples of evil living by which the public might profit. It was their natural veracity, bred in them by a life of hardship, that excited his interest. For them there were no excuses; no kindly shelter obscured their motives. Poverty was their task-master. Defoe did not pronounce more than a judgement of the lips upon their failings. But their courage and resource and tenacity delighted him. He found their society full of good talk, and pleasant stories, and faith in each other, and morality of a home-made kind. Their fortunes had that infinite variety which he praised and relished and beheld with wonder in his own life. These men and women, above all, were free to talk openly of the passions and desires which have moved men and women since the beginning of time, and thus even now they keep their vitality undiminished. There is a dignity in everything that is looked at openly. Even the sordid subject of money, which plays so large a part in their histories, becomes not sordid but tragic when it stands not for ease and consequence but for honour, honesty and life itself. You may object that Defoe is humdrum, but never that he is engrossed with petty things.

He belongs, indeed, to the school of the great plain

writers, whose work is founded upon a knowledge of what is most persistent, though not most seductive, in human nature. The view of London from Hungerford Bridge, grey, serious, massive, and full of the subdued stir of traffic and business, prosaic if it were not for the masts of the ships and the towers and domes of the city, brings him to mind. The tattered girls with violets in their hands at the street corners, and the old weather-beaten women patiently displaying their matches and bootlaces beneath the shelter of arches, seem like characters from his books. He is of the school of Crabbe, and of Gissing, and not merely a fellow pupil in the same stern place of learning, but its founder and master.

Addison†

In July, 1843, Lord Macaulay pronounced the opinion that Joseph Addison had enriched our literature with compositions "that will live as long as the English language." But when Lord Macaulay pronounced an opinion it was not merely an opinion. Even now, at a distance of seventy-six years, the words seem to issue from the mouth of the chosen representative of the people. There is an authority about them, a sonority, a sense of responsibility, which put us in mind of a Prime Minister making a proclamation on behalf of a great empire rather than of a journalist writing about a deceased man of letters for a magazine. The article upon Addison is, indeed, one of the most vigorous of the famous essays. Florid, and at the same time extremely solid, the phrases seem to build up a monument, at once square and lavishly festooned with ornament, which should serve Addison for shelter so long as one stone of Westminster Abbey stands upon another. Yet, though we may have read and admired this particular essay times out of number (as we say when we have read anything three times over), it has never occurred to us, strangely enough, to believe that it is true. That is apt to happen to the admiring reader of Macaulay's essays. While delighting in their richness, force, and variety, and finding every judgement, however emphatic, proper in its place, it seldom occurs to us to connect

† Written in 1919.

these sweeping assertions and undeniable convictions with anything so minute as a human being. So it is with Addison. "If we wish," Macaulay writes, "to find anything more vivid than Addison's best portraits, we must go either to Shakespeare or to Cervantes." "We have not the least doubt that if Addison had written a novel on an extensive plan it would have been superior to any that we possess." His essays, again, "fully entitle him to the rank of a great poet"; and, to complete the edifice, we have Voltaire proclaimed "the prince of buffoons," and together with Swift forced to stoop so low that Addison takes rank above them both as a humorist.

Examined separately, such flourishes of ornament look grotesque enough, but in their place—such is the persuasive power of design—they are part of the decoration; they complete the monument. Whether Addison or another is interred within, it is a very fine tomb. But now that two centuries have passed since the real body of Addison was laid by night under the Abbey floor, we are, through no merit of our own, partially qualified to test the first of the flourishes on that fictitious tombstone to which, though it may be empty, we have done homage, in a formal kind of way, these sixty-seven years. The compositions of Addison will live as long as the English language. Since every moment brings proof that our mother tongue is more lusty and lively than sorts with complete sedateness or chastity, we need only concern ourselves with the vitality of Addison. Neither lusty nor lively is the adjective we should apply to the present condition of the *Tatler* and the *Spectator*. To take a rough test, it is possible to discover how many people in the course of a year borrow Addison's works from the public library, and a particular instance affords us the not very encouraging information that during nine years two people yearly take out the first volume of the *Spectator*. The second volume is less in request than the first. The inquiry is not a cheerful one. From certain marginal comments and pencil marks it seems that these rare dev-

otees seek out only the famous passages and, as their
habit is, score what we are bold enough to consider the
least admirable phrases. No; if Addison lives at all, it is
not in the public libraries. It is in libraries that are markedly private, secluded, shaded by lilac trees and brown
with folios, that he still draws his faint, regular breath.
If any man or woman is going to solace himself with a
page of Addison before the June sun is out of the sky
to-day, it is in some such pleasant retreat as this.

Yet all over England at intervals, perhaps wide ones,
we may be sure that there are people engaged in reading Addison, whatever the year or season. For Addison
is very well worth reading. The temptation to read Pope
on Addison, Macaulay on Addison, Thackeray on Addison, Johnson on Addison rather than Addison himself is
to be resisted, for you will find, if you study the *Tatler*
and the *Spectator*, glance at *Cato*, and run through the
remainder of the six moderate-sized volumes, that Addison is neither Pope's Addison nor anybody else's Addison, but a separate, independent individual still capable
of casting a clear-cut shape of himself upon the consciousness, turbulent and distracted as it is, of nineteen
hundred and nineteen. It is true that the fate of the lesser
shades is always a little precarious. They are so easily
obscured or distorted. It seems so often scarcely worth
while to go through the cherishing and humanising process which is necessary to get into touch with a writer of
the second class who may, after all, have little to give
us. The earth is crusted over them; their features are
obliterated, and perhaps it is not a head of the best period that we rub clean in the end, but only the chip of
an old pot. The chief difficulty with the lesser writers,
however, is not only the effort. It is that our standards
have changed. The things that they like are not the things
that we like; and as the charm of their writing depends
much more upon taste than upon conviction, a change
of manners is often quite enough to put us out of touch
altogether. That is one of the most troublesome barriers

between ourselves and Addison. He attached great importance to certain qualities. He had a very precise notion of what we are used to call "niceness" in man or woman. He was extremely fond of saying that men ought not to be atheists, and that women ought not to wear large petticoats. This directly inspires in us not so much a sense of distaste as a sense of difference. Dutifully, if at all, we strain our imaginations to conceive the kind of audience to whom these precepts were addressed. The *Tatler* was published in 1709; the *Spectator* a year or two later. What was the state of England at that particular moment? Why was Addison so anxious to insist upon the necessity of a decent and cheerful religious belief? Why did he so constantly, and in the main kindly, lay stress upon the foibles of women and their reform? Why was he so deeply impressed with the evils of party government? Any historian will explain; but it is always a misfortune to have to call in the services of any historian. A writer should give us direct certainty; explanations are so much water poured into the wine. As it is, we can only feel that these counsels are addressed to ladies in hoops and gentlemen in wigs—a vanished audience which has learnt its lesson and gone its way and the preacher with it. We can only smile and marvel and perhaps admire the clothes.

And that is not the way to read. To be thinking that dead people deserved these censures and admired this morality, judged the eloquence, which we find so frigid, sublime, the philosophy to us so superficial, profound, to take a collector's joy in such signs of antiquity, is to treat literature as if it were a broken jar of undeniable age but doubtful beauty, to be stood in a cabinet behind glass doors. The charm which still makes *Cato* very readable is much of this nature. When Syphax exclaims,

> So, where our wide Numidian wastes extend,
> Sudden, th' impetuous hurricanes descend,
> Wheel through the air, in circling eddies play,
> Tear up the sands, and sweep whole plains away,

> The helpless traveller, with wild surprise,
> Sees the dry desert all around him rise,
> And smother'd in the dusty whirlwind dies,

we cannot help imagining the thrill in the crowded theatre, the feathers nodding emphatically on the ladies' heads, the gentlemen leaning forward to tap their canes, and every one exclaiming to his neighbour how vastly fine it is and crying "Bravo!" But how can *we* be excited? And so with Bishop Hurd and his notes—his "finely observed," his "wonderfully exact, both in the sentiment and expression," his serene confidence that when "the present humour of idolising Shakespeare is over," the time will come when *Cato* is "supremely admired by all candid and judicious critics." This is all very amusing and productive of pleasant fancies, both as to the faded frippery of our ancestors' minds and the bold opulence of our own. But it is not the intercourse of equals, let alone that other kind of intercourse, which as it makes us contemporary with the author, persuades us that his object is our own. Occasionally in *Cato* one may pick up a few lines that are not obsolete; but for the most part the tragedy which Dr. Johnson thought "unquestionably the noblest production of Addison's genius" has become collector's literature.

Perhaps most readers approach the essays also with some suspicion as to the need of condescension in their minds. The question to be asked is whether Addison, attached as he was to certain standards of gentility, morality, and taste, has not become one of those people of exemplary character and charming urbanity who must never be talked to about anything more exciting than the weather. We have some slight suspicion that the *Spectator* and the *Tatler* are nothing but talk, couched in perfect English, about the number of fine days this year compared with the number of wet the year before. The difficulty of getting on to equal terms with him is shown by the little fable which he introduces into one of the

early numbers of the *Tatler*, of "a young gentleman,
of moderate understanding, but great vivacity, who . . .
had got a little smattering of knowledge, just enough to
make an atheist or a freethinker, but not a philosopher,
or a man of sense." This young gentleman visits his father in the country, and proceeds "to enlarge the narrowness of the country notions; in which he succeeded so
well, that he had seduced the butler by his table-talk,
and staggered his eldest sister. . . . 'Till one day, talking
of his setting dog . . . said 'he did not question but Tray
was as immortal as any one of the family'; and in the
heat of the argument told his father, that for his own
part, 'he expected to die like a dog.' Upon which, the old
man, starting up in a very great passion, cried out, 'Then,
sirrah, you shall live like one'; and taking his cane in his
hand, cudgelled him out of his system. This had so good
an effect upon him, that he took up from that day, fell to
reading good books, and is now a bencher in the Middle-
Temple." There is a good deal of Addison in that story:
his dislike of "dark and uncomfortable prospects"; his
respect for "principles which are the support, happiness,
and glory of all public societies, as well as private persons"; his solicitude for the butler; and his conviction
that to read good books and become a bencher in the
Middle Temple is the proper end for a very vivacious
young gentleman. This Mr. Addison married a countess,
"gave his little senate laws," and, sending for young Lord
Warwick, made that famous remark about seeing how a
Christian can die which has fallen upon such evil days
that our sympathies are with the foolish, and perhaps
fuddled, young peer rather than with the frigid gentleman, not too far gone for a last spasm of self-compla-
cency, upon the bed.

Let us rub off such incrustations, so far as they are due
to the corrosion of Pope's wit or the deposit of mid-
Victorian lachrymosity, and see what, for us in our time,
remains. In the first place, there remains the not despicable virtue, after two centuries of existence, of being

readable. Addison can fairly lay claim to that; and then, slipped in on the tide of the smooth, well-turned prose, are little eddies, diminutive waterfalls, agreeably diversifying the polished surface. We begin to take note of whims, fancies, peculiarities on the part of the essayist which light up the prim, impeccable countenance of the moralist and convince us that, however tightly he may have pursed his lips, his eyes are very bright and not so shallow after all. He is alert to his finger tips. Little muffs, silver garters, fringed gloves draw his attention; he observes with a keen, quick glance, not unkindly, and full rather of amusement than of censure. To be sure, the age was rich in follies. Here were coffee-houses packed with politicians talking of Kings and Emperors and letting their own small affairs go to ruin. Crowds applauded the Italian opera every night without understanding a word of it. Critics discoursed of the unities. Men gave a thousand pounds for a handful of tulip roots. As for women—or "the fair sex," as Addison liked to call them—their follies were past counting. He did his best to count them, with a loving particularity which roused the ill humour of Swift. But he did it very charmingly, with a natural relish for the task, as the following passage shows:

I consider woman as a beautiful romantic animal, that may be adorned with furs and feathers, pearls and diamonds, ores and silks. The lynx shall cast its skin at her feet to make her a tippet; the peacock, parrot, and swan, shall pay contributions to her muff; the sea shall be searched for shells, and the rocks for gems; and every part of nature furnish out its share towards the embellishment of a creature that is the most consummate work of it. All this I shall indulge them in; but as for the petticoat I have been speaking of, I neither can nor will allow it.

In all these matters Addison was on the side of sense and taste and civilisation. Of that little fraternity, often so obscure and yet so indispensable, who in every age keep themselves alive to the importance of art and letters and music, watching, discriminating, denouncing and delighting, Addison was one—distinguished and strangely contemporary with ourselves. It would have been, so one imagines, a great pleasure to take him a manuscript; a great enlightenment, as well as a great honour, to have his opinion. In spite of Pope, one fancies that his would have been criticism of the best order, open-minded and generous to novelty, and yet, in the final resort, unfaltering in its standards. The boldness which is a proof of vigour is shown by his defence of "Chevy Chase." He had so clear a notion of what he meant by the "very spirit and soul of fine writing" as to track it down in an old barbarous ballad or rediscover it in "that divine work" *Paradise Lost.* Moreover, far from being a connoisseur only of the still, settled beauties of the dead, he was aware of the present; a severe critic of its "Gothic taste," vigilant in protecting the rights and honours of the language, and all in favour of simplicity and quiet. Here we have the Addison of Will's and Button's, who, sitting late into the night and drinking more than was good for him, gradually overcame his taciturnity and began to talk. Then he "chained the attention of every one to him." "Addison's conversation," said Pope, "had something in it more charming than I have found in any other man." One can well believe it, for his essays at their best preserve the very cadence of easy yet exquisitely modulated conversation—the smile checked before it has broadened into laughter, the thought lightly turned from frivolity or abstraction, the ideas springing, bright, new, various, with the utmost spontaneity. He seems to speak what comes into his head, and is never at the trouble of raising his voice. But he has described himself in the character of the lute better than any one can do it for him.

The lute is a character directly opposite to the drum, that sounds very finely by itself, or in a very small concert. Its notes are exquisitely sweet, and very low, easily drowned in a multitude of instruments, and even lost among a few, unless you give a particular attention to it. A lute is seldom heard in a company of more than five, whereas a drum will show itself to advantage in an assembly of 500. The lutanists, therefore, are men of a fine genius, uncommon reflection, great affability, and esteemed chiefly by persons of a good taste, who are the only proper judges of so delightful and soft a melody.

Addison was a lutanist. No praise, indeed, could be less appropriate than Lord Macaulay's. To call Addison on the strength of his essays a great poet, or to prophesy that if he had written a novel on an extensive plan it would have been "superior to any that we possess," is to confuse him with the drums and trumpets; it is not merely to overpraise his merits, but to overlook them. Dr. Johnson superbly, and, as his manner is, once and for all has summed up the quality of Addison's poetic genius:

His poetry is first to be considered; of which it must be confessed that it has not often those felicities of diction which give lustre to sentiments, or that vigour of sentiment that animates diction; there is little of ardour, vehemence, or transport; there is very rarely the awfulness of grandeur, and not very often the splendour of elegance. He thinks justly; but he thinks faintly.

The Sir Roger de Coverley papers are those which have the most resemblance, on the surface, to a novel. But their merit consists in the fact that they do not adumbrate, or initiate, or anticipate anything; they exist, perfect, complete, entire in themselves. To read them as if they were a first hesitating experiment containing the seed of greatness to come is to miss the peculiar point of them. They are studies done from the outside by a quiet spectator. When read together they compose a portrait of the Squire and his circle all in characteristic positions —one with his rod, another with his hounds—but each can be detached from the rest without damage to the design or harm to himself. In a novel, where each chapter gains from the one before it or adds to the one that follows it, such separations would be intolerable. The speed, the intricacy, the design, would be mutilated.

These particular qualities are perhaps lacking, but nevertheless Addison's method has great advantages. Each of these essays is very highly finished. The characters are defined by a succession of extremely neat, clean strokes. Inevitably, where the sphere is so narrow—an essay is only three or four pages in length—there is not room for great depth or intricate subtlety. Here, from the *Spectator*, is a good example of the witty and decisive manner in which Addison strikes out a portrait to fill the little frame:

Sombrius is one of these sons of sorrow. He thinks himself obliged in duty to be sad and disconsolate. He looks on a sudden fit of laughter as a breach of his baptismal vow. An innocent jest startles him like blasphemy. Tell him of one who is advanced to a title of honour, he lifts up his hands and eyes; describe a public ceremony, he shakes his head; shew him a gay equipage, he blesses himself. All the little ornaments of life are pomps and vanities. Mirth is wanton, and wit profane. He is scandalized at youth for being lively, and at childhood for being playful. He sits at a christening, or at a marriage-feast, as at a funeral; sighs at the conclusion of a merry story, and grows devout when the rest of the company grow pleasant. After all Sombrius is a religious man, and would have behaved himself very properly, had he lived when Christianity was under a general persecution.

The novel is not a development from that model, for the good reason that no development along these lines is possible. Of its kind such a portrait is perfect; and when we find, scattered up and down the *Spectator* and the *Tatler*, numbers of such little masterpieces with fancies and anecdotes in the same style, some doubt as to the narrowness of such a sphere becomes inevitable. The form of the essay admits of its own particular perfection; and if anything is perfect the exact dimensions of its perfection become immaterial. One can scarcely settle whether, on the whole, one prefers a raindrop to the River Thames. When we have said all that we can say against them—that many are dull, others superficial, the allegories faded, the piety conventional, the morality trite—there still remains the fact that the essays of Addison are perfect essays. Always at the highest point of any art there comes a moment when everything seems in a conspiracy to help the artist, and his achievement becomes a natural felicity on his part of which he seems, to a later age, half-unconscious. So Addison, writing day after day, essay after essay, knew instinctively and exactly how to do it. Whether it was a high thing, or whether it was a low thing, whether an epic is more profound or a lyric more passionate, undoubtedly it is due to Addison that prose is now prosaic—the medium which makes it possible for people of ordinary intelligence to communicate their ideas to the world. Addison is the respectable ancestor of an innumerable progeny. Pick up the first weekly journal and the article upon the "Delights of Summer" or the "Approach of Age" will show his influence. But it will also show, unless the name of Mr. Max Beerbohm, our solitary essayist, is attached to it, that we have lost the art of writing essays. What with our views and our virtues, our passions and profundities, the shapely silver drop, that held the sky in it and so many bright little visions of human life, is now nothing but a hold-all knobbed with luggage packed in a hurry. Even so, the essayist will make an effort, perhaps without knowing it, to write like Addison.

In his temperate and reasonable way Addison more than once amused himself with speculations as to the fate of his writings. He had a just idea of their nature and value. "I have new-pointed all the batteries of ridicule," he wrote. Yet, because so many of his darts had been directed against ephemeral follies, "absurd fashions, ridiculous customs, and affected forms of speech," the time would come, in a hundred years, perhaps, when his essays, he thought, would be "like so many pieces of old plate, where the weight will be regarded, but the fashion lost." Two hundred years have passed; the plate is worn smooth; the pattern almost rubbed out; but the metal is pure silver.

*

The Lives of the Obscure

*

Five shillings, perhaps, will secure a life subscription to this faded, out-of-date, obsolete library, which with a little help from the rates, is chiefly subsidised from the shelves of clergymen's widows, and country gentlemen inheriting more books than their wives like to dust. In the middle of the wide airy room, with windows that look to the sea and let in the shouts of men crying pilchards for sale on the cobbled street below, a row of vases stands, in which specimens of the local flowers droop, each with its name inscribed beneath. The elderly, the marooned, the bored, drift from newspaper to newspaper, or sit holding their heads over back numbers of *The Illustrated London News* and the *Wesleyan Chronicle*. No one has spoken aloud here since the room was opened in 1854. The obscure sleep on the walls, slouching against each other as if they were too drowsy to stand upright. Their backs are flaking off; their titles often vanished. Why disturb their sleep? Why re-open those peaceful graves, the librarian seems to ask, peering over his spectacles, and resenting the duty, which indeed has become laborious, of retrieving from among those nameless tombstones Nos. 1763, 1080, and 606.

I

THE TAYLORS AND THE EDGEWORTHS

For one likes romantically to feel oneself a deliverer
advancing with lights across the waste of years to the
rescue of some stranded ghost—a Mrs. Pilkington, a Rev.
Henry Elman, a Mrs. Ann Gilbert—waiting, appealing,
forgotten, in the growing gloom. Possibly they hear one
coming. They shuffle, they preen, they bridle. Old secrets well up to their lips. The divine relief of communication will soon again be theirs. The dust shifts and
Mrs. Gilbert—but the contact with life is instantly salu-
tary. Whatever Mrs. Gilbert may be doing, she is not
thinking about us. Far from it. Colchester, about the year
1800, was for the young Taylors, as Kensington had been
for their mother, "a very Elysium." There were the
Strutts, the Hills, the Stapletons; there was poetry, philosophy, engraving. For the young Taylors were brought
up to work hard, and if, after a long day's toil upon their
father's pictures, they slipped round to dine with the
Strutts they had a right to their pleasure. Already they
had won prizes in Darton and Harvey's pocketbook. One
of the Strutts knew James Montgomery, and there was
talk, at those gay parties, with the Moorish decorations
and all the cats—for old Ben Strutt was a bit of a character: did not communicate; would not let his daughters
eat meat, so no wonder they died of consumption—there
was talk of printing a joint volume to be called *The
Associate Minstrels*, to which James, if not Robert himself, might contribute. The Stapletons were poetical, too.
Moira and Bithia would wander over the old town wall
at Balkerne Hill reading poetry by moonlight. Perhaps
there was a little too much poetry in Colchester in 1800.
Looking back in the middle of a prosperous and vigorous life, Ann had to lament many broken careers, much
unfulfilled promise. The Stapletons died young, perverted, miserable; Jacob, with his "dark, scorn-speaking

countenance," who had vowed that he would spend the
night looking for Ann's lost bracelet in the street, disappeared, "and I last heard of him vegetating among the
ruins of Rome—himself too much a ruin"; as for the
Hills, their fate was worst of all. To submit to public
baptism was flighty, but to marry Captain M.! Anybody
could have warned pretty Fanny Hill against Captain
M. Yet off she drove with him in his fine phaeton. For
years nothing more was heard of her. Then one night,
when the Taylors had moved to Ongar and old Mr. and
Mrs. Taylor were sitting over the fire, thinking how, as
it was nine o'clock, and the moon was full, they ought,
according to their promise, to look at it and think of
their absent children, there came a knock at the door.
Mrs. Taylor went down to open it. But who was this sad,
shabby-looking woman outside? "Oh, don't you remember the Strutts and the Stapletons, and how you warned
me against Captain M.?" cried Fanny Hill, for it was
Fanny Hill—poor Fanny Hill, all worn and sunk; poor
Fanny Hill, that used to be so sprightly. She was living in a lone house not far from the Taylors, forced to
drudge for her husband's mistress, for Captain M. had
wasted all her fortune, ruined all her life.

Ann married Mr. G., of course—of course. The words
toll persistently through these obscure volumes. For in
the vast world to which the memoir writers admit us
there is a solemn sense of something unescapable, of a
wave gathering beneath the frail flotilla and carrying it
on. One thinks of Colchester in 1800. Scribbling verses,
reading Montgomery—so they begin; the Hills, the Stapletons, the Strutts disperse and disappear as one knew
they would; but here, after long years, is Ann still scribbling, and at last here is the poet Montgomery himself
in her very house, and she begging him to consecrate
her child to poetry by just holding him in his arms, and
he refusing (for he is a bachelor), but taking her for a
walk, and they hear the thunder, and she thinks it the
artillery, and he says in a voice which she will never,

never forget: "Yes! The artillery of Heaven!" It is one
of the attractions of the unknown, their multitude, their
vastness; for, instead of keeping their identity separate,
as remarkable people do, they seem to merge into one
another, their very boards and title-pages and frontis-
pieces dissolving, and their innumerable pages melting
into continuous years so that we can lie back and look
up into the fine mist-like substance of countless lives, and
pass unhindered from century to century, from life to
life. Scenes detach themselves. We watch groups. Here
is young Mr. Elman talking to Miss Biffen at Brighton.
She has neither arms nor legs; a footman carries her
in and out. She teaches miniature painting to his sister.
Then he is in the stage coach on the road to Oxford with
Newman. Newman says nothing. Elman nevertheless reflects that he has known all the great men of his time.
And so back and so forwards, he paces eternally the
fields of Sussex until, grown to an extreme old age, there
he sits in his Rectory thinking of Newman, thinking
of Miss Biffen, and making—it is his great consolation—
string bags for missionaries. And then? Go on looking.
Nothing much happens. But the dim light is exquisitely
refreshing to the eyes. Let us watch little Miss Frend
trotting along the Strand with her father. They meet a
man with very bright eyes. "Mr. Blake," says Mr. Frend.
It is Mrs. Dyer who pours out tea for them in Clifford's
Inn. Mr. Charles Lamb has just left the room. Mrs.
Dyer says she married George because his washerwoman
cheated him so. What do you think George paid for his
shirts, she asks? Gently, beautifully, like the clouds of a
balmy evening, obscurity once more traverses the sky,
an obscurity which is not empty but thick with the
star dust of innumerable lives. And suddenly there is
a rift in it, and we see a wretched little packet-boat
pitching off the Irish coast in the middle of the nineteenth century. There is an unmistakable air of 1840
about the tarpaulins and the hairy monsters in sou'-
westers lurching and spitting over the sloping decks, yet

treating the solitary young woman who stands in shawl and poke bonnet gazing, gazing, not without kindness. No, no, no! She will not leave the deck. She will stand there till it is quite dark, thank you! "Her great love of the sea . . . drew this exemplary wife and mother every now and then irresistibly away from home. No one but her husband knew where she had gone, and her children learnt only later in life that on these occasions, when suddenly she disappeared for a few days, she was taking short sea voyages . . ." a crime which she expiated by months of work among the Midland poor. Then the craving would come upon her, would be confessed in private to her husband, and off she stole again—the mother of Sir George Newnes.

One would conclude that human beings were happy, endowed with such blindness to fate, so indefatigable an interest in their own activities, were it not for those sudden and astonishing apparitions staring in at us, all taut and pale in their determination never to be forgotten, men who have just missed fame, men who have passionately desired redress—men like Haydon, and Mark Pattison, and the Rev. Blanco White. And in the whole world there is probably but one person who looks up for a moment and tries to interpret the menacing face, the furious beckoning fist, before, in the multitude of human affairs, fragments of faces, echoes of voices, flying coattails, and bonnet strings disappearing down the shrubbery walks, one's attention is distracted for ever. What is that enormous wheel, for example, careering downhill in Berkshire in the eighteenth century? It runs faster and faster; suddenly a youth jumps out from within; next moment it leaps over the edge of a chalk pit and is dashed to smithereens. This is Edgeworth's doing—Richard Lovell Edgeworth, we mean, the portentous bore.

For that is the way he has come down to us in his two volumes of memoirs—Byron's bore, Day's friend, Maria's father, the man who almost invented the telegraph, and did, in fact, invent machines for cutting turnips, climb-

ing walls, contracting on narrow bridges and lifting their
wheels over obstacles—a man meritorious, industrious,
advanced, but still, as we investigate his memoirs, mainly
a bore. Nature endowed him with irrepressible energy.
The blood coursed through his veins at least twenty
times faster than the normal rate. His face was red,
round, vivacious. His brain raced. His tongue never
stopped talking. He had married four wives and had
nineteen children, including the novelist Maria. Moreover, he had known every one and done everything. His
energy burst open the most secret doors and penetrated
to the most private apartments. His wife's grandmother,
for instance, disappeared mysteriously every day. Edgeworth blundered in upon her and found her, with her
white locks flowing and her eyes streaming, in prayer
before a crucifix. She was a Roman Catholic then, but
why a penitent? He found out somehow that her husband had been killed in a duel, and she had married the
man who killed him. "The consolations of religion are
fully equal to its terrors," Dick Edgeworth reflected as
he stumbled out again. Then there was the beautiful
young woman in the castle among the forests of Dauph-
iny. Half paralysed, unable to speak above a whisper,
there she lay when Edgeworth broke in and found
her reading. Tapestries flapped on the castle walls; fifty
thousand bats—"odious animals whose stench is uncom-
monly noisome"—hung in clusters in the caves beneath.
None of the inhabitants understood a word she said. But
to the Englishman she talked for hour after hour about
books and politics and religion. He listened; no doubt
he talked. He sat dumbfounded. But what could one do
for her? Alas, one must leave her lying among the tusks,
and the old men, and the cross-bows, reading, reading,
reading. For Edgeworth was employed in turning the
Rhone from its course. He must get back to his job. One
reflection he would make. "I determined on steadily per-
severing in the cultivation of my understanding."

He was impervious to the romance of the situations

in which he found himself. Every experience served only to fortify his character. He reflected, he observed, he improved himself daily. You can improve, Mr. Edgeworth used to tell his children, every day of your life. "He used to say that with this power of improving they might in time be anything, and without it in time they would be nothing." Imperturbable, indefatigable, daily increasing in sturdy self-assurance, he has the gift of the egoist. He brings out, as he bustles and bangs on his way, the diffident, shrinking figures who would otherwise be drowned in darkness. The aged lady, whose private penance he disturbed, is only one of a series of figures who start up on either side of his progress, mute, astonished, showing us in a way that is even now unmistakable, their amazement at this well-meaning man who bursts in upon them at their studies and interrupts their prayers. We see him through their eyes; we see him as he does not dream of being seen. What a tyrant he was to his first wife! How intolerably she suffered! But she never utters a word. It is Dick Edgeworth who tells her story in complete ignorance that he is doing anything of the kind. "It was a singular trait of character in my wife," he observes, "who had never shown any uneasiness at my intimacy with Sir Francis Delaval, that she should take a strong dislike to Mr. Day. A more dangerous and seductive companion than the one, or a more moral and improving companion than the other, could not be found in England." It was, indeed, very singular.

For the first Mrs. Edgeworth was a penniless girl, the daughter of a ruined country gentleman, who sat over his fire picking cinders from the hearth and throwing them into the grate, while from time to time he ejaculated "Hein! Heing!" as yet another scheme for making his fortune came into his head. She had had no education. An itinerant writing-master had taught her to form a few words. When Dick Edgeworth was an undergraduate and rode over from Oxford she fell in love with him and married him in order to escape the poverty and the mystery and the dirt, and to have a husband and children like other women. But with what result? Gigantic wheels ran downhill with the bricklayer's son inside them. Sailing carriages took flight and almost wrecked four stage coaches. Machines did cut turnips, but not very efficiently. Her little boy was allowed to roam the country like a poor man's son, bare-legged, untaught. And Mr. Day, coming to breakfast and staying to dinner, argued incessantly about scientific principles and the laws of nature.

But here we encounter one of the pitfalls of this nocturnal rambling among forgotten worthies. It is so difficult to keep, as we must with highly authenticated people, strictly to the facts. It is so difficult to refrain from making scenes which, if the past could be recalled, might perhaps be found lacking in accuracy. With a character like Thomas Day, in particular, whose history surpasses the bounds of the credible, we find ourselves oozing amazement, like a sponge which has absorbed so much that it can retain no more but fairly drips. Certain scenes have the fascination which belongs rather to the abundance of fiction than to the sobriety of fact. For instance, we conjure up all the drama of poor Mrs. Edgeworth's daily life; her bewilderment, her loneliness, her despair, how she must have wondered whether any one really wanted machines to climb walls, and assured the gentlemen that turnips were better cut simply with a knife, and so blundered and floundered and been snubbed that she dreaded the almost daily arrival of the tall young man with his pompous, melancholy face, marked by the smallpox, his profusion of uncombed black hair, and his finical cleanliness of hands and person. He talked fast, fluently, incessantly, for hours at a time about philosophy and nature, and M. Rousseau. Yet it was her house; she had to see to his meals, and, though he ate as though he were half asleep, his appetite was enormous. But it was no use complaining to her husband. Edgeworth said, "She lamented about trifles." He went on to say: "The lamenting of a female with whom we live does not render home delightful." And then, with his obtuse open-mindedness, he asked her what she had to complain of? Did he ever leave her alone? In the five or six years of their married life he had slept from home not more than five or six times. Mr. Day could corroborate that. Mr. Day corroborated everything that Mr. Edgeworth said. He egged him on with his experiments. He told him to leave his son without education. He did not care a rap what the people of Henley said. In short, he was at the bottom of all the absurdities and extravagances which made Mrs. Edgeworth's life a burden to her.

Yet let us choose another scene—one of the last that poor Mrs. Edgeworth was to behold. She was returning from Lyons, and Mr. Day was her escort. A more singular figure, as he stood on the deck of the packet which took them to Dover, very tall, very upright, one finger in the breast of his coat, letting the wind blow his hair out, dressed absurdly, though in the height of fashion, wild, romantic, yet at the same time authoritative and pompous, could scarcely be imagined; and this strange creature, who loathed women, was in charge of a lady who was about to become a mother, had adopted two orphan girls, and had set himself to win the hand of Miss Elizabeth Sneyd by standing between boards for six hours daily in order to learn to dance. Now and again he pointed his toe with rigid precision; then, waking from the congenial dream into which the dark clouds, the flying waters, and the shadow of England upon the horizon had thrown him, he rapped out an order in the smart, affected tones of a man of the world. The sailors stared, but they obeyed. There was something sincere about him, something proudly indifferent to what you thought; yes, something comforting and humane, too, so that Mrs. Edgeworth for her part was determined never to laugh at him again. But men were strange; life was difficult, and with a sigh of bewilderment, perhaps of re-

lief, poor Mrs. Edgeworth landed at Dover, was brought
to bed of a daughter, and died.

Day meanwhile proceeded to Lichfield. Elizabeth
Sneyd, of course, refused him—gave a great cry, people
said; exclaimed that she had loved Day the blackguard,
but hated Day the gentleman, and rushed from the room.
And then, they said, a terrible thing happened. Mr. Day,
in his rage, bethought him of the orphan, Sabrina Syd-
ney, whom he had bred to be his wife; visited her at
Sutton Coldfield; flew into a passion at the sight of her;
fired a pistol at her skirts, poured melted sealing wax
over her arms, and boxed her ears. "No; I could never
have done that," Mr. Edgeworth used to say, when people described the scene. And whenever to the end of his
life he thought of Thomas Day he fell silent. So great,
so passionate, so inconsistent—his life had been a tragedy,
and in thinking of his friend, the best friend he had ever
had, Richard Edgeworth fell silent.

It is almost the only occasion upon which silence is
recorded of him. To muse, to repent, to contemplate
were foreign to his nature. His wife and friends and
children are silhouetted with extreme vividness upon a
broad disc of interminable chatter. Upon no other background could we realise so clearly the sharp fragment of
his first wife, or the shades and depths which make up
the character, at once humane and brutal, advanced and
hidebound of the inconsistent philosopher, Thomas Day.
But his power is not limited to people; landscapes,
groups, societies seem, even as he describes them, to split
off from him, to be projected away, so that we are able
to run just ahead of him and anticipate his coming. They
are brought out all the more vividly by the extreme incongruity which so often marks his comment and stamps
his presence; they live with a peculiar beauty, fantastic,
solemn, mysterious, in contrast with Edgeworth, who is
none of these things. In particular, he brings before us
a garden in Cheshire, the garden of a parsonage, an ancient but commodious parsonage.

One pushed through a white gate and found oneself in a grass court, small but well kept, with roses growing in the hedges and grapes hanging from the walls. But what, in the name of wonder, were those objects in the middle of the grass plot? Through the dusk of an autumn evening there shone out an enormous white globe. Round it at various distances were others of different sizes—the planets and their satellites, it seemed. But who could have placed them there, and why? The house was silent; the windows shut; nobody was stirring. Then, furtively peeping from behind a curtain, appeared for a second the face of an elderly man, handsome, dishevelled, distraught. It vanished.

In some mysterious way, human beings inflict their own vagaries upon nature. Moths and birds must have flitted more silently through the little garden; over everything must have brooded the same fantastic peace. Then, red-faced, garrulous, inquisitive, in burst Richard Lovell Edgeworth. He looked at the globes; he satisfied himself that they were of "accurate design and workmanlike construction." He knocked at the door. He knocked and knocked. No one came. At length, as his impatience was overcoming him, slowly the latch was undone, gradually the door was opened; a clergyman, neglected, unkempt, but still a gentleman, stood before him. Edgeworth named himself, and they retired to a parlour littered with books and papers and valuable furniture now fallen to decay. At last, unable to control his curiosity any longer, Edgeworth asked what were the globes in the garden? Instantly the clergyman displayed extreme agitation. It was his son who had made them, he exclaimed; a boy of genius, a boy of the greatest industry, and of virtue and acquirements far beyond his age. But he had died. His wife had died. Edgeworth tried to turn the conversation, but in vain. The poor man rushed on passionately, incoherently about his son, his genius, his death. "It struck me that his grief had injured his understanding," said Edgeworth, and he was becoming

more and more uncomfortable when the door opened
and a girl of fourteen or fifteen, entering with a tea-tray
in her hand, suddenly changed the course of his host's
conversation. Indeed, she was beautiful; dressed in white;
her nose a shade too prominent, perhaps—but no, her
proportions were exquisitely right. "She is a scholar and
an artist!" the clergyman exclaimed as she left the room.
But why did she leave the room? If she was his daughter
why did she not preside at the tea-table? Was she his
mistress? Who was she? And why was the house in this
state of litter and decay? Why was the front door
locked? Why was the clergyman apparently a prisoner,
and what was his secret story? Questions began to
crowd into Edgeworth's head as he sat drinking his tea;
but he could only shake his head and make one last reflection, "I feared that something was not right," as he
shut the white wicket gate behind him, and left alone for
ever in the untidy house among the planets and their
satellites, the mad clergyman and the lovely girl.

II
LAETITIA PILKINGTON

Let us bother the librarian once again. Let us ask him to
reach down, dust, and hand over to us that little brown
book over there, the Memoirs of Mrs. Pilkington, three
volumes bound in one, printed by Peter Hoey in Dublin,
MDCCLXXVI. The deepest obscurity shades her retreat; the dust lies heavy on her tomb—one board is
loose, that is to say, and nobody has read her since early
in the last century when a reader, presumably a lady,
whether disgusted by her obscenity or stricken by the
hand of death, left off in the middle and marked her
place with a faded list of goods and groceries. If ever a
woman wanted a champion, it is obviously Laetitia Pilkington. Who then was she?

Can you imagine a very extraordinary cross between
Moll Flanders and Lady Ritchie, between a rolling and

rollicking woman of the town and a lady of breeding
and refinement? Laetitia Pilkington (1712-1759) was
something of the sort—shady, shifty, adventurous, and
yet, like Thackeray's daughter, like Miss Mitford, like
Madame de Sévigné and Jane Austen and Maria Edgeworth, so imbued with the old traditions of her sex that
she wrote, as ladies talk, to give pleasure. Throughout
her *Memoirs*, we can never forget that it is her wish to
entertain, her unhappy fate to sob. Dabbing her eyes and
controlling her anguish, she begs us to forgive an odious
breach of manners which only the suffering of a lifetime,
the intolerable persecutions of Mr. P——n, the malig-
nant, she must say the h——h, spite of Lady C——t can
excuse. For who should know better than the Earl of
Killmallock's great-granddaughter that it is the part of a
lady to hide her sufferings? Thus Laetitia is in the great
tradition of English women of letters. It is her duty to
entertain; it is her instinct to conceal. Still, though her
room near the Royal Exchange is threadbare, and the
table is spread with old play-bills instead of a cloth, and
the butter is served in a shoe, and Mr. Worsdale has used
the teapot to fetch small beer that very morning, still
she presides, still she entertains. Her language is a trifle
coarse, perhaps. But who taught her English? The great
Doctor Swift.

In all her wanderings, which were many and in her
failings, which were great, she looked back to those early
Irish days when Swift had pinched her into propriety of
speech. He had beaten her for fumbling at a drawer: he
had daubed her cheeks with burnt cork to try her temper; he had bade her pull off her shoes and stockings and
stand against the wainscot and let him measure her. At
first she had refused; then she had yielded. "Why," said
the Dean, "I suspected you had either broken Stockings
or foul toes, and in either case should have delighted to
expose you." Three feet two inches was all she measured,
he declared, though, as Laetitia complained, the weight
of Swift's hand on her head had made her shrink to half

her size. But she was foolish to complain. Probably she owed her intimacy to that very fact—she was only three feet two. Swift had lived a lifetime among the giants; now there was a charm in dwarfs. He took the little creature into his library. " 'Well,' said he, 'I have brought you here to show you all the Money I got when I was in the Ministry, but don't steal any of it.' 'I won't, indeed, Sir,' said I; so he opened a Cabinet, and showed me a whole parcel of empty drawers. 'Bless me,' says he, 'the Money is flown.' " There was a charm in her surprise; there was a charm in her humility. He could beat her and bully her, make her shout when he was deaf, force her husband to drink the lees of the wine, pay their cab fares, stuff guineas into a piece of gingerbread, and relent surprisingly, as if there were something grimly pleasing to him in the thought of so foolish a midget setting up to have a life and a mind of her own. For with Swift she was herself; it was the effect of his genius. She had to pull off her stockings if he told her to. So, though his satire terrified her, and she found it highly unpleasant to dine at the Deanery and see him watching, in the great glass which hung before him for that purpose, the butler stealing beer at the sideboard, she knew that it was a privilege to walk with him in his garden; to hear him talk of Mr. Pope and quote Hudibras; and then be hustled back in the rain to save coach hire, and then to sit chatting in the parlour with Mrs. Brent, the housekeeper, about the Dean's oddity and charity, and how the sixpence he saved on the coach he gave to the lame old man who sold gingerbread at the corner, while the Dean dashed up the front stairs and down the back so violently that she was afraid he would fall and hurt himself.

But memories of great men are no infallible specific. They fall upon the race of life like beams from a lighthouse. They flash, they shock, they reveal, they vanish. To remember Swift was of little avail to Laetitia when the troubles of life came thick about her. Mr. Pilkington left her for Widow W—rr—n. Her father—her dear father—died. The sheriff's officers insulted her. She was deserted in an empty house with two children to provide for. The tea chest was secured, the garden gate locked, and the bills left unpaid. And still she was young and attractive and gay, with an inordinate passion for scribbling verses and an incredible hunger for reading books. It was this that was her undoing. The book was fascinating and the hour late. The gentleman would not lend it, but would stay till she had finished. They sat in her bedroom. It was highly indiscreet, she owned. Suddenly twelve watchmen broke through the kitchen window, and Mr. Pilkington appeared with a cambric handkerchief tied about his neck. Swords were drawn and heads broken. As for her excuse, how could one expect Mr. Pilkington and the twelve watchmen to believe that? Only reading! Only sitting up late to finish a new book! Mr. Pilkington and the watchmen interpreted the situation as such men would. But lovers of learning, she is persuaded, will understand her passion and deplore its consequences.

And now what was she to do? Reading had played her false, but still she could write. Ever since she could form her letters, indeed, she had written, with incredible speed and considerable grace, odes, addresses, apostrophes to Miss Hoadley, to the Recorder of Dublin, to Dr. Delville's place in the country. "Hail, happy Delville, blissful seat!" "Is there a man whose fixed and steady gaze——" —the verses flowed without the slightest difficulty on the slightest occasion. Now, therefore, crossing to England, she set up, as her advertisement had it, to write letters upon any subject, except the law, for twelve pence ready money, and no trust given. She lodged opposite White's Chocolate House, and there, in the evening, as she watered her flowers on the leads, the noble gentlemen in the window across the road drank her health, sent her over a bottle of burgundy; and later she heard old Colonel —— crying, "Poke after me, my

lord, poke after me," as he shepherded the D—— of
M—lb—gh up her dark stairs. That lovely gentleman,
who honoured his title by wearing it, kissed her, compli-
mented her, opened his pocket-book, and left her with a
banknote for fifty pounds upon Sir Francis Child. Such
tributes stimulated her pen to astonishing outbursts of
impromptu gratitude. If, on the other hand, a gentleman refused to buy or a lady hinted impropriety, this
same flowery pen writhed and twisted in agonies of hate
and vituperation. "Had I said that your F——r died Blas-
pheming the Almighty," one of her accusations begins,
but the end is unprintable. Great ladies were accused of
every depravity, and the clergy, unless their taste in poetry was above reproach, suffered an incessant castiga-
tion. Mr. Pilkington, she never forgot, was a clergyman.

Slowly but surely the Earl of Killmallock's great-
granddaughter descended in the social scale. From St.
James's Street and its noble benefactors she migrated to
Green Street to lodge with Lord Stair's *valet de chambre*
and his wife, who washed for persons of distinction. She,
who had dallied with dukes, was glad for company's sake
to take a hand at quadrille with footmen and laundresses
and Grub Street writers, who, as they drank porter,
sipped green tea, and smoked tobacco, told stories of the
utmost scurrility about their masters and mistresses. The
spiciness of their conversation made amends for the vulgarity of their manners. From them Laetitia picked up
those anecdotes of the great which sprinkled her pages
with dashes and served her purpose when subscribers
failed and landladies grew insolent. Indeed, it was a hard
life—to trudge to Chelsea in the snow wearing nothing
but a chintz gown and be put off with a beggarly half-
crown by Sir Hans Sloane; next to tramp to Ormond
Street and extract two guineas from the odious Dr.
Meade, which, in her glee, she tossed in the air and lost
in a crack of the floor; to be insulted by footmen; to
sit down to a dish of boiling water because her land-
lady must not guess that a pinch of tea was beyond her

means. Twice on moonlight nights, with the lime trees in flower, she wandered in St. James's Park and contemplated suicide in Rosamond's Pond. Once, musing among the tombs in Westminster Abbey, the door was locked on her, and she had to spend the night in the pulpit wrapped in a carpet from the Communion Table to protect herself from the assaults of rats. "I long to listen to the young-ey'd cherubims!" she exclaimed. But a very different fate was in store for her. In spite of Mr. Colley Cibber, and Mr. Richardson, who supplied her first with gilt-edged notepaper and then with baby linen, those harpies, her landladies, after drinking her ale, devouring her lobsters, and failing often for years at a time to comb their hair, succeeded in driving Swift's friend, and the Earl's great-granddaughter, to be imprisoned with common debtors in the Marshalsea.

Bitterly she cursed her husband who had made her a lady of adventure instead of what nature intended, "a harmless household dove." More and more wildly she ransacked her brains for anecdotes, memories, scandals, views about the bottomless nature of the sea, the inflammable character of the earth—anything that would fill a page and earn her a guinea. She remembered that she had eaten plovers' eggs with Swift. "Here, Hussey," said he, "is a Plover's egg. King William used to give crowns apiece for them. . . ." Swift never laughed, she remembered. He used to suck in his cheeks instead of laughing. And what else could she remember? A great many gentlemen, a great many landladies; how the window was thrown up when her father died, and her sister came downstairs with the sugar-basin, laughing. All had been bitterness and struggle, except that she had loved Shakespeare, known Swift, and kept through all the shifts and shades of an adventurous career a gay spirit, something of a lady's breeding, and the gallantry which, at the end of her short life, led her to crack her joke and enjoy her duck with death at her heart and duns at her pillow.

III

MISS ORMEROD*

The trees stood massively in all their summer foliage spotted and grouped upon a meadow which sloped gently down from the big white house. There were unmistakable signs of the year 1835 both in the trees and in the sky, for modern trees are not nearly so voluminous as these ones, and the sky of those days had a kind of pale diffusion in its texture which was different from the more concentrated tone of the skies we know.

Mr. George Ormerod stepped from the drawing-room window of Sedbury House, Gloucestershire, wearing a tall furry hat and white trousers strapped under his instep; he was closely, though deferentially, followed by a lady wearing a yellow-spotted dress over a crinoline, and behind her, singly and arm in arm, came nine children in nankeen jackets and long white drawers. They were going to see the water let out of a pond.

The youngest child, Eleanor, a little girl with a pale face, rather elongated features, and black hair, was left by herself in the drawing-room, a large sallow apartment with pillars, two chandeliers, for some reason enclosed in holland bags, and several octagonal tables some of inlaid wood and others of greenish malachite. At one of these little Eleanor Ormerod was seated in a high chair.

"Now, Eleanor," said her mother, as the party assembled for the expedition to the pond, "here are some pretty beetles. Don't touch the glass. Don't get down from your chair, and when we come back little George will tell you all about it."

So saying, Mrs. Ormerod placed a tumbler of water containing about half a dozen great water grubs in the middle of the malachite table, at a safe distance from the child, and followed her husband down the slope of old-

---

* Founded upon the Life of Eleanor Ormerod, by Robert Wallace Murray. 1904.

fashioned turf towards a cluster of extremely old-fashioned sheep; opening, directly she stepped on to the terrace, a tiny parasol of bottle green silk with a bottle green fringe, though the sky was like nothing so much as a flock bed covered with a counterpane of white dimity.

The plump pale grubs gyrated slowly round and round in the tumbler. So simple an entertainment must surely soon have ceased to satisfy. Surely Eleanor would shake the tumbler, upset the grubs, and scramble down from her chair. Why, even a grown person can hardly watch those grubs crawling down the glass wall, then floating to the surface, without a sense of boredom not untinged with disgust. But the child sat perfectly still. Was it her custom, then, to be entertained by the gyrations of grubs? Her eyes were reflective, even critical. But they shone with increasing excitement. She beat one hand upon the edge of the table. What was the reason? One of the grubs had ceased to float: he lay at the bottom; the rest, descending, proceeded to tear him to pieces.

"And how has little Eleanor enjoyed herself?" asked Mr. Ormerod, in rather a deep voice, stepping into the room and with a slight air of heat and of fatigue upon his face.

"Papa," said Eleanor, almost interrupting her father in her eagerness to impart her observation, "I saw one of the grubs fall down and the rest came and ate him!"

"Nonsense, Eleanor," said Mr. Ormerod. "You are not telling the truth." He looked severely at the tumbler in which the beetles were still gyrating as before.

"Papa, it was true!"

"Eleanor, little girls are not allowed to contradict their fathers," said Mrs. Ormerod, coming in through the window, and closing her green parasol with a snap.

"Let this be a lesson," Mr. Ormerod began, signing to the other children to approach, when the door opened, and the servant announced,

"Captain Fenton."

Captain Fenton "was at times thought to be tedious in his recurrence to the charge of the Scots Greys in which he had served at the battle of Waterloo."

But what is this crowd gathered round the door of the George Hotel in Chepstow? A faint cheer rises from the bottom of the hill. Up comes the mail coach, horses steaming, panels mud-splashed. "Make way! Make way!" cries the ostler and the vehicle dashes into the courtyard, pulls up sharp before the door. Down jumps the coachman, the horses are led off, and a fine team of spanking greys is harnessed with incredible speed in their stead. Upon all this—coachman, horses, coach, and passengers—the crowd looked with gaping admiration every Wednesday evening all through the year. But to-day, the twelfth of March, 1852, as the coachman settled his rug, and stretched his hands for the reins, he observed that instead of being fixed upon him, the eyes of the people of Chepstow darted this way and that. Heads were jerked. Arms flung out. Here a hat swooped in a semi-circle. Off drove the coach almost unnoticed. As it turned the corner all the outside passengers craned their necks, and one gentleman rose to his feet and shouted, "There! there! there!" before he was bowled into eternity. It was an insect—a red-winged insect. Out the people of Chepstow poured into the high road; down the hill they ran; always the insect flew in front of them; at length by Chepstow Bridge a young man, throwing his bandanna over the blade of an oar, captured it alive and presented it to a highly respectable elderly gentleman who now came puffing upon the scene—Samuel Budge, doctor, of Chepstow. By Samuel Budge it was presented to Miss Ormerod; by her sent to a professor at Oxford. And he, declaring it "a fine specimen of the rose underwinged locust" added the gratifying information that it "was the first of the kind to be captured so far west."

And so, at the age of twenty-four Miss Eleanor Ormerod was thought the proper person to receive the gift of a locust.

When Eleanor Ormerod appeared at archery meetings and croquet tournaments young men pulled their whiskers and young ladies looked grave. It was so difficult to make friends with a girl who could talk of nothing but black beetles and earwigs—"Yes, that's what she likes, isn't it queer?—Why, the other day Ellen, Mama's maid, heard from Jane, who's under-kitchenmaid at Sedbury House, that Eleanor tried to boil a beetle in the kitchen saucepan and he wouldn't die, and swam round and round, and she got into a terrible state and sent the groom all the way to Gloucester to fetch chloroform —all for an insect, my dear!—and she gives the cottagers shillings to collect beetles for her—and she spends hours in her bedroom cutting them up—and she climbs trees like a boy to find wasps' nests—oh, you can't think what they don't say about her in the village—for she does look so odd, dressed anyhow, with that great big nose and those bright little eyes, so like a caterpillar herself, I always think—but of course she's wonderfully clever and very good, too, both of them. Georgiana has a lending library for the cottagers, and Eleanor never misses a service—but there she is—that short pale girl in the large bonnet. Do go and talk to her, for I'm sure I'm too stupid, but you'd find plenty to say—" But neither Fred nor Arthur, Henry nor William found anything to say—

". . . probably the lecturer would have been equally well pleased had none of her own sex put in an appearance."

This comment upon a lecture delivered in the year 1889 throws some light, perhaps, upon archery meetings in the 'fifties.

It being nine o'clock on a February night some time about 1862 all the Ormerods were in the library; Mr. Ormerod making architectural designs at a table; Mrs. Ormerod lying on a sofa making pencil drawings upon

grey paper; Eleanor making a model of a snake to serve
as a paper weight; Georgiana making a copy of the font
in Tidenham Church; some of the others examining
books with beautiful illustrations; while at intervals
someone rose, unlocked the wire book case, took down a
volume for instruction or entertainment, and perused it
beneath the chandelier.

Mr. Ormerod required complete silence for his studies. His word was law, even to the dogs, who, in the absence of their master, instinctively obeyed the eldest
male person in the room. Some whispered colloquy
there might be between Mrs. Ormerod and her daughters—

"The draught under the pew was really worse than
ever this morning, Mama—"

"And we could only unfasten the latch in the chancel
because Eleanor happened to have her ruler with her—"

"—hm—m—m. Dr. Armstrong—Hm—m—m—"

"—Anyhow things aren't as bad with us as they are at
Kinghampton. They say Mrs. Briscoe's Newfoundland
dog follows her right up to the chancel rails when she
takes the sacrament—"

"And the turkey is still sitting on its eggs in the pulpit."

—"The period of incubation for a turkey is between
three and four weeks"—said Eleanor, thoughtfully looking up from her cast of the snake and forgetting, in the
interest of her subject, to speak in a whisper.

"Am I to be allowed no peace in my own house?" Mr.
Ormerod exclaimed angrily, rapping with his ruler on
the table, upon which Mrs. Ormerod half shut one eye
and squeezed a little blob of Chinese white on to her
high light, and they remained silent until the servants
came in, when everyone, with the exception of Mrs. Ormerod, fell on their knees. For she, poor lady, suffered
from a chronic complaint and left the family party for-
ever a year or two later, when the green sofa was moved
into the corner, and the drawings given to her nieces in

memory of her. But Mr. Ormerod went on making architectural drawings at nine p.m. every night (save on Sundays when he read a sermon) until he too lay upon the green sofa, which had not been used since Mrs. Ormerod lay there, but still looked much the same. "We deeply felt the happiness of ministering to his welfare," Miss Ormerod wrote, "for he would not hear of our leaving him for even twenty-four hours and he objected to visits from my brothers excepting occasionally for a short time. They, not being used to the gentle ways necessary for an aged invalid, worried him . . . the Thursday following, the 9th October, 1873, he passed gently away at the mature age of eighty-seven years." Oh, graves in country churchyards—respectable burials—mature old gentlemen—D.C.L., LL.D., F.R.S., F.S.A.—lots of letters come after your names, but lots of women are buried with you!

There remained the Hessian Fly and the Bot—mysterious insects! Not, one would have thought, among God's most triumphant creations, and yet—if you see them under a microscope!—the Bot, obese, globular, obscene; the Hessian, booted, spurred, whiskered, cadaverous. Next slip under the glass an innocent grain; behold it pockmarked and livid; or take this strip of hide, and note those odious pullulating lumps—well, what does the landscape look like then?

The only palatable object for the eye to rest on in acres of England is a lump of Paris Green. But English people won't use microscopes; you can't make them use Paris Green either—or if they do, they let it drip. Dr. Ritzema Bos is a great stand-by. For they won't take a woman's word. And indeed, though for the sake of the Ox Warble one must stretch a point, there are matters, questions of stock infestation, things one has to go into —things a lady doesn't even like to see, much less discuss, in print—"these, I say, I intend to leave entirely to the Veterinary surgeons. My brother—oh, he's dead now

—a very good man—for whom I collected wasps' nests
—lived at Brighton and wrote about wasps—he, I say,
wouldn't let me learn anatomy, never liked me to do
more than take sections of teeth."

Ah, but Eleanor, the Bot and the Hessian have more
power over you than Mr. Edward Ormerod himself.
Under the microscope you clearly perceive that these
insects have organs, orifices, excrement; they do, most
emphatically, copulate. Escorted on the one side by the
Bos or Warble, on the other by the Hessian Fly, Miss
Ormerod advanced statelily, if slowly, into the open.
Never did her features show more sublime than when
lit up by the candour of her avowal. "This is excrement; these, though Ritzema Bos is positive to the contrary, are the generative organs of the male. I've proved
it." Upon her head the hood of Edinburgh most fitly
descended; pioneer of purity even more than of Paris
Green.

"If you're sure I'm not in your way," said Miss Lipscomb
unstrapping her paint box and planting her tripod firmly
in the path, "—I'll try to get a picture of those lovely
hydrangeas against the sky— What flowers you have in
Penzance!"

The market gardener crossed his hands on his hoe,
slowly twined a piece of bass round his finger, looked at
the sky, said something about the sun, also about the
prevalence of lady artists, and then, with a nod of his
head, observed sententiously that it was to a lady that
he owed everything he had.

"Ah?" said Miss Lipscomb, flattered, but already
much occupied with her composition.

"A lady with a queer-sounding name," said Mr. Pas-
coe, "but that's the lady I've called my little girl after—
I don't think there's such another in Christendom."

Of course it was Miss Ormerod, equally of course
Miss Lipscomb was the sister of Miss Ormerod's family
doctor; and so she did no sketching that morning, but

left with a handsome bunch of grapes instead—for every flower had drooped, ruin had stared him in the face—he had written, not believing one bit what they told him—to the lady with the queer name, back there came a book "In-ju-ri-ous In-sects," with the page turned down, perhaps by her very hand, also a letter which he kept at home under the clock, but he knew every word by heart, since it was due to what she said there that he wasn't a ruined man—and the tears ran down his face and Miss Lipscomb, clearing a space on the lodging-house table, wrote the whole story to her brother.

"The prejudice against Paris Green certainly seems to be dying down," said Miss Ormerod when she read it. —"But now," she sighed rather heavily, being no longer young and much afflicted with the gout, "now it's the sparrows."

One might have thought that *they* would have left her alone—innocent dirt-grey birds, taking more than their share of the breakfast crumbs, otherwise inoffensive. But once you look through a microscope—once you see the Hessian and the Bot as they really are—there's no peace for an elderly lady pacing her terrace on a fine May morning. For example, why, when there are crumbs enough for all, do only the sparrows get them? Why not swallows or martins? Why—oh, here come the servants for prayers—

"Forgive us our trespasses as we forgive them that trespass against us. . . . For thine is the Kingdom and the power and the glory, for ever and ever. Amen—"

"The Times, ma'am—"

"Thank you, Dixon. . . . The Queen's birthday! We must drink her Majesty's health in the old white port, Dixon. Home Rule—tut—tut—tut. All that madman Gladstone. My father would have thought the world was coming to an end, and I'm not at all sure that it isn't. I must talk to Dr. Lipscomb—"

Yet all the time in the tail of her eye she saw myriads of sparrows, and retiring to the study proclaimed in a pamphlet of which 36,000 copies were gratuitously distributed that the sparrow is a pest.

"When he eats an insect," she said to her sister Georgiana, "which isn't often, it's one of the few insects that one wants to keep—one of the very few," she added with a touch of acidity natural to one whose investigations have all tended to the discredit of the insect race.

"But there'll be some very unpleasant consequences to face," she concluded—"Very unpleasant indeed."

Happily the port was now brought in, the servants assembled; and Miss Ormerod, rising to her feet, gave the toast "Her Blessed Majesty." She was extremely loyal, and moreover she liked nothing better than a glass of her father's old white port. She kept his pigtail, too, in a box.

Such being her disposition it went hard with her to analyse the sparrow's crop, for the sparrow she felt, symbolises something of the homely virtue of English domestic life, and to proclaim it stuffed with deceit was disloyal to much that she, and her fathers before her, held dear. Sure enough the clergy—the Rev. J. E. Walker—denounced her for her brutality; "God Save the Sparrow!" exclaimed the Animal's Friend; and Miss Carrington, of the Humanitarian League, replied in a leaflet described by Miss Ormerod as "spirity, discourteous, and inaccurate."

"Well," said Miss Ormerod to her sister, "it did me no harm before to be threatened to be shot at, also hanged in effigy, and other little attentions."

"Still it was very disagreeable, Eleanor—more disagreeable I believe, to me than to you," said Georgiana. Soon Georgiana died. She had however finished the beautiful series of insect diagrams at which she worked every morning in the dining-room and they were presented to Edinburgh University. But Eleanor was never the same woman after that.

Deer forest fly—flour moths—weevils—grouse and cheese flies—beetles—foreign correspondents—eel worms—ladybirds—wheat midges—resignation from the Royal

Agricultural Society—gall mites—boot beetles—Announcement of honorary degree to be conferred—feelings of appreciation and anxiety—paper on wasps—last annual report—warnings of serious illness—proposed pension—gradual loss of strength— Finally Death.

That is life, so they say.

"It does no good to keep people waiting for an answer," sighed Miss Ormerod, "though I don't feel as able as I did since that unlucky accident at Waterloo. And no one realises what the strain of the work is—often I'm the only lady in the room, and the gentlemen so learned, though I've always found them most helpful, most generous in every way. But I'm growing old, Miss Hartwell, that's what it is. That's what led me to be thinking of this difficult matter of flour infestation in the middle of the road so that I didn't see the horse until he had poked his nose into my ear. . . . Then there's this nonsense about a pension. What could possess Mr. Barron to think of such a thing? I should feel inexpressibly lowered if I accepted a pension. Why, I don't altogether like writing LL.D. after my name, though Georgie would have liked it. All I ask is to be let go on in my own quiet way. Now where is Messrs. Langridge's sample? We must take that first. 'Gentlemen, I have examined your sample and find . . .'"

"If any one deserves a thorough good rest it's you, Miss Ormerod," said Dr. Lipscomb, who had grown a little white over the ears. "I should say the farmers of England ought to set up a statue to you, bring offerings of corn and wine—make you a kind of Goddess, eh—what was her name?"

"Not a very shapely figure for a Goddess," said Miss Ormerod with a little laugh. "I should enjoy the wine though. You're not going to cut me off my one glass of port surely?"

"You must remember," said Dr. Lipscomb, shaking his head, "how much your life means to others."

"Well, I don't know about that," said Miss Ormerod,

pondering a little. "To be sure, I've chosen my epitaph. 'She introduced Paris Green into England,' and there might be a word or two about the Hessian fly—that, I do believe, was a good piece of work."

"No need to think about epitaphs yet," said Dr. Lipscomb.

"Our lives are in the hands of the Lord," said Miss Ormerod simply.

Dr. Lipscomb bent his head and looked out of the window. Miss Ormerod remained silent.

"English entomologists care little or nothing for objects of practical importance," she exclaimed suddenly. "Take this question of flour infestation—I can't say how many grey hairs that hasn't grown me."

"Figuratively speaking, Miss Ormerod," said Dr. Lipscomb, for her hair was still raven black.

"Well, I do believe all good work is done in concert," Miss Ormerod continued. "It is often a great comfort to me to think that."

"It's beginning to rain," said Dr. Lipscomb. "How will your enemies like that, Miss Ormerod?"

"Hot or cold, wet or dry, insects always flourish!" cried Miss Ormerod, energetically sitting up in bed.

"Old Miss Ormerod is dead," said Mr. Drummond, opening The Times on Saturday, July 20th, 1901.

"Old Miss Ormerod?" asked Mrs. Drummond.

*

Jane Austen

*

It is probable that if Miss Cassandra Austen had had her way, we should have had nothing of Jane Austen's except her novels. To her elder sister alone did she write freely; to her alone she confided her hopes and, if rumour is true, the one great disappointment of her life; but when Miss Cassandra Austen grew old, and the growth of her sister's fame made her suspect that a time might come when strangers would pry and scholars speculate, she burnt, at great cost to herself, every letter that could gratify their curiosity, and spared only what she judged too trivial to be of interest.

Hence our knowledge of Jane Austen is derived from a little gossip, a few letters, and her books. As for the gossip, gossip which has survived its day is never despicable; with a little rearrangement it suits our purpose admirably. For example, Jane "is not at all pretty and very prim, unlike a girl of twelve . . . Jane is whimsical and affected," says little Philadelphia Austen of her cousin. Then we have Mrs. Mitford, who knew the Austens as girls and thought Jane "the prettiest, silliest, most affected, husband-hunting butterfly she ever remembers." Next, there is Miss Mitford's anonymous friend "who visits her now [and] says that she has stiffened into the most perpendicular, precise, taciturn piece of 'single blessedness' that ever existed, and that, until *Pride and Prejudice* showed what a precious gem was

hidden in that unbending case, she was no more regarded
in society than a poker or firescreen. . . . The case is
very different now," the good lady goes on; "she is still
a poker—but a poker of whom everybody is afraid. . . .
A wit, a delineator of character, who does not talk is
terrific indeed!" On the other side, of course, there are
the Austens, a race little given to panegyric of themselves, but nevertheless, they say, her brothers "were
very fond and very proud of her. They were attached
to her by her talents, her virtues, and her engaging manners, and each loved afterwards to fancy a resemblance
in some niece or daughter of his own to the dear sister
Jane, whose perfect equal they yet never expected to
see." Charming but perpendicular, loved at home but
feared by strangers, biting of tongue but tender of heart
—these contrasts are by no means incompatible, and
when we turn to the novels we shall find ourselves stumbling there too over the same complexities in the writer.

To begin with, that prim little girl whom Philadelphia found so unlike a child of twelve, whimsical and
affected, was soon to be the authoress of an astonishing
and unchildish story, *Love and Freindship*,* which, incredible though it appears, was written at the age of
fifteen. It was written, apparently, to amuse the schoolroom; one of the stories in the same book is dedicated
with mock solemnity to her brother; another is neatly
illustrated with water-colour heads by her sister. There
are jokes which, one feels, were family property; thrusts
of satire, which went home because all little Austens
made mock in common of fine ladies who "sighed and
fainted on the sofa."

Brothers and sisters must have laughed when Jane read
out loud her last hit at the vices which they all abhorred.
"I die a martyr to my grief for the loss of Augustius.
One fatal swoon has cost me my life. Beware of Swoons,
Dear Laura. . . . Run mad as often as you chuse, but

* *Love and Freindship*, Chatto and Windus.

do not faint. . . ." And on she rushed, as fast as she could write and quicker than she could spell, to tell the incredible adventures of Laura and Sophia, of Philander and Gustavus, of the gentleman who drove a coach between Edinburgh and Stirling every other day, of the theft of the fortune that was kept in the table drawer, of the starving mothers and the sons who acted Macbeth. Undoubtedly, the story must have roused the schoolroom to uproarious laughter. And yet, nothing is more obvious than that this girl of fifteen, sitting in her private corner of the common parlour, was writing not to draw a laugh from brother and sisters, and not for home consumption. She was writing for everybody, for nobody, for our age, for her own; in other words, even at that early age Jane Austen was writing. One hears it in the rhythm and shapeliness and severity of the sentences. "She was nothing more than a mere good tempered, civil, and obliging young woman; as such we could scarcely dislike her—she was only an object of contempt." Such a sentence is meant to outlast the Christmas holidays. Spirited, easy, full of fun, verging with freedom upon sheer nonsense,—*Love and Freindship* is all that, but what is this note which never merges in the rest, which sounds distinctly and penetratingly all through the volume? It is the sound of laughter. The girl of fifteen is laughing, in her corner, at the world.

Girls of fifteen are always laughing. They laugh when Mr. Binney helps himself to salt instead of sugar. They almost die of laughing when old Mrs. Tomkins sits down upon the cat. But they are crying the moment after. They have no fixed abode from which they see that there is something eternally laughable in human nature, some quality in men and women that for ever excites our satire. They do not know that Lady Greville who snubs, and poor Maria who is snubbed, are permanent features of every ballroom. But Jane Austen knew it from her birth upwards. One of those fairies who

perch upon cradles must have taken her a flight through
the world directly she was born. When she was laid in
the cradle again she knew not only what the world
looked like, but had already chosen her kingdom. She
had agreed that if she might rule over that territory,
she would covet no other. Thus at fifteen she had few
illusions about other people and none about herself.
Whatever she writes is finished and turned and set in its
relation, not to the parsonage, but to the universe. She
is impersonal; she is inscrutable. When the writer, Jane
Austen, wrote down in the most remarkable sketch in
the book a little of Lady Greville's conversation, there is
no trace of anger at the snub which the clergyman's
daughter, Jane Austen, once received. Her gaze passes
straight to the mark, and we know precisely where,
upon the map of human nature, that mark is. We know
because Jane Austen kept to her compact; she never
trespassed beyond her boundaries. Never, even at the
emotional age of fifteen, did she round upon herself in
shame, obliterate a sarcasm in a spasm of compassion, or
blur an outline in a mist of rhapsody. Spasms and rhapsodies, she seems to have said, pointing with her stick,
end *there;* and the boundary line is perfectly distinct.
But she does not deny that moons and mountains and
castles exist—on the other side. She has even one romance of her own. It is for the Queen of Scots. She
really admired her very much. "One of the first characters in the world," she called her, "a bewitching Princess whose only friend was then the Duke of Norfolk,
and whose only ones now Mr. Whitaker, Mrs. Lefroy,
Mrs. Knight and myself." With these words her passion
is neatly circumscribed, and rounded with a laugh. It is
amusing to remember in what terms the young Brontës
wrote, not very much later, in their northern parsonage,
about the Duke of Wellington.

The prim little girl grew up. She became "the prettiest, silliest, most affected husband-hunting butterfly"
Mrs. Mitford ever remembered, and, incidentally, the

authoress of a novel called *Pride and Prejudice*, which, written stealthily under cover of a creaking door, lay for many years unpublished. A little later, it is thought, she began another story, *The Watsons*, and being for some reason dissatisfied with it, left it unfinished. Unfinished and unsuccessful, it may throw more light upon its writer's genius than the polished masterpiece blazing in universal fame. Her difficulties are more apparent in it, and the method she took to overcome them less artfully concealed. To begin with, the stiffness and the bareness of the first chapters prove that she was one of those writers who lay their facts out rather baldly in the first version and then go back and back and back and cover them with flesh and atmosphere. How it would have been done we cannot say—by what suppressions and insertions and artful devices. But the miracle would have been accomplished; the dull history of fourteen years of family life would have been converted into another of those exquisite and apparently effortless introductions; and we should never have guessed what pages of preliminary drudgery Jane Austen forced her pen to go through. Here we perceive that she was no conjuror after all. Like other writers, she had to create the atmosphere in which her own peculiar genius could bear fruit. Here she fumbles; here she keeps us waiting. Suddenly, she has done it; now things can happen as she likes things to happen. The Edwards' are going to the ball. The Tomlinsons' carriage is passing; she can tell us that Charles is "being provided with his gloves and told to keep them on"; Tom Musgrove retreats to a remote corner with a barrel of oysters and is famously snug. Her genius is freed and active. At once our senses quicken; we are possessed with the peculiar intensity which she alone can impart. But of what is it all composed? Of a ball in a country town; a few couples meeting and taking hands in an assembly room; a little eating and drinking; and for catastrophe, a boy being snubbed by one young lady and kindly treated by another. There is no tragedy and no heroism. Yet for some reason the little scene is moving out of all proportion to its surface solemnity. We have been made to see that if Emma acted so in the ball-room, how considerate, how tender, inspired by what sincerity of feeling she would have shown herself in those graver crises of life which, as we watch her, come inevitably before our eyes. Jane Austen is thus a mistress of much deeper emotion than appears upon the surface. She stimulates us to supply what is not there. What she offers is, apparently, a trifle, yet is composed of something that expands in the reader's mind and endows with the most enduring form of life scenes which are outwardly trivial. Always the stress is laid upon character. How, we are made to wonder, will Emma behave when Lord Osborne and Tom Musgrove make their call at five minutes before three, just as Mary is bringing in the tray and the knife-case? It is an extremely awkward situation. The young men are accustomed to much greater refinement. Emma may prove herself ill-bred, vulgar, a nonentity. The turns and twists of the dialogue keep us on the tenterhooks of suspense. Our attention is half upon the present moment, half upon the future. And when, in the end, Emma behaves in such a way as to vindicate our highest hopes of her, we are moved as if we had been made witnesses of a matter of the highest importance. Here, indeed, in this unfinished and in the main inferior story are all the elements of Jane Austen's greatness. It has the permanent quality of literature. Think away the surface animation, the likeness to life, and there remains to provide a deeper pleasure, an exquisite discrimination of human values. Dismiss this too from the mind and one can dwell with extreme satisfaction upon the more abstract art which, in the ball-room scene, so varies the emotions and proportions the parts that it is possible to enjoy it, as one enjoys poetry, for itself, and not as a link which carries the story this way and that.

But the gossip says of Jane Austen that she was per-

pendicular, precise, and taciturn—"a poker of whom
everybody is afraid." Of this too there are traces; she
could be merciless enough; she is one of the most consistent satirists in the whole of literature. Those first
angular chapters of *The Watsons* prove that hers was
not a prolific genius; she had not, like Emily Brontë,
merely to open the door to make herself felt. Humbly
and gaily she collected the twigs and straws out of
which the nest was to be made and placed them neatly
together. The twigs and straws were a little dry and a
little dusty in themselves. There was the big house and
the little house; a tea party, a dinner party, and an occasional picnic; life was hedged in by valuable connec-
tions and adequate incomes; by muddy roads, wet feet,
and a tendency on the part of the ladies to get tired; a
little money supported it, a little consequence, and the
education commonly enjoyed by upper middle-class families living in the country. Vice, adventure, passion were
left outside. But of all this prosiness, of all this little-
ness, she evades nothing, and nothing is slurred over.
Patiently and precisely she tells us how they "made no
stop anywhere till they reached Newbury, where a com-
fortable meal, uniting dinner and supper, wound up the
enjoyments and fatigues of the day." Nor does she pay
to conventions merely the tribute of lip homage; she
believes in them besides accepting them. When she is
describing a clergyman, like Edmund Bertram, or a sailor,
in particular, she appears debarred by the sanctity of
his office from the free use of her chief tool, the comic
genius, and is apt therefore to lapse into decorous panegyric or matter-of-fact description. But these are ex-
ceptions; for the most part her attitude recalls the
anonymous ladies' ejaculation—"A wit, a delineator of
character, who does not talk is terrific indeed!" She
wishes neither to reform nor to annihilate; she is silent;
and that is terrific indeed. One after another she creates
her fools, her prigs, her worldlings, her Mr. Collins',
her Sir Walter Elliotts, her Mrs. Bennetts. She encircles

them with the lash of a whip-like phrase which, as it
runs round them, cuts out their silhouettes for ever. But
there they remain; no excuse is found for them and no
mercy shown them. Nothing remains of Julia and Maria
Bertram when she has done with them; Lady Bertram is
left "sitting and calling to Pug and trying to keep him
from the flower beds" eternally. A divine justice is
meted out; Dr. Grant, who begins by liking his goose
tender, ends by bringing on "apoplexy and death, by
three great institutionary dinners in one week." Sometimes it seems as if her creatures were born merely to
give Jane Austen the supreme delight of slicing their
heads off. She is satisfied; she is content; she would not
alter a hair on anybody's head, or move one brick or
one blade of grass in a world which provides her with
such exquisite delight.

Nor, indeed, would we. For even if the pangs of outraged vanity, or the heat of moral wrath, urged us to
improve away a world so full of spite, pettiness, and
folly, the task is beyond our powers. People are like that
—the girl of fifteen knew it; the mature woman proves
it. At this very moment some Lady Bertram finds it almost too trying to keep Pug from the flower beds; she
sends Chapman to help Miss Fanny, a little late. The
discrimination is so perfect, the satire so just that,
consistent though it is, it almost escapes our notice.
No touch of pettiness, no hint of spite, rouses us from
our contemplation. Delight strangely mingles with our
amusement. Beauty illumines these fools.

That elusive quality is indeed often made up of very
different parts, which it needs a peculiar genius to bring
together. The wit of Jane Austen has for partner the
perfection of her taste. Her fool is a fool, her snob is a
snob, because he departs from the model of sanity and
sense which she has in mind, and conveys to us unmistakably even while she makes us laugh. Never did any
novelist make more use of an impeccable sense of human
values. It is against the disc of an unerring heart, an un-

failing good taste, an almost stern morality, that she shows up those deviations from kindness, truth, and sincerity which are among the most delightful things in English literature. She depicts a Mary Crawford in her mixture of good and bad entirely by this means. She lets her rattle on against the clergy, or in favour of a baronetage and ten thousand a year with all the ease and spirit possible; but now and again she strikes one note of her own, very quietly, but in perfect tune, and at once all Mary Crawford's chatter, though it continues to amuse, rings flat. Hence the depth, the beauty, the complexity of her scenes. From such contrasts there comes a beauty, a solemnity even which are not only as remarkable as her wit, but an inseparable part of it. In *The Watsons* she gives us a foretaste of this power; she makes us wonder why an ordinary act of kindness, as she describes it, becomes so full of meaning. In her masterpieces, the same gift is brought to perfection. Here is nothing out of the way; it is midday in Northamptonshire; a dull young man is talking to rather a weakly young woman on the stairs as they go up to dress for dinner, with housemaids passing. But, from triviality, from commonplace, their words become suddenly full of meaning, and the moment for both one of the most memorable in their lives. It fills itself; it shines; it glows; it hangs before us, deep, trembling, serene for a second; next, the housemaid passes, and this drop in which all the happiness of life has collected gently subsides again to become part of the ebb and flow of ordinary existence.

What more natural then, with this insight into their profundity, than that Jane Austen should have chosen to write of the trivialities of day to day existence, of parties, picnics, and country dances? No "suggestions to alter her style of writing" from the Prince Regent or Mr. Clarke could tempt her; no romance, no adventure, no politics or intrigue could hold a candle to life on a country-house staircase as she saw it. Indeed, the Prince Regent and his librarian had run their heads

against a very formidable obstacle; they were trying to
tamper with an incorruptible conscience, to disturb an
infallible discretion. The child who formed her sentences
so finely when she was fifteen never ceased to form
them, and never wrote for the Prince Regent or his Librarian, but for the world at large. She knew exactly
what her powers were, and what material they were
fitted to deal with as material should be dealt with by
a writer, whose standard of finality was high. There were
impressions that lay outside her province; emotions that
by no stretch or artifice could be properly coated and
covered by her own resources. For example, she could
not make a girl talk enthusiastically of banners and
chapels. She could not throw herself wholeheartedly
into a romantic moment. She had all sorts of devices for
evading scenes of passion. Nature and its beauties she
approached in a sidelong way of her own. She describes
a beautiful night without once mentioning the moon.
Nevertheless, as we read the few formal phrases about
"the brilliancy of an unclouded night and the contrast
of the deep shade of the woods" the night is at once as
"solemn, and soothing, and lovely" as she tells us, quite
simply, that it was.

The balance of her gifts was singularly perfect.
Among her finished novels there are no failures, and
among her many chapters few that sink markedly below
the level of the others. But, after all, she died at the age
of forty-two. She died at the height of her powers. She
was still subject to those changes which often make the
final period of a writer's career the most interesting of
all. Vivacious, irrepressible, gifted with an invention of
great vitality, there can be no doubt that she would have
written more, had she lived, and it is tempting to consider whether she would not have written differently.
The boundaries were marked; moons, mountains, and
castles lay on the other side. But was she not sometimes
tempted to trespass for a minute? Was she not begin-

ning, in her own gay and brilliant manner, to contemplate a little voyage of discovery?

Let us take *Persuasion*, the last completed novel, and look by its light at the books she might have written had she lived. There is a peculiar beauty and a peculiar dullness in *Persuasion*. The dullness is that which so often marks the transition stage between two different periods. The writer is a little bored. She has grown too familiar with the ways of her world; she no longer notes them freshly. There is an asperity in her comedy which suggests that she has almost ceased to be amused by the vanities of a Sir Walter or the snobbery of a Miss Elliott. The satire is harsh, and the comedy crude. She is no longer so freshly aware of the amusements of daily life. Her mind is not altogether on her object. But, while we feel that Jane Austen has done this before, and done it better, we also feel that she is trying to do something which she has never yet attempted. There is a new element in *Persuasion*, the quality, perhaps, that made Dr. Whewell fire up and insist that it was "the most beautiful of her works." She is beginning to discover that the world is larger, more mysterious, and more romantic than she had supposed. We feel it to be true of herself when she says of Anne: "She had been forced into prudence in her youth, she learned romance as she grew older—the natural sequel of an unnatural beginning." She dwells frequently upon the beauty and the melancholy of nature, upon the autumn where she had been wont to dwell upon the spring. She talks of the "influence so sweet and so sad of autumnal months in the country." She marks "the tawny leaves and withered hedges." "One does not love a place the less because one has suffered in it," she observes. But it is not only in a new sensibility to nature that we detect the change. Her attitude to life itself is altered. She is seeing it, for the greater part of the book, through the eyes of a woman who, unhappy herself, has a special sympathy for the happiness and unhappiness of others, which, until the very end, she is forced to comment upon in silence. Therefore the observation is less of facts and more of feelings than is usual. There is an expressed emotion in the scene at the concert and in the famous talk about woman's constancy which proves not merely the biographical fact that Jane Austen had loved, but the aesthetic fact that she was no longer afraid to say so. Experience, when it was of a serious kind, had to sink very deep, and to be thoroughly disinfected by the passage of time, before she allowed herself to deal with it in fiction. But now, in 1817, she was ready. Outwardly, too, in her circumstances, a change was imminent. Her fame had grown very slowly. "I doubt," wrote Mr. Austen Leigh, "whether it would be possible to mention any other author of note whose personal obscurity was so complete." Had she lived a few more years only, all that would have been altered. She would have stayed in London, dined out, lunched out, met famous people, made new friends, read, travelled, and carried back to the quiet country cottage a hoard of observations to feast upon at leisure.

And what effect would all this have had upon the six novels that Jane Austen did not write? She would not have written of crime, of passion, or of adventure. She would not have been rushed by the importunity of publishers or the flattery of friends into slovenliness or insincerity. But she would have known more. Her sense of security would have been shaken. Her comedy would have suffered. She would have trusted less (this is already perceptible in *Persuasion*) to dialogue and more to reflection to give us a knowledge of her characters. Those marvellous little speeches which sum up, in a few minutes' chatter, all that we need in order to know an Admiral Croft or a Mrs. Musgrove for ever, that shorthand, hit-or-miss method which contains chapters of analysis and psychology, would have become too crude to hold all that she now perceived of the complexity of human nature. She would have devised a method, clear and composed as ever, but deeper and more suggestive, for conveying not only what people say, but what they leave unsaid; not only what they are, but what life is. She would have stood farther away from her characters, and seen them more as a group, less as individuals. Her satire, while it played less incessantly, would have been more stringent and severe. She would have been the forerunner of Henry James and of Proust—but enough. Vain are these speculations: the most perfect artist among women, the writer whose books are immortal, died "just as she was beginning to feel confidence in her own success."

Modern Fiction

In making any survey, even the freest and loosest, of modern fiction it is difficult not to take it for granted that the modern practice of the art is somehow an improvement upon the old. With their simple tools and primitive materials, it might be said, Fielding did well and Jane Austen even better, but compare their opportunities with ours! Their masterpieces certainly have a strange air of simplicity. And yet the analogy between literature and the process, to choose an example, of making motor cars scarcely holds good beyond the first glance. It is doubtful whether in the course of the centuries, though we have learnt much about making machines, we have learnt anything about making literature. We do not come to write better; all that we can be said to do is to keep moving, now a little in this direction, now in that, but with a circular tendency should the whole course of the track be viewed from a sufficiently lofty pinnacle. It need scarcely be said that we make no claim to stand, even momentarily, upon that vantage ground. On the flat, in the crowd, half blind with dust, we look back with envy to those happier warriors, whose battle is won and whose achievements wear so serene an air of accomplishment that we can scarcely refrain from whispering that the fight was not so fierce for them as for us. It is for the historian of literature to decide; for him to say if we are now beginning or end-ing or standing in the middle of a great period of prose fiction, for down in the plain little is visible. We only know that certain gratitudes and hostilities inspire us; that certain paths seem to lead to fertile land, others to the dust and the desert; and of this perhaps it may be worth while to attempt some account.

Our quarrel, then, is not with the classics, and if we speak of quarrelling with Mr. Wells, Mr. Bennett, and Mr. Galsworthy it is partly that by the mere fact of their existence in the flesh their work has a living, breathing, every-day imperfection which bids us take what liberties with it we choose. But it is also true that, while we thank them for a thousand gifts, we reserve our unconditional gratitude for Mr. Hardy, for Mr. Conrad, and in a much lesser degree for the Mr. Hudson, of *The Purple Land*, *Green Mansions*, and *Far Away and Long Ago*. Mr. Wells, Mr. Bennett, and Mr. Galsworthy have excited so many hopes and disappointed them so persistently that our gratitude largely takes the form of thanking them for having shown us what they might have done but have not done; what we certainly could not do, but as certainly, perhaps, do not wish to do. No single phrase will sum up the charge or grievance which we have to bring against a mass of work so large in its volume and embodying so many qualities, both admirable and the reverse. If we tried to formulate our meaning in one word we should say that these three writers are materialists. It is because they are concerned not with the spirit but with the body that they have disappointed us, and left us with the feeling that the sooner English fiction turns its back upon them, as politely as may be, and marches, if only into the desert, the better for its soul. Naturally, no single word reaches the centre of three separate targets. In the case of Mr. Wells it falls notably wide of the mark. And yet even with him it indicates to our thinking the fatal alloy in his genius, the great clod of clay that has got itself mixed up with the purity of his inspiration. But Mr. Bennett is perhaps the worst culprit of the three, inasmuch as he is by far the best workman. He can make a book so well constructed and solid in its craftsmanship that it is difficult for the most exacting of critics to see through what chink or crevice decay can creep in. There is not so much as a draught between the frames of the windows, or a crack in the boards. And yet—if life should refuse to live there? That is a risk which the creator of *The Old Wives' Tale*, George Cannon, Edwin Clayhanger, and hosts of other figures, may well claim to have surmounted. His characters live abundantly, even unexpectedly, but it remains to ask how do they live, and what do they live for? More and more they seem to us, deserting even the well-built villa in the Five Towns, to spend their time in some softly padded first-class railway carriage, pressing bells and buttons innumerable; and the destiny to which they travel so luxuriously becomes more and more unquestionably an eternity of bliss spent in the very best hotel in Brighton. It can scarcely be said of Mr. Wells that he is a materialist in the sense that he takes too much delight in the solidity of his fabric. His mind is too generous in its sympathies to allow him to spend much time in making things shipshape and substantial. He is a materialist from sheer goodness of heart, taking upon his shoulders the work that ought to have been discharged by Government officials, and in the plethora of his ideas and facts scarcely having leisure to realise, or forgetting to think important, the crudity and coarseness of his human beings. Yet what more damaging criticism can there be both of his earth and of his Heaven than that they are to be inhabited here and hereafter by his Joans and his Peters? Does not the inferiority of their natures tarnish whatever institutions and ideals may be provided for them by the generosity of their creator? Nor, profoundly though we respect the integrity and humanity of Mr. Galsworthy, shall we find what we seek in his pages.

If we fasten, then, one label on all these books, on

which is one word, materialists, we mean by it that they write of unimportant things; that they spend immense skill and immense industry making the trivial and the transitory appear the true and the enduring.

We have to admit that we are exacting, and, further, that we find it difficult to justify our discontent by explaining what it is that we exact. We frame our question differently at different times. But it reappears most persistently as we drop the finished novel on the crest of a sigh— Is it worth while? What is the point of it all? Can it be that owing to one of those little deviations which the human spirit seems to make from time to time Mr. Bennett has come down with his magnificent apparatus for catching life just an inch or two on the wrong side? Life escapes; and perhaps without life nothing else is worth while. It is a confession of vagueness to have to make use of such a figure as this, but we scarcely better the matter by speaking, as critics are prone to do, of reality. Admitting the vagueness which afflicts all criticism of novels, let us hazard the opinion that for us at this moment the form of fiction most in vogue more often misses than secures the thing we seek. Whether we call it life or spirit, truth or reality, this, the essential thing, has moved off, or on, and refuses to be contained any longer in such ill-fitting vestments as we provide. Nevertheless, we go on perseveringly, conscientiously, constructing our two and thirty chapters after a design which more and more ceases to resemble the vision in our minds. So much of the enormous labour of proving the solidity, the likeness to life, of the story is not merely labour thrown away but labour misplaced to the extent of obscuring and blotting out the light of the conception. The writer seems constrained, not by his own free will but by some powerful and unscrupulous tyrant who has him in thrall to provide a plot, to provide comedy, tragedy, love, interest, and an air of probability embalming the whole so impeccable that if all his figures were to come to life they would find themselves

dressed down to the last button of their coats in the
fashion of the hour. The tyrant is obeyed; the novel is
done to a turn. But sometimes, more and more often as
time goes by, we suspect a momentary doubt, a spasm of
rebellion, as the pages fill themselves in the customary
way. Is life like this? Must novels be like this?

Look within and life, it seems, is very far from being
"like this." Examine for a moment an ordinary mind on
an ordinary day. The mind receives a myriad impressions
—trivial, fantastic, evanescent, or engraved with the
sharpness of steel. From all sides they come, an incessant
shower of innumerable atoms; and as they fall, as they
shape themselves into the life of Monday or Tuesday,
the accent falls differently from of old; the moment of
importance came not here but there; so that if a writer
were a free man and not a slave, if he could write what
he chose, not what he must, if he could base his work
upon his own feeling and not upon convention, there
would be no plot, no comedy, no tragedy, no love interest or catastrophe in the accepted style, and perhaps
not a single button sewn on as the Bond Street tailors
would have it. Life is not a series of gig lamps sym-
metrically arranged; but a luminous halo, a semi-trans-
parent envelope surrounding us from the beginning of
consciousness to the end. Is it not the task of the novelist to convey this varying, this unknown and uncir-
cumscribed spirit, whatever aberration or complexity it
may display, with as little mixture of the alien and external as possible? We are not pleading merely for courage and sincerity; we are suggesting that the proper
stuff of fiction is a little other than custom would have
us believe it.

It is, at any rate, in some such fashion as this that we
seek to define the quality which distinguishes the work
of several young writers, among whom Mr. James Joyce
is the most notable, from that of their predecessors.
They attempt to come closer to life, and to preserve
more sincerely and exactly what interests and moves

them, even if to do so they must discard most of the conventions which are commonly observed by the novelist. Let us record the atoms as they fall upon the mind in the order in which they fall, let us trace the pattern, however disconnected and incoherent in appearance, which each sight or incident scores upon the consciousness. Let us not take it for granted that life exists more fully in what is commonly thought big than in what is commonly thought small. Any one who has read *The Portrait of the Artist as a Young Man* or, what promises to be a far more interesting work, *Ulysses,** now appearing in the *Little Review*, will have hazarded some theory of this nature as to Mr. Joyce's intention. On our part, with such a fragment before us, it is hazarded rather than affirmed; but whatever the intention of the whole there can be no question but that it is of the utmost sincerity and that the result, difficult or unpleasant as we may judge it, is undeniably important. In contrast with those whom we have called materialists Mr. Joyce is spiritual; he is concerned at all costs to reveal the flickerings of that innermost flame which flashes its messages through the brain, and in order to preserve it he disregards with complete courage whatever seems to him adventitious, whether it be probability, or coherence or any other of these signposts which for generations have served to support the imagination of a reader when called upon to imagine what he can neither touch nor see. The scene in the cemetery, for instance, with its brilliancy, its sordidity, its incoherence, its sudden lightning flashes of significance, does undoubtedly come so close to the quick of the mind that, on a first reading at any rate, it is difficult not to acclaim a masterpiece. If we want life itself here, surely we have it. Indeed, we find ourselves fumbling rather awkwardly if we try to say what else we wish, and for what reason a work of such originality yet fails to compare, for we must take

* Written April 1919.

high examples, with *Youth* or *The Mayor of Caster-bridge*. It fails because of the comparative poverty of the writer's mind, we might say simply and have done with it. But it is possible to press a little further and wonder whether we may not refer our sense of being in a bright yet narrow room, confined and shut in, rather than enlarged and set free, to some limitation imposed by the method as well as by the mind. Is it the method that inhibits the creative power? Is it due to the method that we feel neither jovial nor magnanimous, but centred in a self which, in spite of its tremor of susceptibility, never embraces or creates what is outside itself and beyond? Does the emphasis laid, perhaps didactically, upon indecency, contribute to the effect of something angular and isolated? Or is it merely that in any effort of such originality it is much easier, for contemporaries especially, to feel what it lacks than to name what it gives? In any case it is a mistake to stand outside examining "methods." Any method is right, every method is right, that expresses what we wish to express, if we are writers; that brings us closer to the novelist's intention if we are readers. This method has the merit of bringing us closer to what we were prepared to call life itself; did not the reading of *Ulysses* suggest how much of life is excluded or ignored, and did it not come with a shock to open *Tristram Shandy* or even *Pendennis* and be by them convinced that there are not only other aspects of life, but more important ones into the bargain.

However this may be, the problem before the novelist at present, as we suppose it to have been in the past, is to contrive means of being free to set down what he chooses. He has to have the courage to say that what interests him is no longer "this" but "that": out of "that" alone must he construct his work. For the moderns "that," the point of interest, lies very likely in the dark places of psychology. At once, therefore, the accent falls a little differently; the emphasis is upon something hitherto ignored; at once a different outline of form be-

Modern Fiction157

comes necessary, difficult for us to grasp, incomprehensible to our predecessors. No one but a modern, perhaps no one but a Russian, would have felt the interest of the situation which Tchekov has made into the short story which he calls "Gusev." Some Russian soldiers lie ill on board a ship which is taking them back to Russia. We are given a few scraps of their talk and some of their thoughts; then one of them dies and is carried away; the talk goes on among the others for a time, until Gusev himself dies, and looking "like a carrot or a radish" is thrown overboard. The emphasis is laid upon such unexpected places that at first it seems as if there were no emphasis at all; and then, as the eyes accustom themselves to twilight and discern the shapes of things in a room we see how complete the story is, how profound, and how truly in obedience to his vision Tchekov has chosen this, that, and the other, and placed them together to compose something new. But it is impossible to say "this is comic," or "that is tragic," nor are we certain, since short stories, we have been taught, should be brief and conclusive, whether this, which is vague and inconclusive, should be called a short story at all.

The most elementary remarks upon modern English fiction can hardly avoid some mention of the Russian influence, and if the Russians are mentioned one runs the risk of feeling that to write of any fiction save theirs is waste of time. If we want understanding of the soul and heart where else shall we find it of comparable profundity? If we are sick of our own materialism the least considerable of their novelists has by right of birth a natural reverence for the human spirit. "Learn to make yourself akin to people. . . . But let this sympathy be not with the mind—for it is easy with the mind—but with the heart, with love towards them." In every great Russian writer we seem to discern the features of a saint, if sympathy for the sufferings of others, love towards them, endeavour to reach some goal worthy of the most exacting demands of the spirit constitute saintliness. It is the saint in them which confounds us with a feeling of our own irreligious triviality, and turns so many of our famous novels to tinsel and trickery. The conclusions of the Russian mind, thus comprehensive and compassionate, are inevitably, perhaps, of the utmost sadness. More accurately indeed we might speak of the inconclusiveness of the Russian mind. It is the sense that there is no answer, that if honestly examined life presents question after question which must be left to sound on and on after the story is over in hopeless interrogation that fills us with a deep, and finally it may be with a resentful, despair. They are right perhaps; unquestionably they see further than we do and without our gross impediments of vision. But perhaps we see something that escapes them, or why should this voice of protest mix itself with our gloom? The voice of protest is the voice of another and an ancient civilisation which seems to have bred in us the instinct to enjoy and fight rather than to suffer and understand. English fiction from Sterne to Meredith bears witness to our natural delight in humour and comedy, in the beauty of earth, in the activities of the intellect, and in the splendour of the body. But any deductions that we may draw from the comparison of two fictions so immeasurably far apart are futile save indeed as they flood us with a view of the infinite possibilities of the art and remind us that there is no limit to the horizon, and that nothing—no "method," no experiment, even of the wildest—is forbidden, but only falsity and pretence. "The proper stuff of fiction" does not exist; everything is the proper stuff of fiction, every feeling, every thought; every quality of brain and spirit is drawn upon; no perception comes amiss. And if we can imagine the art of fiction come alive and standing in our midst, she would undoubtedly bid us break her and bully her, as well as honour and love her, for so her youth is renewed and her sovereignty assured.

*

Jane Eyre and Wuthering Heights†

*

Of the hundred years that have passed since Charlotte
Brontë was born, she, the centre now of so much leg-
end, devotion, and literature, lived but thirty-nine. It
is strange to reflect how different those legends might
have been had her life reached the ordinary human span.
She might have become, like some of her famous contemporaries, a figure familiarly met with in London and
elsewhere, the subject of pictures and anecdotes innumerable, the writer of many novels, of memoirs possibly, removed from us well within the memory of the
middle-aged in all the splendour of established fame. She
might have been wealthy, she might have been prosperous. But it is not so. When we think of her we have to
imagine some one who had no lot in our modern world;
we have to cast our minds back to the 'fifties of the last
century, to a remote parsonage upon the wild Yorkshire
moors. In that parsonage, and on those moors, unhappy
and lonely, in her poverty and her exaltation, she remains
for ever.

These circumstances, as they affected her character,
may have left their traces on her work. A novelist, we
reflect, is bound to build up his structure with much
very perishable material which begins by lending it reality and ends by cumbering it with rubbish. As we open
Jane Eyre once more we cannot stifle the suspicion that

† Written in 1916.

we shall find her world of imagination as antiquated, mid-Victorian, and out of date as the parsonage on the moor, a place only to be visited by the curious, only preserved by the pious. So we open *Jane Eyre;* and in two pages every doubt is swept clean from our minds.

Folds of scarlet drapery shut in my view to the right hand; to the left were the clear panes of glass, protecting, but not separating me from the drear November day. At intervals, while turning over the leaves of my book, I studied the aspect of that winter afternoon. Afar, it offered a pale blank of mist and cloud; near, a scene of wet lawn and storm-beat shrub, with ceaseless rain sweeping away wildly before a long and lamentable blast.

There is nothing there more perishable than the moor itself, or more subject to the sway of fashion than the "long and lamentable blast." Nor is this exhilaration short-lived. It rushes us through the entire volume, without giving us time to think, without letting us lift our eyes from the page. So intense is our absorption that if some one moves in the room the movement seems to take place not there but up in Yorkshire. The writer has us by the hand, forces us along her road, makes us see what she sees, never leaves us for a moment or allows us to forget her.* At the end we are steeped through and through with the genius, the vehemence, the indig-

* Charlotte and Emily Brontë had much the same sense of colour. ". . . we saw—ah! it was beautiful—a splendid place carpeted with crimson, and crimson-covered chairs and tables, and a pure white ceiling bordered by gold, a shower of glass drops hanging in silver chains from the centre, and shimmering with little soft tapers" (*Wuthering Heights*). Yet it was merely a very pretty drawing-room, and within it a boudoir, both spread with white carpets, on which seemed laid brilliant garlands of flowers; both ceiled with snowy mouldings of white grapes and vine leaves, beneath which glowed in rich contrast crimson couches and ottomans; while the ornaments on the pale Parian mantelpiece were of sparkling Bohemia glass, ruby red; and between the windows large mirrors repeated the general blending of snow and fire.

nation of Charlotte Brontë. Remarkable faces, figures of strong outline and gnarled feature have flashed upon us in passing; but it is through her eyes that we have seen them. Once she is gone, we seek for them in vain. Think of Rochester and we have to think of Jane Eyre. Think of the moor, and again, there is Jane Eyre. Think of the drawing-room, even, those "white carpets on which seemed laid brilliant garlands of flowers," that "pale Parian mantelpiece" with its Bohemia glass of "ruby red" and the "general blending of snow and fire"—what is all that except Jane Eyre?

The drawbacks of being Jane Eyre are not far to seek. Always to be a governess and always to be in love is a serious limitation in a world which is full, after all, of people who are neither one nor the other. The characters of a Jane Austen or of a Tolstoi have a million facets compared with these. They live and are complex by means of their effect upon many different people who serve to mirror them in the round. They move hither and thither whether their creators watch them or not, and the world in which they live seems to us an independent world which we can visit, now that they have created it, by ourselves. Thomas Hardy is more akin to Charlotte Brontë in the power of his personality and the narrowness of his vision. But the differences are vast. As we read *Jude the Obscure* we are not rushed to a finish; we brood and ponder and drift away from the text in plethoric trains of thought which build up round the characters an atmosphere of question and suggestion of which they are themselves, as often as not, unconscious. Simple peasants as they are, we are forced to confront them with destinies and questionings of the hugest import, so that often it seems as if the most important characters in a Hardy novel are those which have no names. Of this power, of this speculative curiosity, Charlotte Brontë has no trace. She does not attempt to solve the problems of human life; she is even unaware that such problems exist; all her force, and it is the more tremendous for being constricted, goes into the assertion, "I love," "I hate," "I suffer."

For the self-centred and self-limited writers have a power denied the more catholic and broad-minded. Their impressions are close packed and strongly stamped between their narrow walls. Nothing issues from their minds which has not been marked with their own impress. They learn little from other writers, and what they adopt they cannot assimilate. Both Hardy and Charlotte Brontë appear to have founded their styles upon a stiff and decorous journalism. The staple of their prose is awkward and unyielding. But both with labour and the most obstinate integrity by thinking every thought until it has subdued words to itself, have forged for themselves a prose which takes the mould of their minds entire; which has, into the bargain, a beauty, a power, a swiftness of its own. Charlotte Brontë, at least, owed nothing to the reading of many books. She never learnt the smoothness of the professional writer, or acquired his ability to stuff and sway his language as he chooses. "I could never rest in communication with strong, discreet, and refined minds, whether male or female," she writes, as any leader-writer in a provincial journal might have written; but gathering fire and speed goes on in her own authentic voice "till I had passed the outworks of conventional reserve and crossed the threshold of confidence, and won a place by their hearts' very hearthstone." It is there that she takes her seat; it is the red and fitful glow of the heart's fire which illumines her page. In other words, we read Charlotte Brontë not for exquisite observation of character—her characters are vigorous and elementary; not for comedy—hers is grim and crude; not for a philosophic view of life—hers is that of a country parson's daughter; but for her poetry. Probably that is so with all writers who have, as she has, an overpowering personality, who, as we should say in real life, have only to open the door to make themselves felt. There is in them some untamed ferocity perpetually at war with the accepted order of things which makes them desire to create instantly rather than to observe patiently. This very ardour, rejecting half shades and other minor impediments, wings its way past the daily conduct of ordinary people and allies itself with their more inarticulate passions. It makes them poets, or, if they choose to write in prose, intolerant of its restrictions. Hence it is that both Emily and Charlotte are always invoking the help of nature. They both feel the need of some more powerful symbol of the vast and slumbering passions in human nature than words or actions can convey. It is with a description of a storm that Charlotte ends her finest novel *Villette*. "The skies hang full and dark—a wrack sails from the west; the clouds cast themselves into strange forms." So she calls in nature to describe a state of mind which could not otherwise be expressed. But neither of the sisters observed nature accurately as Dorothy Wordsworth observed it, or painted it minutely as Tennyson painted it. They seized those aspects of the earth which were most akin to what they themselves felt or imputed to their characters, and so their storms, their moors, their lovely spaces of summer weather are not ornaments applied to decorate a dull page or display the writer's powers of observation—they carry on the emotion and light up the meaning of the book.

The meaning of a book, which lies so often apart from what happens and what is said and consists rather in some connection which things in themselves different have had for the writer, is necessarily hard to grasp. Especially this is so when, like the Brontës, the writer is poetic, and his meaning inseparable from his language, and itself rather a mood than a particular observation. *Wuthering Heights* is a more difficult book to understand than *Jane Eyre*, because Emily was a greater poet than Charlotte. When Charlotte wrote she said with eloquence and splendour and passion "I love," "I hate," "I suffer." Her experience, though more intense, is on a level with our own. But there is no "I" in *Wuthering*

Heights. There are no governesses. There are no employ-
ers. There is love, but it is not the love of men and
women. Emily was inspired by some more general conception. The impulse which urged her to create was not
her own suffering or her own injuries. She looked out
upon a world cleft into gigantic disorder and felt within
her the power to unite it in a book. That gigantic ambition is to be felt throughout the novel—a struggle, half
thwarted but of superb conviction, to say something
through the mouths of her characters which is not
merely "I love" or "I hate," but "we, the whole human
race" and "you, the eternal powers . . ." the sentence
remains unfinished. It is not strange that it should be so;
rather it is astonishing that she can make us feel what
she had it in her to say at all. It surges up in the half-
articulate words of Catherine Earnshaw, "If all else per-
ished and *he* remained, I should still continue to be; and
if all else remained and he were annihilated, the universe
would turn to a mighty stranger; I should not seem part
of it." It breaks out again in the presence of the dead.
"I see a repose that neither earth nor hell can break, and
I feel an assurance of the endless and shadowless hereafter—the eternity they have entered—where life is
boundless in its duration, and love in its sympathy and
joy in its fulness." It is this suggestion of power under-
lying the apparitions of human nature, and lifting them
up into the presence of greatness that gives the book its
huge stature among other novels. But it was not enough
for Emily Brontë to write a few lyrics, to utter a cry,
to express a creed. In her poems she did this once and
for all, and her poems will perhaps outlast her novel.
But she was novelist as well as poet. She must take upon
herself a more laborious and a more ungrateful task. She
must face the fact of other existences, grapple with the
mechanism of external things, build up, in recognisable
shape, farms and houses and report the speeches of men
and women who existed independently of herself. And
so we reach these summits of emotion not by rant or

rhapsody but by hearing a girl sing old songs to herself as she rocks in the branches of a tree; by watching the moor sheep crop the turf; by listening to the soft wind breathing through the grass. The life at the farm with all its absurdities and its improbability is laid open to us. We are given every opportunity of comparing *Wuthering Heights* with a real farm and Heathcliff with a real man. How, we are allowed to ask, can there be truth or insight or the finer shades of emotion in men and women who so little resemble what we have seen ourselves? But even as we ask it we see in Heathcliff the brother that a sister of genius might have seen; he is impossible, we say, but nevertheless no boy in literature has so vivid an existence as his. So it is with the two Catherines; never could women feel as they do or act in their manner, we say. All the same, they are the most lovable women in English fiction. It is as if she could tear up all that we know human beings by, and fill these unrecognisable transparences with such a gust of life that they transcend reality. Hers, then, is the rarest of all powers. She could free life from its dependence on facts; with a few touches indicate the spirit of a face so that it needs no body; by speaking of the moor make the wind blow and the thunder roar.

*

George Eliot

*

To read George Eliot attentively is to become aware how little one knows about her. It is also to become aware of the credulity, not very creditable to one's insight, with which, half consciously and partly maliciously, one had accepted the late Victorian version of a deluded woman who held phantom sway over subjects even more deluded than herself. At what moment, and by what means her spell was broken it is difficult to ascertain. Some people attribute it to the publication of her *Life*. Perhaps George Meredith, with his phrase about the "mercurial little showman" and the "errant woman" on the dais, gave point and poison to the arrows of thousands incapable of aiming them so accurately, but delighted to let fly. She became one of the butts for youth to laugh at, the convenient symbol of a group of serious people who were all guilty of the same idolatry and could be dismissed with the same scorn. Lord Acton had said that she was greater than Dante; Herbert Spencer exempted her novels, as if they were not novels, when he banned all fiction from the London Library. She was the pride and paragon of her sex. Moreover, her private record was not more alluring than her public. Asked to describe an afternoon at the Priory, the story-teller always intimated that the memory of those serious Sunday afternoons had come to tickle his sense of humour. He had been so much alarmed by the grave lady in her low chair; he had been so anxious to say the intelligent thing. Certainly, the talk had been very serious, as a note in the fine clear hand of the great novelist bore witness. It was dated on the Monday morning, and she accused herself of having spoken without due forethought of Marivaux when she meant another; but no doubt, she said, her listener had already supplied the correction. Still, the memory of talking about Marivaux to George Eliot on a Sunday afternoon was not a romantic memory. It had faded with the passage of the years. It had not become picturesque.

Indeed, one cannot escape the conviction that the long, heavy face with its expression of serious and sullen and almost equine power has stamped itself depressingly upon the minds of people who remember George Eliot, so that it looks out upon them from her pages. Mr. Gosse has lately described her as he saw her driving through London in a victoria—

a large, thick-set sybil, dreamy and immobile, whose massive features, somewhat grim when seen in profile, were incongruously bordered by a hat, always in the height of Paris fashion, which in those days commonly included an immense ostrich feather.

Lady Ritchie, with equal skill, has left a more intimate indoor portrait:

She sat by the fire in a beautiful black satin gown, with a green shaded lamp on the table beside her, where I saw German books lying and pamphlets and ivory paper-cutters. She was very quiet and noble, with two steady little eyes and a sweet voice. As I looked I felt her to be a friend, not exactly a personal friend, but a good and benevolent impulse.

A scrap of her talk is preserved. "We ought to respect our influence," she said. "We know by our own experience how very much others affect our lives, and we must remember that we in turn must have the same effect upon others." Jealously treasured, committed to memory, one can imagine recalling the scene, repeating the words, thirty years later and suddenly, for the first time, bursting into laughter.

In all these records one feels that the recorder, even when he was in the actual presence, kept his distance and kept his head, and never read the novels in later years with the light of a vivid, or puzzling, or beautiful personality dazzling in his eyes. In fiction, where so much of personality is revealed, the absence of charm is a great lack; and her critics, who have been, of course, mostly of the opposite sex, have resented, half consciously perhaps, her deficiency in a quality which is held to be supremely desirable in women. George Eliot was not charming; she was not strongly feminine; she had none of those eccentricities and inequalities of temper which give to so many artists the endearing simplicity of children. One feels that to most people, as to Lady Ritchie, she was "not exactly a personal friend, but a good and benevolent impulse." But if we consider these portraits more closely we shall find that they are all the portraits of an elderly celebrated woman, dressed in black satin, driving in her victoria, a woman who has been through her struggle and issued from it with a profound desire to be of use to others, but with no wish for intimacy, save with the little circle who had known her in the days of her youth. We know very little about the days of her youth; but we do know that the culture, the philosophy, the fame, and the influence were all built upon a very humble foundation—she was the grand-daughter of a carpenter.

The first volume of her life is a singularly depressing record. In it we see her raising herself with groans and struggles from the intolerable boredom of petty provincial society (her father had risen in the world and become more middle class, but less picturesque) to be the assistant editor of a highly intellectual London review, and the esteemed companion of Herbert Spencer. The stages are painful as she reveals them in the sad soliloquy in which Mr. Cross condemned her to tell the story of her life. Marked in early youth as one "sure to get something up very soon in the way of a clothing club," she proceeded to raise funds for restoring a church by making a chart of ecclesiastical history; and that was followed by a loss of faith which so disturbed her father that he refused to live with her. Next came the struggle with the translation of Strauss, which, dismal and "soul-stupefying" in itself, can scarcely have been made less so by the usual feminine tasks of ordering a household and nursing a dying father, and the distressing conviction, to one so dependent upon affection, that by becoming a blue-stocking she was forfeiting her brother's respect. "I used to go about like an owl," she said, "to the great disgust of my brother." "Poor thing," wrote a friend who saw her toiling through Strauss with a statue of the risen Christ in front of her, "I do pity her sometimes, with her pale sickly face and dreadful headaches, and anxiety, too, about her father." Yet, though we cannot read the story without a strong desire that the stages of her pilgrimage might have been made, if not more easy, at least more beautiful, there is a dogged determination in her advance upon the citadel of culture which raises it above our pity. Her development was very slow and very awkward, but it had the irresistible impetus behind it of a deep-seated and noble ambition. Every obstacle at length was thrust from her path. She knew every one. She read everything. Her astonishing intellectual vitality had triumphed. Youth was over, but youth had been full of suffering. Then, at the age of thirty-five, at the height of her powers, and in the fullness of her freedom, she made the decision which was of such profound moment to her and still matters even to us, and went to Weimar, alone with George Henry Lewes.

The books which followed so soon after her union testify in the fullest manner to the great liberation which had come to her with personal happiness. In themselves they provide us with a plentiful feast. Yet at the thresh-

old of her literary career one may find in some of the
circumstances of her life influences that turned her mind
to the past, to the country village, to the quiet and
beauty and simplicity of childish memories and away
from herself and the present. We understand how it was
that her first book was *Scenes of Clerical Life*, and not
Middlemarch. Her union with Lewes had surrounded
her with affection, but in view of the circumstances and
of the conventions it had also isolated her. "I wish it to
be understood," she wrote in 1857, "that I should never
invite any one to come and see me who did not ask
for the invitation." She had been "cut off from what is
called the world," she said later, but she did not regret
it. By becoming thus marked, first by circumstances and
later, inevitably, by her fame, she lost the power to move
on equal terms unnoted among her kind; and the loss for
a novelist was serious. Still, basking in the light and sunshine of *Scenes of Clerical Life*, feeling the large mature
mind spreading itself with a luxurious sense of freedom
in the world of her "remotest past," to speak of loss
seems inappropriate. Everything to such a mind was
gain. All experience filtered down through layer after
layer of perception and reflection, enriching and nour-
ishing. The utmost we can say, in qualifying her attitude
towards fiction by what little we know of her life, is
that she had taken to heart certain lessons not usually
learnt early, if learnt at all, among which, perhaps, the
most branded upon her was the melancholy virtue of
tolerance; her sympathies are with the everyday lot, and
play most happily in dwelling upon the homespun of
ordinary joys and sorrows. She has none of that romantic intensity which is connected with a sense of one's
own individuality, unsated and unsubdued, cutting its
shape sharply upon the background of the world. What
were the loves and sorrows of a snuffy old clergyman,
dreaming over his whisky, to the fiery egotism of Jane
Eyre? The beauty of those first books, *Scenes of Clerical Life*, *Adam Bede*, *The Mill on the Floss*, is very great.

It is impossible to estimate the merit of the Poysers, the Dodsons, the Gilfils, the Bartons, and the rest with all their surroundings and dependencies, because they have put on flesh and blood and we move among them, now bored, now sympathetic, but always with that unquestioning acceptance of all that they say and do, which we accord to the great originals only. The flood of memory and humour which she pours so spontaneously into one figure, one scene after another, until the whole fabric of ancient rural England is revived, has so much in common with a natural process that it leaves us with little consciousness that there is anything to criticise. We accept; we feel the delicious warmth and release of spirit which the great creative writers alone procure for us. As one comes back to the books after years of absence they pour out, even against our expectation, the same store of energy and heat, so that we want more than anything to idle in the warmth as in the sun beating down from the red orchard wall. If there is an element of unthinking abandonment in thus submitting to the humours of Midland farmers and their wives, that, too, is right in the circumstances. We scarcely wish to analyse what we feel to be so large and deeply human. And when we consider how distant in time the world of Shepperton and Hayslope is, and how remote the minds of farmer and agricultural labourers from those of most of George Eliot's readers, we can only attribute the ease and pleasure with which we ramble from house to smithy, from cottage parlour to rectory garden, to the fact that George Eliot makes us share their lives, not in a spirit of condescension or of curiosity, but in a spirit of sympathy. She is no satirist. The movement of her mind was too slow and cumbersome to lend itself to comedy. But she gathers in her large grasp a great bunch of the main elements of human nature and groups them loosely together with a tolerant and wholesome understanding which, as one finds upon re-reading, has not only kept her figures fresh and free, but has given

them an unexpected hold upon our laughter and tears.
There is the famous Mrs. Poyser. It would have been
easy to work her idiosyncrasies to death, and, as it is,
perhaps, George Eliot gets her laugh in the same place
a little too often. But memory, after the book is shut,
brings out, as sometimes in real life, the details and subtleties which some more salient characteristic has pre-
vented us from noticing at the time. We recollect that
her health was not good. There were occasions upon
which she said nothing at all. She was patience itself
with a sick child. She doted upon Totty. Thus one can
muse and speculate about the greater number of George
Eliot's characters and find, even in the least important,
a roominess and margin where those qualities lurk which
she has no call to bring from their obscurity.

But in the midst of all this tolerance and sympathy
there are, even in the early books, moments of greater
stress. Her humour has shown itself broad enough to
cover a wide range of fools and failures, mothers and
children, dogs and flourishing midland fields, farmers,
sagacious or fuddled over their ale, horse-dealers, inn-
keepers, curates, and carpenters. Over them all broods
a certain romance, the only romance that George Eliot
allowed herself—the romance of the past. The books are
astonishingly readable and have no trace of pomposity
or pretence. But to the reader who holds a large stretch
of her early work in view it will become obvious that
the mist of recollection gradually withdraws. It is not
that her power diminishes, for, to our thinking, it is at
its highest in the mature *Middlemarch*, the magnificent
book which with all its imperfections is one of the few
English novels written for grown-up people. But the
world of fields and farms no longer contents her. In
real life she had sought her fortunes elsewhere; and
though to look back into the past was calming and con-
soling, there are, even in the early works, traces of that
troubled spirit, that exacting and questioning and baffled presence who was George Eliot herself. In *Adam*

Bede there is a hint of her in Dinah. She shows herself far more openly and completely in Maggie in *The Mill on the Floss*. She is Janet in *Janet's Repentance*, and Romola, and Dorothea seeking wisdom and finding one scarcely knows what in marriage with Ladislaw. Those who fall foul of George Eliot do so, we incline to think, on account of her heroines; and with good reason; for there is no doubt that they bring out the worst of her, lead her into difficult places, make her self-conscious, didactic, and occasionally vulgar. Yet if you could delete the whole sisterhood you would leave a much smaller and a much inferior world, albeit a world of greater artistic perfection and far superior jollity and comfort. In accounting for her failure, in so far as it was a failure, one recollects that she never wrote a story until she was thirty-seven, and that by the time she was thirty-seven she had come to think of herself with a mixture of pain and something like resentment. For long she preferred not to think of herself at all. Then, when the first flush of creative energy was exhausted and self-confidence had come to her, she wrote more and more from the personal standpoint, but she did so without the unhesitating abandonment of the young. Her self-consciousness is always marked when her heroines say what she herself would have said. She disguised them in every possible way. She granted them beauty and wealth into the bargain; she invented, more improbably, a taste for brandy. But the disconcerting and stimulating fact remained that she was compelled by the very power of her genius to step forth in person upon the quiet bucolic scene.

The noble and beautiful girl who insisted upon being born into the Mill on the Floss is the most obvious example of the ruin which a heroine can strew about her. Humour controls her and keeps her lovable so long as she is small and can be satisfied by eloping with the gipsies or hammering nails into her doll; but she develops; and before George Eliot knows what has happened she has a full-grown woman on her hands demanding what neither gipsies nor dolls, nor St. Ogg's itself is capable of giving her. First Philip Wakem is produced, and later Stephen Guest. The weakness of the one and the coarseness of the other have often been pointed out; but both, in their weakness and coarseness, illustrate not so much George Eliot's inability to draw the portrait of a man, as the uncertainty, the infirmity, and the fumbling which shook her hand when she had to conceive a fit mate for a heroine. She is in the first place driven beyond the home world she knew and loved, and forced to set foot in middle-class drawing-rooms where young men sing all the summer morning and young women sit embroidering smoking-caps for bazaars. She feels herself out of her element, as her clumsy satire of what she calls "good society" proves.

Good society has its claret and its velvet carpets, its dinner engagements six weeks deep, its opera, and its faëry ball rooms . . . gets its science done by Faraday and its religion by the superior clergy who are to be met in the best houses; how should it have need of belief and emphasis?

There is no trace of humour or insight there, but only the vindictiveness of a grudge which we feel to be personal in its origin. But terrible as the complexity of our social system is in its demands upon the sympathy and discernment of a novelist straying across the boundaries, Maggie Tulliver did worse than drag George Eliot from her natural surroundings. She insisted upon the introduction of the great emotional scene. She must love; she must despair; she must be drowned clasping her brother in her arms. The more one examines the great emotional scenes the more nervously one anticipates the brewing and gathering and thickening of the cloud which will burst upon our heads at the moment of crisis in a shower of disillusionment and verbosity. It is partly that her hold upon dialogue, when it is not dialect, is slack; and partly that she seems to shrink with an elderly dread of fatigue from the effort of emotional concentration. She allows her heroines to talk too much. She has little verbal felicity. She lacks the unerring taste which chooses one sentence and compresses the heart of the scene within that. "Whom are you going to dance with?" asked Mr. Knightley, at the Westons' ball. "With you, if you will ask me," said Emma; and she has said enough. Mrs. Casaubon would have talked for an hour and we should have looked out of the window.

Yet, dismiss the heroines without sympathy, confine George Eliot to the agricultural world of her "remotest past," and you not only diminish her greatness but lose her true flavour. That greatness is here we can have no doubt. The width of the prospect, the large strong outlines of the principal features, the ruddy light of the early books, the searching power and reflective richness of the later tempt us to linger and expatiate beyond our limits. But it is upon the heroines that we would cast a final glance. "I have always been finding out my religion since I was a little girl," says Dorothea Casaubon. "I used to pray so much—now I hardly ever pray. I try not to have desires merely for myself. . . ." She is speaking for them all. That is their problem. They cannot live without religion, and they start out on the search for one when they are little girls. Each has the deep feminine passion for goodness, which makes the place where she stands in aspiration and agony the heart of the book —still and cloistered like a place of worship, but that she no longer knows to whom to pray. In learning they seek their goal; in the ordinary tasks of womanhood; in the wider service of their kind. They do not find what they seek, and we cannot wonder. The ancient consciousness of woman, charged with suffering and sensibility, and for so many ages dumb, seems in them to have brimmed and overflowed and uttered a demand for something—they scarcely know what—for something that is perhaps incompatible with the facts of human existence. George Eliot had far too strong an intelligence to tamper with those facts, and too broad a humour to mitigate the truth because it was a stern one. Save for the supreme courage of their endeavour, the struggle ends, for her heroines, in tragedy, or in a compromise that is even more melancholy. But their story is the incomplete version of the story of George Eliot herself. For her, too, the burden and the complexity of womanhood were not enough; she must reach beyond the sanctuary and pluck for herself the strange bright fruits of art and knowledge. Clasping them as few women have ever clasped them, she would not renounce her own inheritance—the difference of view, the difference of standard—nor accept an inappropriate reward. Thus we behold her, a memorable figure, inordinately praised and shrinking from her fame, despondent, reserved, shuddering back into the arms of love as if there alone were satisfaction and, it might be, justification, at the same time reaching out with "a fastidious yet hungry ambition" for all that life could offer the free and inquiring mind and confronting her feminine aspirations with the real world of men. Triumphant was the issue for her, whatever it may have been for her creations, and as we recollect all that she dared and achieved, how with every obstacle against her—sex and health and convention—she sought more knowledge and more freedom till the body, weighted with its double burden, sank worn out, we must lay upon her grave whatever we have it in our power to bestow of laurel and rose.

The Russian Point of View

Doubtful as we frequently are whether either the French
or the Americans, who have so much in common with
us, can yet understand English literature, we must admit graver doubts whether, for all their enthusiasm, the
English can understand Russian literature. Debate might
protract itself indefinitely as to what we mean by "understand." Instances will occur to everybody of American writers in particular who have written with the
highest discrimination of our literature and of ourselves;
who have lived a lifetime among us, and finally have
taken legal steps to become subjects of King George.
For all that, have they understood us, have they not remained to the end of their days foreigners? Could any
one believe that the novels of Henry James were written
by a man who had grown up in the society which he
describes, or that his criticism of English writers was
written by a man who had read Shakespeare without
any sense of the Atlantic Ocean and two or three hundred years on the far side of it separating his civilisation
from ours? A special acuteness and detachment, a sharp
angle of vision the foreigner will often achieve; but not
that absence of self-consciousness, that ease and fellowship and sense of common values which make for intimacy, and sanity, and the quick give and take of familiar
intercourse.

Not only have we all this to separate us from Russian

literature, but a much more serious barrier—the difference of language. Of all those who feasted upon Tolstoi,
Dostoevsky, and Tchekov during the past twenty years,
not more than one or two perhaps have been able to
read them in Russian. Our estimate of their qualities has
been formed by critics who have never read a word
of Russian, or seen Russia, or even heard the language
spoken by natives; who have had to depend, blindly and
implicitly, upon the work of translators.

What we are saying amounts to this, then, that we
have judged a whole literature stripped of its style.
When you have changed every word in a sentence from
Russian to English, have thereby altered the sense a little, the sound, weight, and accent of the words in relation to each other completely, nothing remains except
a crude and coarsened version of the sense. Thus treated,
the great Russian writers are like men deprived by an
earthquake or a railway accident not only of all their
clothes, but also of something subtler and more important—their manners, the idiosyncrasies of their characters. What remains is, as the English have proved by the
fanaticism of their admiration, something very powerful
and very impressive, but it is difficult to feel sure, in
view of these mutilations, how far we can trust ourselves
not to impute, to distort, to read into them an emphasis
which is false.

They have lost their clothes, we say, in some terrible
catastrophe, for some such figure as that describes the
simplicity, the humanity, startled out of all effort to
hide and disguise its instincts, which Russian literature,
whether it is due to translation, or to some more
profound cause, makes upon us. We find these qualities
steeping it through, as obvious in the lesser writers as in
the greater. "Learn to make yourselves akin to people. I
would even like to add: make yourself indispensable to
them. But let this sympathy be not with the mind—for
it is easy with the mind—but with the heart, with love
towards them." "From the Russian," one would say in-

stantly, wherever one chanced on that quotation. The simplicity, the absence of effort, the assumption that in a world bursting with misery the chief call upon us is to understand our fellow-sufferers, "and not with the mind —for it is easy with the mind—but with the heart"—this is the cloud which broods above the whole of Russian literature, which lures us from our own parched brilliancy and scorched thoroughfares to expand in its shade —and of course with disastrous results. We become awkward and self-conscious; denying our own qualities, we write with an affectation of goodness and simplicity which is nauseating in the extreme. We cannot say "Brother" with simple conviction. There is a story by Mr. Galsworthy in which one of the characters so addresses another (they are both in the depths of misfortune). Immediately everything becomes strained and affected. The English equivalent for "Brother" is "Mate" —a very different word, with something sardonic in it, an indefinable suggestion of humour. Met though they are in the depths of misfortune the two Englishmen who thus accost each other will, we are sure, find a job, make their fortunes, spend the last years of their lives in luxury, and leave a sum of money to prevent poor devils from calling each other "Brother" on the Embankment. But it is common suffering, rather than common happiness, effort, or desire that produces the sense of brotherhood. It is the "deep sadness" which Dr. Hagberg Wright finds typical of the Russian people that creates their literature.

A generalisation of this kind will, of course, even if it has some degree of truth when applied to the body of literature, be changed profoundly when a writer of genius sets to work on it. At once other questions arise. It is seen that an "attitude" is not simple; it is highly complex. Men reft of their coats and their manners, stunned by a railway accident, say hard things, harsh things, unpleasant things, difficult things, even if they say them with the abandonment and simplicity which catastrophe

has bred in them. Our first impressions of Tchekov are
not of simplicity but of bewilderment. What is the point
of it, and why does he make a story out of this? we ask
as we read story after story. A man falls in love with a
married woman, and they part and meet, and in the end
are left talking about their position and by what means
they can be free from "this intolerable bondage."

" 'How? How?' he asked, clutching his head. . . .
And it seemed as though in a little while the solution
would be found and then a new and splendid life would
begin." That is the end. A postman drives a student to
the station and all the way the student tries to make the
postman talk, but he remains silent. Suddenly the postman says unexpectedly, "It's against the regulations to
take any one with the post." And he walks up and down
the platform with a look of anger on his face. "With
whom was he angry? Was it with people, with poverty,
with the autumn nights?" Again, that story ends.

But is it the end, we ask? We have rather the feeling
that we have overrun our signals; or it is as if a tune had
stopped short without the expected chords to close it.
These stories are inconclusive, we say, and proceed to
frame a criticism based upon the assumption that stories
ought to conclude in a way that we recognise. In so doing we raise the question of our own fitness as readers.
Where the tune is familiar and the end emphatic—lovers
united, villains discomfited, intrigues exposed—as it is in
most Victorian fiction, we can scarcely go wrong, but
where the tune is unfamiliar and the end a note of interrogation or merely the information that they went on
talking, as it is in Tchekov, we need a very daring and
alert sense of literature to make us hear the tune, and in
particular those last notes which complete the harmony.
Probably we have to read a great many stories before we
feel, and the feeling is essential to our satisfaction, that
we hold the parts together, and that Tchekov was not
merely rambling disconnectedly, but struck now this

note, now that with intention, in order to complete his meaning.

We have to cast about in order to discover where the emphasis in these strange stories rightly comes. Tchekov's own words give us a lead in the right direction. ". . . such a conversation as this between us," he says, "would have been unthinkable for our parents. At night they did not talk, but slept sound; we, our generation, sleep badly, are restless, but talk a great deal, and are always trying to settle whether we are right or not." Our literature of social satire and psychological finesse both sprang from that restless sleep, that incessant talking; but after all, there is an enormous difference between Tchekov and Henry James, between Tchekov and Bernard Shaw. Obviously—but where does it arise? Tchekov, too, is aware of the evils and injustices of the social state; the condition of the peasants appals him, but the reformer's zeal is not his—that is not the signal for us to stop. The mind interests him enormously; he is a most subtle and delicate analyst of human relations. But again, no; the end is not there. Is it that he is primarily interested not in the soul's relation with other souls, but with the soul's relation to health—with the soul's relation to goodness? These stories are always showing us some affectation, pose, insincerity. Some woman has got into a false relation; some man has been perverted by the inhumanity of his circumstances. The soul is ill; the soul is cured; the soul is not cured. Those are the emphatic points in his stories.

Once the eye is used to these shades, half the "conclusions" of fiction fade into thin air; they show like transparences with a light behind them—gaudy, glaring, superficial. The general tidying up of the last chapter, the marriage, the death, the statement of values so sonorously trumpeted forth, so heavily underlined, become of the most rudimentary kind. Nothing is solved, we feel; nothing is rightly held together. On the other hand, the method which at first seemed so casual, inconclusive, and occupied with trifles, now appears the result of an exquisitely original and fastidious taste, choosing boldly, arranging infallibly, and controlled by an honesty for which we can find no match save among the Russians themselves. There may be no answer to these questions, but at the same time let us never manipulate the evidence so as to produce something fitting, decorous, agreeable to our vanity. This may not be the way to catch the ear of the public; after all, they are used to louder music, fiercer measures; but as the tune sounded, so he has written it. In consequence, as we read these little stories about nothing at all, the horizon widens; the soul gains an astonishing sense of freedom.

In reading Tchekov we find ourselves repeating the word "soul" again and again. It sprinkles his pages. Old drunkards use it freely; ". . . you are high up in the service, beyond all reach, but haven't real soul, my dear boy . . . there's no strength in it." Indeed, it is the soul that is the chief character in Russian fiction. Delicate and subtle in Tchekov, subject to an infinite number of humours and distempers, it is of greater depth and volume in Dostoevsky, liable to violent diseases and raging fevers, but still the predominant concern. Perhaps that is why it needs so great an effort on the part of an English reader to read *The Brothers Karamazov* or *The Possessed* a second time. The "soul" is alien to him. It is even antipathetic. It has little sense of humour and no sense of comedy. It is formless. It has slight connection with the intellect. It is confused, diffuse, tumultuous, incapable, it seems, of submitting to the control of logic or the discipline of poetry. The novels of Dostoevsky are seething whirlpools, gyrating sandstorms, waterspouts which hiss and boil and suck us in. They are composed purely and wholly of the stuff of the soul. Against our wills we are drawn in, whirled round, blinded, suffocated, and at the same time filled with a giddy rapture. Out of Shakespeare there is no more exciting reading. We open the door and find ourselves in a room full of Russian generals, the tutors of Russian generals, their step-daughters and cousins and crowds of miscellaneous people who are all talking at the tops of their voices about their most private affairs. But where are we? Surely it is the part of a novelist to inform us whether we are in an hotel, a flat, or hired lodging. Nobody thinks of explaining. We are souls, tortured, unhappy souls, whose only business it is to talk, to reveal, to confess, to draw up at whatever rending of flesh and nerve those crabbed sins which crawl on the sand at the bottom of us. But, as we listen, our confusion slowly settles. A rope is flung to us; we catch hold of a soliloquy; holding on by the skin of our teeth, we are rushed through the water; feverishly, wildly, we rush on and on, now submerged, now in a moment of vision understanding more than we have ever understood before, and receiving such revelations as we are wont to get only from the press of life at its fullest. As we fly we pick it all up—the names of the people, their relationships, that they are staying in an hotel at Roulettenburg, that Polina is involved in an intrigue with the Marquis de Grieux—but what unimportant matters these are compared with the soul! It is the soul that matters, its passion, its tumult, its astonishing medley of beauty and vileness. And if our voices suddenly rise into shrieks of laughter, or if we are shaken by the most violent sobbing, what more natural?—it hardly calls for remark. The pace at which we are living is so tremendous that sparks must rush off our wheels as we fly. Moreover, when the speed is thus increased and the elements of the soul are seen, not separately in scenes of humour or scenes of passion as our slower English minds conceive them, but streaked, involved, inextricably confused, a new panorama of the human mind is revealed. The old divisions melt into each other. Men are at the same time villains and saints; their acts are at once beautiful and despicable. We love and we hate at the same time. There is none of that precise division between good and bad to which we are used. Often those for whom we feel most affection are the greatest criminals, and the most abject sinners move us to the strongest admiration as well as love.

Dashed to the crest of the waves, bumped and battered on the stones at the bottom, it is difficult for an English reader to feel at ease. The process to which he is accustomed in his own literature is reversed. If we wished to tell the story of a General's love affair (and we should find it very difficult in the first place not to laugh at a General), we should begin with his house; we should solidify his surroundings. Only when all was ready should we attempt to deal with the General himself. Moreover, it is not the samovar but the teapot that rules in England; time is limited; space crowded; the influence of other points of view, of other books, even of other ages, makes itself felt. Society is sorted out into lower, middle, and upper classes, each with its own traditions, its own manners, and, to some extent, its own language. Whether he wishes it or not, there is a constant pressure upon an English novelist to recognise these barriers, and, in consequence, order is imposed on him and some kind of form; he is inclined to satire rather than to compassion, to scrutiny of society rather than understanding of individuals themselves.

No such restraints were laid on Dostoevsky. It is all the same to him whether you are noble or simple, a tramp or a great lady. Whoever you are, you are the vessel of this perplexed liquid, this cloudy, yeasty, precious stuff, the soul. The soul is not restrained by barriers. It overflows, it floods, it mingles with the souls of others. The simple story of a bank clerk who could not pay for a bottle of wine spreads, before we know what is happening, into the lives of his father-in-law and the five mistresses whom his father-in-law treated abominably, and the postman's life, and the charwoman's, and the Princesses' who lodged in the same block of flats; for nothing is outside Dostoevsky's province; and when he is tired, he does not stop, he goes on. He cannot restrain himself. Out it tumbles upon us, hot, scalding, mixed, marvellous, terrible, oppressive—the human soul.

There remains the greatest of all novelists—for what else can we call the author of *War and Peace*? Shall we find Tolstoi, too, alien, difficult, a foreigner? Is there some oddity in his angle of vision which, at any rate until we have become disciples and so lost our bearings, keeps us at arm's length in suspicion and bewilderment? From his first words we can be sure of one thing at any rate—here is a man who sees what we see, who proceeds, too, as we are accustomed to proceed, not from the inside outwards, but from the outside inwards. Here is a world in which the postman's knock is heard at eight o'clock, and people go to bed between ten and eleven. Here is a man, too, who is no savage, no child of nature; he is educated; he has had every sort of experience. He is one of those born aristocrats who have used their privileges to the full. He is metropolitan, not suburban. His senses, his intellect, are acute, powerful, and well nourished. There is something proud and superb in the attack of such a mind and such a body upon life. Nothing seems to escape him. Nothing glances off him unrecorded. Nobody, therefore, can so convey the excitement of sport, the beauty of horses, and all the fierce desirability of the world to the senses of a strong young man. Every twig, every feather sticks to his magnet. He notices the blue or red of a child's frock; the way a horse shifts its tail; the sound of a cough; the action of a man trying to put his hands into pockets that have been sewn up. And what his infallible eye reports of a cough or a trick of the hands his infallible brain refers to something hidden in the character so that we know his people, not only by the way they love and their views on politics and the immortality of the soul, but also by the way they sneeze and choke. Even in a translation we feel that we have been set on a mountain-top and had a telescope put into our hands. Everything is astonishingly clear and absolutely sharp. Then, suddenly, just as we are exulting, breathing deep, feeling at once braced and purified, some detail—perhaps the head of a man—comes at us out of the picture in an alarming way, as if extruded by the very intensity of its life. "Suddenly a strange thing happened to me: first I ceased to see what was around me; then his face seemed to vanish till only the eyes were left, shining over against mine; next the eyes seemed to be in my own head, and then all became confused—I could see nothing and was forced to shut my eyes, in order to break loose from the feeling of pleasure and fear which his gaze was producing in me. . . ." Again and again we share Masha's feelings in *Family Happiness*. One shuts one's eyes to escape the feeling of pleasure and fear. Often it is pleasure that is uppermost. In this very story there are two descriptions, one of a girl walking in a garden at night with her lover, one of a newly married couple prancing down their drawing-room, which so convey the feeling of intense happiness that we shut the book to feel it better. But always there is an element of fear which makes us, like Masha, wish to escape from the gaze which Tolstoi fixes on us. Does it arise from the sense, which in real life might harass us, that such happiness as he describes is too intense to last, that we are on the edge of disaster? Or is it not that the very intensity of our pleasure is somehow questionable and forces us to ask, with Pozdnyshev in the *Kreutzer Sonata*, "But why live?" Life dominates Tolstoi as the soul dominates Dostoevsky. There is always at the centre of all the brilliant and flashing petals of the flower this scorpion, "Why live?" There is always at the centre of the book some Olenin, or Pierre, or Levin who gathers into himself all experience, turns the world round between his fingers, and never ceases to ask even as he enjoys it, what is the meaning of it, and what should be our aims. It is not the priest who shatters our desires most effectively; it is the man who has known them, and loved them himself. When he derides them, the world indeed turns to dust and ashes beneath our feet. Thus fear mingles with our pleasure, and of the three great Russian writers, it is Tolstoi who most enthralls us and most repels.

But the mind takes its bias from the place of its birth, and no doubt, when it strikes upon a literature so alien as the Russian, flies off at a tangent far from the truth.

*

Outlines

*

I

MISS MITFORD

Speaking truthfully, *Mary Russell Mitford and Her Surroundings* is not a good book. It neither enlarges the mind nor purifies the heart. There is nothing in it about Prime Ministers and not very much about Miss Mitford. Yet, as one is setting out to speak the truth, one must own that there are certain books which can be read without the mind and without the heart, but still with considerable enjoyment. To come to the point, the great merit of these scrapbooks, for they can scarcely be called biographies, is that they license mendacity. One cannot believe what Miss Hill says about Miss Mitford, and thus one is free to invent Miss Mitford for oneself. Not for a second do we accuse Miss Hill of telling lies. That infirmity is entirely ours. For example: "Alresford was the birthplace of one who loved nature as few have loved her, and whose writings 'breathe the air of the hayfields and the scent of the hawthorn boughs,' and seem to waft to us 'the sweet breezes that blow over ripened cornfields and daisied meadows.'" It is perfectly true that Miss Mitford was born at Alresford, and yet, when it is put like that, we doubt whether she was ever born at all. Indeed she was, says Miss Hill; she was born "on the 16th December, 1787. 'A pleasant house in truth it was,' Miss Mitford writes. 'The breakfast-room . . . was a lofty and

spacious apartment.' " So Miss Mitford was born in the
breakfast-room about eight-thirty on a snowy morning
between the Doctor's second and third cups of tea. "Par-
don me," said Mrs. Mitford, turning a little pale, but not
omitting to add the right quantity of cream to her husband's tea, "I feel . . ." That is the way in which Mendacity begins. There is something plausible and even ingenious in her approaches. The touch about the cream,
for instance, might be called historical, for it is well
known that when Mary won £20,000 in the Irish lottery,
the Doctor spent it all upon Wedgwood china, the winning number being stamped upon the soup plates in the
middle of an Irish harp, the whole being surmounted by
the Mitford arms, and encircled by the motto of Sir
John Bertram, one of William the Conqueror's knights,
from whom the Mitfords claimed descent. "Observe,"
says Mendacity, "with what an air the Doctor drinks his
tea, and how she, poor lady, contrives to curtsey as she
leaves the room." Tea? I inquire, for the Doctor, though
a fine figure of a man, is already purple and profuse, and
foams like a crimson cock over the frill of his fine laced
shirt. "Since the ladies have left the room," Mendacity
begins, and goes on to make up a pack of lies with the
sole object of proving that Dr. Mitford kept a mistress
in the purlieus of Reading and paid her money on the
pretence that he was investing it in a new method of
lighting and heating houses invented by the Marquis de
Chavannes. It came to the same thing in the end—to the
King's Bench Prison, that is to say; but instead of allowing us to recall the literary and historical associations of
the place, Mendacity wanders off to the window and dis-
tracts us again by the platitudinous remark that it is still
snowing. There is something very charming in an ancient
snowstorm. The weather has varied almost as much in
the course of generations as mankind. The snow of those
days was more formally shaped and a good deal softer
than the snow of ours, just as an eighteenth-century cow
was no more like our cows than she was like the florid

and fiery cows of Elizabethan pastures. Sufficient attention has scarcely been paid to this aspect of literature,
which, it cannot be denied, has its importance.

Our brilliant young men might do worse, when in
search of a subject, than devote a year or two to cows in
literature, snow in literature, the daisy in Chaucer and
in Coventry Patmore. At any rate, the snow falls heavily. The Portsmouth mail-coach has already lost its way;
several ships have foundered, and Margate pier has been
totally destroyed. At Hatfield Peveral twenty sheep have
been buried, and though one supports itself by gnawing
wurzels which it has found near it, there is grave reason
to fear that the French king's coach has been blocked on
the road to Colchester. It is now the 16th of February,
1808.

Poor Mrs. Mitford! Twenty-one years ago she left the
breakfast-room, and no news has yet been received of her
child. Even Mendacity is a little ashamed of itself, and,
picking up *Mary Russell Mitford and Her Surroundings*,
assures us that everything will come right if we possess
ourselves in patience. The French king's coach was on its
way to Bocking; at Bocking lived Lord and Lady Charles
Murray-Aynsley; and Lord Charles was shy. Lord
Charles had always been shy. Once when Mary Mitford was five years old—sixteen years, that is, before the
sheep were lost and the French king went to Bocking—
Mary "threw him into an agony of blushing by running
up to his chair in mistake for that of my papa." He had
indeed to leave the room. Miss Hill, who, somewhat
strangely, finds the society of Lord and Lady Charles
pleasant, does not wish to quit it without "introducing an
incident in connection with them which took place in the
month of February, 1808." But is Miss Mitford concerned
in it? we ask, for there must be an end of trifling. To
some extent, that is to say, Lady Charles was a cousin of
the Mitfords, and Lord Charles was shy. Mendacity is
quite ready to deal with "the incident" even on these
terms; but, we repeat, we have had enough of trifling.

Miss Mitford may not be a great woman; for all we know she was not even a good one; but we have certain responsibilities as a reviewer which we are not going to evade.

There is, to begin with, English literature. A sense of the beauty of nature has never been altogether absent, however much the cow may change from age to age, from English poetry. Nevertheless, the difference between Pope and Wordsworth in this respect is very considerable. *Lyrical Ballads* was published in 1798; *Our Village* in 1824. One being in verse and the other in prose, it is not necessary to labour a comparison which contains, however, not only the elements of justice, but the seeds of many volumes. Like her great predecessor, Miss Mitford much preferred the country to the town; and thus, perhaps, it may not be inopportune to dwell for a moment upon the King of Saxony, Mary Anning, and the ichthyosaurus. Let alone the fact that Mary Anning and Mary Mitford had a Christian name in common, they are further connected by what can scarcely be called a fact, but may, without hazard, be called a probability. Miss Mitford was looking for fossils at Lyme Regis only fifteen years before Mary Anning found one. The King of Saxony visited Lyme in 1844, and seeing the head of an ichthyosaurus in Mary Anning's window, asked her to drive to Pinny and explore the rocks. While they were looking for fossils, an old woman seated herself in the King's coach—was she Mary Mitford? Truth compels us to say that she was not; but there is no doubt, and we are not trifling when we say it, that Mary Mitford often expressed a wish that she had known Mary Anning, and it is singularly unfortunate to have to state that she never did. For we have reached the year 1844; Mary Mitford is fifty-seven years of age, and so far, thanks to Mendacity and its trifling ways, all we know of her is that she did not know Mary Anning, had not found an ichthyosaurus, had not been out in a snowstorm, and had not seen the King of France.

It is time to wring the creature's neck, and begin again at the very beginning.

What considerations, then, had weight with Miss Hill when she decided to write *Mary Russell Mitford and Her Surroundings?* Three emerge from the rest, and may be held of paramount importance. In the first place, Miss Mitford was a lady; in the second, she was born in the year 1787; and in the third, the stock of female characters who lend themselves to biographic treatment by their own sex is, for one reason or another, running short. For instance, little is known of Sappho, and that little is not wholly to her credit. Lady Jane Grey has merit, but is undeniably obscure. Of George Sand, the more we know the less we approve. George Eliot was led into evil ways which not all her philosophy can excuse. The Brontës, however highly we rate their genius, lacked that indefinable something which marks the lady; Harriet Martineau was an atheist; Mrs. Browning was a married woman; Jane Austen, Fanny Burney, and Maria Edgeworth have been done already; so that, what with one thing and another, Mary Russell Mitford is the only woman left.

There is no need to labour the extreme importance of the date when we see the word "surroundings" on the back of a book. Surroundings, as they are called, are invariably eighteenth-century surroundings. When we come, as of course we do, to that phrase which relates how "as we looked upon the steps leading down from the upper room, we fancied we saw the tiny figure jumping from step to step," it would be the grossest outrage upon our sensibilities to be told that those steps were Athenian, Elizabethan, or Parisian. They were, of course, eighteenth-century steps, leading down from the old panelled room into the shady garden, where, tradition has it, William Pitt played marbles, or, if we like to be bold, where on still summer days we can almost fancy that we hear the drums of Bonaparte on the coast of France. Bonaparte is the limit of the imagination on one side, as

Monmouth is on the other; it would be fatal if the imagination took to toying with Prince Albert or sporting with King John. But fancy knows her place, and there is no need to labour the point that her place is the eighteenth century. The other point is more obscure. One must be a lady. Yet what that means, and whether we like what it means, may both be doubtful. If we say that Jane Austen was a lady and that Charlotte Brontë was not one, we do as much as need be done in the way of definition, and commit ourselves to neither side.

It is undoubtedly because of their reticence that Miss Hill is on the side of the ladies. They sigh things off and they smile things off, but they never seize the silver table by the legs or dash the teacups on the floor. It is in many ways a great convenience to have a subject who can be trusted to live a long life without once raising her voice. Sixteen years is a considerable stretch of time, but of a lady it is enough to say, "Here Mary Mitford passed sixteen years of her life and here she got to know and love not only their own beautiful grounds but also every turn of the surrounding shady lanes." Her loves were vegetable, and her lanes were shady. Then, of course, she was educated at the school where Jane Austen and Mrs. Sherwood had been educated. She visited Lyme Regis, and there is mention of the Cobb. She saw London from the top of St. Paul's, and London was much smaller then than it is now. She changed from one charming house to another, and several distinguished literary gentlemen paid her compliments and came to tea. When the dining-room ceiling fell down it did not fall on her head, and when she took a ticket in a lottery she did win the prize. If in the foregoing sentences there are any words of more than two syllables, it is our fault and not Miss Hill's; and to do that writer justice, there are not many whole sentences in the book which are neither quoted from Miss Mitford nor supported by the authority of Mr. Crissy.

But how dangerous a thing is life! Can one be sure

that anything not wholly made of mahogany will to the
very end stand empty in the sun? Even cupboards have
their secret springs, and when, inadvertently we are
sure, Miss Hill touches this one, out, terrible to relate,
topples a stout old gentleman. In plain English, Miss
Mitford had a father. There is nothing actually improper
in that. Many women have had fathers. But Miss Mitford's father was kept in a cupboard; that is to say, he
was not a nice father. Miss Hill even goes so far as to
conjecture that when "an imposing procession of neighbours and friends" followed him to the grave, "we
cannot help thinking that this was more to show sympathy and respect for Miss Mitford than from special respect for him." Severe as the judgement is, the glutton-
ous, bibulous, amorous old man did something to deserve
it. The less said about him the better. Only, if from your
earliest childhood your father has gambled and specu-
lated, first with your mother's fortune, then with your
own, spent your earnings, driven you to earn more, and
spent that too; if in old age he has lain upon a sofa and
insisted that fresh air is bad for daughters, if, dying at
length, he has left debts that can only be paid by selling
everything you have or sponging upon the charity of
friends—then even a lady sometimes raises her voice.
Miss Mitford herself spoke out once. "It was grief to go;
there I had toiled and striven and tasted as deeply of bitter anxiety, of fear, and of hope as often falls to the lot
of woman." What language for a lady to use! for a lady,
too, who owns a teapot. There is a drawing of the teapot at the bottom of the page. But it is now of no avail;
Miss Mitford has smashed it to smithereens. That is the
worst of writing about ladies; they have fathers as well
as teapots. On the other hand, some pieces of Dr. Mitford's Wedgwood dinner service are still in existence,
and a copy of Adam's Geography, which Mary won as a
prize at school, is "in our temporary possession." If
there is nothing improper in the suggestion, might not
the next book be devoted entirely to them?

II
DR. BENTLEY

As we saunter through those famous courts where Dr. Bentley once reigned supreme we sometimes catch sight of a figure hurrying on its way to Chapel or Hall which, as it disappears, draws our thoughts enthusiastically after it. For that man, we are told, has the whole of Sophocles at his finger-ends; knows Homer by heart; reads Pindar as we read the *Times;* and spends his life, save for these short excursions to eat and pray, wholly in the company of the Greeks. It is true that the infirmities of our education prevent us from appreciating his emendations as they deserve; his life's work is a sealed book to us; none the less, we treasure up the last flicker of his black gown, and feel as if a bird of Paradise had flashed by us, so bright is his spirit's raiment, and in the murk of a November evening we had been privileged to see it winging its way to roost in fields of amaranth and beds of moly. Of all men, great scholars are the most mysterious, the most august. Since it is unlikely that we shall ever be admitted to their intimacy, or see much more of them than a black gown crossing a court at dusk, the best we can do is to read their lives—for example, the *Life of Dr. Bentley* by Bishop Monk.

There we shall find much that is odd and little that is reassuring. The greatest of our scholars, the man who read Greek as the most expert of us read English not merely with an accurate sense of meaning and grammar but with a sensibility so subtle and widespread that he perceived relations and suggestions of language which enabled him to fetch up from oblivion lost lines and inspire new life into the little fragments that remained, the man who should have been steeped in beauty (if what they say of the Classics is true) as a honey-pot is ingrained with sweetness was, on the contrary, the most quarrelsome of mankind.

"I presume that there are not many examples of an individual who has been a party in six distinct suits before the Court of King's Bench within the space of three years," his biographer remarks; and adds that Bentley won them all. It is difficult to deny his conclusion that though Dr. Bentley might have been a first-rate lawyer or a great soldier "such a display suited any character rather than that of a learned and dignified clergyman." Not all these disputes, however, sprung from his love of literature. The charges against which he had to defend himself were directed against him as Master of Trinity College, Cambridge. He was habitually absent from chapel; his expenditure upon building and upon his household was excessive; he used the college seal at meetings which did not consist of the statutable number of sixteen, and so on. In short, the career of the Master of Trinity was one continuous series of acts of aggression and defiance, in which Dr. Bentley treated the Society of Trinity College as a grown man might treat an importunate rabble of street boys. Did they dare to hint that the staircase at the Lodge which admitted four persons abreast was quite wide enough?—did they refuse to sanction his expenditure upon a new one? Meeting them in the Great Court one evening after chapel he proceeded urbanely to question them. They refused to budge. Whereupon, with a sudden alteration of colour and voice, Bentley demanded whether "they had forgotten his rusty sword?" Mr. Michael Hutchinson and some others, upon whose backs the weight of that weapon would have first descended, brought pressure upon their seniors. The bill for £350 was paid and their preferment secured. But Bentley did not wait for this act of submission to finish his staircase.

So it went on, year after year. Nor was the arrogance of his behaviour always justified by the splendour or utility of the objects he had in view—the creation of the Backs, the erection of an observatory, the foundation of a laboratory. More trivial desires were gratified with the

same tyranny. Sometimes he wanted coal; sometimes
bread and ale; and then Madame Bentley, sending her
servant with a snuff-box in token of authority, got from
the butteries at the expense of the college a great deal
more of these commodities than the college thought that
Dr. Bentley ought to require. Again, when he had four
pupils to lodge with him who paid him handsomely for
their board, it was drawn from the College, at the command of the snuff-box, for nothing. The principles of
"delicacy and good feeling" which the Master might have
been expected to observe (great scholar as he was,
steeped in the wine of the classics) went for nothing.
His argument that the "few College loaves" upon which
the four young patricians were nourished were amply
repaid by the three sash windows which he had put into
their rooms at his own expense failed to convince the
Fellows. And when, on Trinity Sunday 1719, the Fellows found the famous College ale not to their liking,
they were scarcely satisfied when the butler told them
that it had been brewed by the Master's orders, from
the Master's malt, which was stored in the Master's gran-
ary, and though damaged by "an insect called the weevil"
had been paid for at the very high rates which the Master demanded.

Still these battles over bread and beer are trifles and
domestic trifles at that. His conduct in his profession
will throw more light upon our inquiry. For, released
from brick and building, bread and beer, patricians and
their windows, it may be found that he expanded in the
atmosphere of Homer, Horace, and Manilius, and proved
in his study the benign nature of those influences which
have been wafted down to us through the ages. But there
the evidence is even less to the credit of the dead languages. He acquitted himself magnificently, all agree, in
the great controversy about the letters of Phalaris. His
temper was excellent and his learning prodigious. But
that triumph was succeeded by a series of disputes which
force upon us the extraordinary spectacle of men of

learning and genius, of authority and divinity, brawling
about Greek and Latin texts, and calling each other names
for all the world like bookies on a racecourse or washer-
women in a back street. For this vehemence of temper
and virulence of language were not confined to Bentley alone; they appear unhappily characteristic of the
profession as a whole. Early in life, in the year 1691, a
quarrel was fastened upon him by his brother chaplain
Hody for writing Malelas, not as Hody preferred,
Malela. A controversy in which Bentley displayed learning and wit, and Hody accumulated endless pages of bitter argument against the letter *s* ensued. Hody was
worsted, and "there is too much reason to believe, that
the offence given by this trivial cause was never afterwards healed." Indeed, to mend a line was to break a
friendship. James Gronovius of Leyden—"*homunculus
eruditione mediocri, ingenio nullo*," as Bentley called
him—attacked Bentley for ten years because Bentley had
succeeded in correcting a fragment of Callimachus where
he had failed.

But Gronovius was by no means the only scholar who
resented the success of a rival with a rancour that grey
hairs and forty years spent in editing the classics failed
to subdue. In all the chief towns of Europe lived men like
the notorious de Pauw of Utrecht, "a person who has
justly been considered the pest and disgrace of letters,"
who, when a new theory or new edition appeared,
banded themselves together to deride and humiliate the
scholar. ". . . all his writings," Bishop Monk remarks of
de Pauw, "prove him to be devoid of candour, good
faith, good manners, and every gentlemanly feeling: and
while he unites all the defects and bad qualities that were
ever found in a critic or commentator, he adds one peculiar to himself, an incessant propensity to indecent allusions." With such tempers and such habits it is not
strange that the scholars of those days sometimes ended
lives made intolerable by bitterness, poverty, and neglect
by their own hands, like Johnson, who after a lifetime

spent in the detection of minute errors of construction, went mad and drowned himself in the meadows near Nottingham. On May 20, 1712, Trinity College was shocked to find that the professor of Hebrew, Dr. Sike, had hanged himself "some time this evening, before candlelight, in his sash." When Kuster died, it was reported that he, too, had killed himself. And so, in a sense, he had. For when his body was opened "there was found a cake of sand along the lower region of his belly. This, I take it, was occasioned by his sitting nearly double, and writing on a very low table, surrounded with three or four circles of books placed on the ground, which was the situation we usually found him in." The minds of poor schoolmasters, like John Ker of the dissenting Academy, who had had the high gratification of dining with Dr. Bentley at the Lodge, when the talk fell upon the use of the word *equidem,* were so distorted by a lifetime of neglect and study that they went home, collected all uses of the word *equidem* which contradicted the Doctor's opinion, returned to the Lodge, anticipating in their simplicity a warm welcome, met the Doctor issuing to dine with the Archbishop of Canterbury, followed him down the street in spite of his indifference and annoyance, and, being refused even a word of farewell, went home to brood over their injuries and wait the day of revenge.

But the bickerings and animosities of the smaller fry were magnified, not obliterated, by the Doctor himself in the conduct of his own affairs. The courtesy and good temper which he had shown in his early controversies had worn away. ". . . a course of violent animosities and the indulgence of unrestrained indignation for many years had impaired both his taste and judgement in controversy," and he condescended, though the subject in dispute was the Greek Testament, to call his antagonist "maggot," "vermin," "gnawing rat," and "cabbage head," to refer to the darkness of his complexion, and to insinuate that his wits were crazed, which charge he supported by dwelling on the fact that his brother, a clergyman, wore a beard to his girdle.

Violent, pugnacious, and unscrupulous, Dr. Bentley survived these storms and agitations, and remained, though suspended from his degrees and deprived of his mastership, seated at the Lodge imperturbably. Wearing a broad-brimmed hat indoors to protect his eyes, smoking his pipe, enjoying his port, and expounding to his friends his doctrine of the digamma, Bentley lived those eighty years which, he said, were long enough "to read everything which was worth reading," "*Et tunc*," he added, in his peculiar manner,

> *Et tunc magna mei sub terris ibit imago.*

A small square stone marked his grave in Trinity College, but the Fellows refused to record upon it the fact that he had been their Master.

But the strangest sentence in this strange story has yet to be written, and Bishop Monk writes it as if it were a commonplace requiring no comment. "For a person who was neither a poet, nor possessed of poetical taste to venture upon such a task was no common presumption." The task was to detect every slip of language in *Paradise Lost*, and all instances of bad taste and incorrect imagery. The result was notoriously lamentable. Yet in what, we may ask, did it differ from those in which Bentley was held to have acquitted himself magnificently? And if Bentley was incapable of appreciating the poetry of Milton, how can we accept his verdict upon Horace and Homer? And if we cannot trust implicitly to scholars, and if the study of Greek is supposed to refine the manners and purify the soul—but enough. Our scholar has returned from Hall; his lamp is lit; his studies are resumed; and it is time that our profane speculations should have an end. Besides, all this happened many, many years ago.

III
LADY DOROTHY NEVILL

She had stayed, in a humble capacity, for a week in the ducal household. She had seen the troops of highly decorated human beings descending in couples to eat, and ascending in couples to bed. She had, surreptitiously, from a gallery, observed the Duke himself dusting the miniatures in the glass cases, while the Duchess let her crochet fall from her hands as if in utter disbelief that the world had need of crochet. From an upper window she had seen, as far as eye could reach, gravel paths swerving round isles of greenery and losing themselves in little woods designed to shed the shade without the severity of forests; she had watched the ducal carriage bowling in and out of the prospect, and returning a different way from the way it went. And what was her verdict? "A lunatic asylum."

It is true that she was a lady's-maid, and that Lady Dorothy Nevill, had she encountered her on the stairs, would have made an opportunity to point out that that is a very different thing from being a lady.

My mother never failed to point out the folly of workwomen, shop-girls, and the like calling each other "Ladies." All this sort of thing seemed to her to be mere vulgar humbug, and she did not fail to say so.

What can we point out to Lady Dorothy Nevill? that with all her advantages she had never learned to spell? that she could not write a grammatical sentence? that she lived for eighty-seven years and did nothing but put food into her mouth and slip gold through her fingers? But delightful though it is to indulge in righteous indignation, it is misplaced if we agree with the lady's-maid that high birth is a form of congenital insanity, that the sufferer merely inherits the diseases of his ancestors, and endures them, for the most part very stoically, in one of those comfortably padded lunatic asylums which are known, euphemistically, as the stately homes of England.

Moreover, the Walpoles are not ducal. Horace Walpole's mother was a Miss Shorter; there is no mention of Lady Dorothy's mother in the present volume, but her great-grandmother was Mrs. Oldfield the actress, and, to her credit, Lady Dorothy was "exceedingly proud" of the fact. Thus she was not an extreme case of aristocracy; she was confined rather to a bird-cage than to an asylum; through the bars she saw people walking at large, and once or twice she made a surprising little flight into the open air. A gayer, brighter, more vivacious specimen of the caged tribe can seldom have existed; so that one is forced at times to ask whether what we call living in a cage is not the fate that wise people, condemned to a single sojourn upon earth, would choose. To be at large is, after all, to be shut out; to waste most of life in accumulating the money to buy and the time to enjoy what the Lady Dorothys find clustering and glowing about their cradles when their eyes first open—, as hers opened in the year 1826 at number eleven Berkeley Square. Horace Walpole had lived there. Her father, Lord Orford, gambled it away in one night's play the year after she was born. But Wolterton Hall, in Norfolk, was full of carving and mantelpieces, and there were rare trees in the garden, and a large and famous lawn. No novelist could wish a more charming and even romantic environment in which to set the story of two little girls, growing up, wild yet secluded, reading Bossuet with their governess, and riding out on their ponies at the head of the tenantry on polling day. Nor can one deny that to have had the author of the following letter among one's ancestors would have been a source of inordinate pride. It is addressed to the Norwich Bible Society, which had invited Lord Orford to become its president:

I have long been addicted to the Gaming Table. I have lately taken to the Turf. I fear I frequently blaspheme. But I have never distributed religious tracts. All this was known to you and your Society. Notwithstanding which you think me a fit person to be your president. God forgive your hypocrisy.

It was not Lord Orford who was in the cage on that occasion. But, alas! Lord Orford owned another country house, Ilsington Hall, in Dorsetshire, and there Lady Dorothy came in contact first with the mulberry tree, and later with Mr. Thomas Hardy; and we get our first glimpse of the bars. We do not pretend to the ghost of an enthusiasm for Sailors' Homes in general; no doubt mulberry trees are much nicer to look at; but when it comes to calling people "vandals" who cut them down to build houses, and to having footstools made from the wood, and to carving upon those footstools inscriptions which testify that "often and often has King George III taken his tea" under this very footstool, then we want to protest—"Surely you must mean Shakespeare?" But as her subsequent remarks upon Mr. Hardy tend to prove, Lady Dorothy does not mean Shakespeare. She "warmly appreciated" the works of Mr. Hardy, and used to complain "that the county families were too stupid to appreciate his genius at its proper worth." George the Third drinking his tea; the county families failing to appreciate Mr. Hardy: Lady Dorothy is undoubtedly behind the bars.

Yet no story more aptly illustrates the barrier which we perceive hereafter between Lady Dorothy and the outer world than the story of Charles Darwin and the blankets. Among her recreations Lady Dorothy made a hobby of growing orchids, and thus got into touch with "the great naturalist." Mrs. Darwin, inviting her to stay with them, remarked with apparent simplicity that she had heard that people who moved much in London society were fond of being tossed in blankets. "I am afraid," her letter ended, "we should hardly be able to offer you anything of that sort." Whether in fact the necessity of tossing Lady Dorothy in a blanket had been seriously debated at Down, or whether Mrs. Darwin ob-

scurely hinted her sense of some incongruity between
her husband and the lady of the orchids, we do not
know. But we have a sense of two worlds in collision;
and it is not the Darwin world that emerges in fragments. More and more do we see Lady Dorothy hopping
from perch to perch, picking at groundsel here, and at
hempseed there, indulging in exquisite trills and roulades,
and sharpening her beak against a lump of sugar in a
large, airy, magnificently equipped bird-cage. The cage
was full of charming diversions. Now she illuminated
leaves which had been macerated to skeletons; now she
interested herself in improving the breed of donkeys;
next she took up the cause of silkworms, almost threatened Australia with a plague of them, and "actually succeeded in obtaining enough silk to make a dress"; again
she was the first to discover that wood, gone green with
decay, can be made, at some expense, into little boxes;
she went into the question of funguses and established
the virtues of the neglected English truffle; she imported
rare fish; spent a great deal of energy in vainly trying
to induce storks and Cornish choughs to breed in Sussex;
painted on china; emblazoned heraldic arms, and, attach-
ing whistles to the tails of pigeons, produced wonderful
effects "as of an aerial orchestra" when they flew through
the air. To the Duchess of Somerset belongs the credit
of investigating the proper way of cooking guinea-pigs;
but Lady Dorothy was one of the first to serve up a dish
of these little creatures at luncheon in Charles Street.

But all the time the door of the cage was ajar. Raids
were made into what Mr. Nevill calls "Upper Bohemia";
from which Lady Dorothy returned with "authors,
journalists, actors, actresses, or other agreeable and
amusing people." Lady Dorothy's judgement is proved
by the fact that they seldom misbehaved, and some indeed became quite domesticated, and wrote her "very
gracefully turned letters." But once or twice she made
a flight beyond the cage herself. "These horrors," she
said, alluding to the middle class, "are so clever and we

are so stupid; but then look how well they are educated, while our children learn nothing but how to spend their parents' money!" She brooded over the fact. Something was going wrong. She was too shrewd and too honest not to lay the blame partly at least upon her own class. "I suppose she can just about read?" she said of one lady calling herself cultured; and of another, "She is indeed curious and well adapted to open bazaars." But to our thinking her most remarkable flight took place a year or two before her death, in the Victoria and Albert Museum:

I do so agree with you [she wrote]—though I ought not to say so—that the upper class are very—I don't know what to say—but they seem to take no interest in anything—but golfing, etc. One day I was at the Victoria and Albert Museum, just a few sprinkles of legs, for I am sure they looked too frivolous to have bodies and souls attached to them—but what softened the sight to my eyes were 2 little Japs poring over each article with a handbook . . . our bodies, of course, giggling and looking at nothing. Still worse, not one soul of the higher class visible: in fact I never heard of any one of them knowing of the place, and for this we are spending millions—it is all too painful.

It was all too painful, and the guillotine, she felt, loomed ahead. That catastrophe she was spared, for who could wish to cut off the head of a pigeon with a whistle attached to its tail? But if the whole bird-cage had been overturned and the aerial orchestra sent screaming and fluttering through the air, we can be sure, as Mr. Joseph Chamberlain told her, that her conduct would have been "a credit to the British aristocracy."

IV
ARCHBISHOP THOMSON

The origin of Archbishop Thomson was obscure. His great-uncle "may reasonably be supposed" to have been "an ornament to the middle classes." His aunt married a gentleman who was present at the murder of Gustavus III of Sweden and his father met his death at the age of eighty-seven by treading on a cat in the early hours of the morning. The physical vigour which this anecdote implies was combined in the Archbishop with powers of intellect which promised success in whatever profession he adopted. At Oxford it seemed likely that he would devote himself to philosophy or science. While reading for his degree he found time to write the *Outlines of the Laws of Thought*, which "immediately became a recognised text-book for Oxford classes." But though poetry, philosophy, medicine, and the law held out their temptations he put such thoughts aside, or never entertained them, having made up his mind from the first to dedicate himself to Divine service. The measure of his success in the more exalted sphere is attested by the following facts: Ordained deacon in 1842 at the age of twenty-three, he became Dean and Bursar of Queen's College, Oxford, in 1845; Provost in 1855, Bishop of Gloucester and Bristol in 1861, and Archbishop of York in 1862. Thus at the early age of forty-three he stood next in rank to the Archbishop of Canterbury himself; and it was commonly though erroneously expected that he would in the end attain to that dignity also.

It is a matter of temperament and belief whether you read this list with respect or with boredom; whether you look upon an archbishop's hat as a crown or as an extinguisher. If, like the present reviewer, you are ready to hold the simple faith that the outer order corresponds to the inner—that a vicar is a good man, a canon a better man, and an archbishop the best man of all—you will find the study of the Archbishop's life one of extreme fascination. He has turned aside from poetry and philosophy and law, and specialised in virtue. He has dedicated himself to the service of the Divine. His spiritual proficiency has been such that he has developed from deacon to dean, from dean to bishop, and from bishop to archbishop in the short space of twenty years.

As there are only two archbishops in the whole of England the inference seems to be that he is the second best man in England; his hat is the proof of it. Even in a material sense his hat was one of the largest; it was larger than Mr. Gladstone's; larger than Thackeray's; larger than Dickens'; it was in fact, so his hatter told him and we are inclined to agree, an "eight full." Yet he began much as other men begin. He struck an undergraduate in a fit of temper and was rusticated; he wrote a text-book of logic and rowed a very good oar. But after he was ordained his diary shows that the specialising process had begun. He thought a great deal about the state of his soul; about "the monstrous tumour of Simony"; about Church reform; and about the meaning of Christianity. "Self-renunciation," he came to the conclusion, "is the foundation of Christian Religion and Christian Morals. . . . The highest wisdom is that which can enforce and cultivate this self-renunciation. Hence (against Cousin) I hold that religion is higher far than philosophy." There is one mention of chemists and capillarity, but science and philosophy were, even at this early stage, in danger of being crowded out. Soon the diary takes a different tone. "He seems," says his biographer, "to have had no time for committing his thoughts to paper"; he records his engagements only, and he dines out almost every night. Sir Henry Taylor, whom he met at one of these parties, described him as "simple, solid, good, capable, and pleasing." Perhaps it was his solidity combined with his "eminently scientific" turn of mind, his blandness as well as his bulk, that impressed some of these great people with the confidence that in him the Church had found a very necessary champion. His "brawny logic" and massive frame seemed to fit him to grapple with a task that taxed the strongest—how, that is, to reconcile the scientific discoveries of the age with religion, and even prove them "some of its strongest witnesses for the truth." If any one could do this Thomson could; his practical ability, unhampered by any mystical

or dreaming tendency, had already proved itself in the
conduct of the business affairs of his College. From
Bishop he became almost instantly Archbishop; and in
becoming Archbishop he became Primate of England,
Governor of the Charterhouse and King's College, London, patron of one hundred and twenty livings, with the
Archdeaconries of York, Cleveland, and the East Riding in his gift, and the Canonries and Prebends in York
Minster. Bishopthorpe itself was an enormous palace;
he was immediately faced by the "knotty question" of
whether to buy all the furniture—"much of it only poor
stuff"—or to furnish the house anew, which would cost
a fortune. Moreover there were seven cows in the park;
but these, perhaps, were counterbalanced by nine children in the nursery. Then the Prince and Princess of
Wales came to stay, and the Archbishop took upon himself the task of furnishing the Princess's apartments. He
went up to London and bought eight Moderator lamps,
two Spanish figures holding candles, and reminded himself of the necessity of buying "soap for Princess." But
meanwhile far more serious matters claimed every ounce
of his strength. Already he had been exhorted to "wield
the sure lance of your brawny logic against the sophis-
tries" of the authors of *Essays and Reviews*, and had
responded in a work called *Aids to Faith*. Near at hand
the town of Sheffield, with its large population of imperfectly educated working men, was a breeding ground
of scepticism and discontent. The Archbishop made it
his special charge. He was fond of watching the rolling
of armour plate, and constantly addressed meetings of
working men. "Now what are these Nihilisms, and So-
cialisms, and Communisms, and Fenianisms, and Secret
Societies—what do they all mean?" he asked. "Selfish-
ness," he replied, and "assertion of one class against the
rest is at the bottom of them all." There was a law of
nature, he said, by which wages went up and wages went
down. "You must accept the declivity as well as the

ascent. . . . If we could only get people to learn that,
then things would go on a great deal better and
smoother." And the working men of Sheffield responded
by giving him five hundred pieces of cutlery mounted
in sterling silver. But presumably there were a certain
number of knives among the spoons and the forks.

Bishop Colenso, however, was far more troublesome
than the working men of Sheffield; and the Ritualists
vexed him so persistently that even his vast strength felt
the strain. The questions which were referred to him for
decision were peculiarly fitted to tease and annoy even
a man of his bulk and his blandness. Shall a drunkard
found dead in a ditch, or a burglar who has fallen
through a skylight, be given the benefit of the Burial
Service? he was asked. The question of lighted candles
was "most difficult"; the wearing of coloured stoles and
the administration of the mixed chalice taxed him con-
siderably; and finally there was the Rev. John Purchas,
who, dressed in cope, alb, biretta and stole "cross-wise,"
lit candles and extinguished them "for no special reason";
filled a vessel with black powder and rubbed it into the
foreheads of his congregation; and hung over the Holy
Table "a figure, image, or stuffed skin of a dove, in a flying attitude." The Archbishop's temper, usually so positive and imperturbable, was gravely ruffled. "Will there
ever come a time when it will be thought a crime to
have striven to keep the Church of England as representing the common sense of the Nation?" he asked. "I
suppose it may, but I shall not see it. I have gone through
a good deal, but I do not repent of having done my
best." If, for a moment, the Archbishop himself could
ask such a question, we must confess to a state of complete bewilderment. What has become of our superla-
tively good man? He is harassed and cumbered; spends
his time settling questions about stuffed pigeons and coloured petticoats; writes over eighty letters before breakfast sometimes; scarcely has time to run over to Paris

and buy his daughter a bonnet; and in the end has to ask himself whether one of these days his conduct will not be considered a crime.

Was it a crime? And if so, was it his fault? Did he not start out in the belief that Christianity had something to do with renunciation and was not entirely a matter of common sense? If honours and obligations, pomps and possessions, accumulated and encrusted him, how, being an Archbishop, could he refuse to accept them? Princesses must have their soap; palaces must have their furniture; children must have their cows. And, pathetic though it seems, he never completely lost his interest in science. He wore a pedometer; he was one of the first to use a camera; he believed in the future of the type-writer; and in his last years he tried to mend a broken clock. He was a delightful father too; he wrote witty, terse, sensible letters; his good stories were much to the point; and he died in harness. Certainly he was a very able man, but if we insist upon goodness—is it easy, is it possible, for a good man to be an Archbishop?

*

The Patron and the Crocus

*

Young men and women beginning to write are generally given the plausible but utterly impracticable advice to write what they have to write as shortly as possible, as clearly as possible, and without other thought in their minds except to say exactly what is in them. Nobody ever adds on these occasions the one thing needful: "And be sure you choose your patron wisely," though that is the gist of the whole matter. For a book is always written for somebody to read, and, since the patron is not merely the paymaster, but also in a very subtle and insidious way the instigator and inspirer of what is written, it is of the utmost importance that he should be a desirable man.

But who, then, is the desirable man—the patron who will cajole the best out of the writer's brain and bring to birth the most varied and vigorous progeny of which he is capable? Different ages have answered the question differently. The Elizabethans, to speak roughly, chose the aristocracy to write for and the playhouse public. The eighteenth-century patron was a combination of coffee-house wit and Grub Street bookseller. In the nineteenth century the great writers wrote for the half-crown magazines and the leisured classes. And looking back and applauding the splendid results of these different alliances, it all seems enviably simple, and plain as a pikestaff compared with our own predicament—for whom

should we write? For the present supply of patrons
is of unexampled and bewildering variety. There is the
daily Press, the weekly Press, the monthly Press; the
English public and the American public; the best-seller
public and the worst-seller public; the high-brow public
and the red-blood public; all now organised self-conscious entities capable through their various mouthpieces
of making their needs known and their approval or dis-
pleasure felt. Thus the writer who has been moved by
the sight of the first crocus in Kensington Gardens has,
before he sets pen to paper, to choose from a crowd of
competitors the particular patron who suits him best. It
is futile to say, "Dismiss them all; think only of your
crocus," because writing is a method of communication;
and the crocus is an imperfect crocus until it has been
shared. The first man or the last may write for himself
alone, but he is an exception and an unenviable one at
that, and the gulls are welcome to his works if the gulls
can read them.

Granted, then, that every writer has some public or
other at the end of his pen, the high-minded will say
that it should be a submissive public, accepting obedi-
ently whatever he likes to give it. Plausible as the theory
sounds, great risks are attached to it. For in that case
the writer remains conscious of his public, yet is superior to it—an uncomfortable and unfortunate combination, as the works of Samuel Butler, George Meredith, and
Henry James may be taken to prove. Each despised the
public; each desired a public; each failed to attain a public; and each wreaked his failure upon the public by a
succession, gradually increasing in intensity, of angulari-
ties, obscurities, and affectations which no writer whose
patron was his equal and friend would have thought it
necessary to inflict. Their crocuses in consequence are
tortured plants, beautiful and bright, but with something
wry-necked about them, malformed, shrivelled on the
one side, overblown on the other. A touch of the sun
would have done them a world of good. Shall we then

rush to the opposite extreme and accept (if in fancy alone) the flattering proposals which the editors of the *Times* and the *Daily News* may be supposed to make us —"Twenty pounds down for your crocus in precisely fifteen hundred words, which shall blossom upon every breakfast table from John o' Groats to the Land's End before nine o'clock to-morrow morning with the writer's name attached"?

But will one crocus be enough, and must it not be a very brilliant yellow to shine so far, to cost so much, and to have one's name attached to it? The Press is undoubtedly a great multiplier of crocuses. But if we look at some of these plants, we shall find that they are only very distantly related to the original little yellow or purple flower which pokes up through the grass in Kensington Gardens about this time of year. The newspaper crocus is amazing but still a very different plant. It fills precisely the space allotted to it. It radiates a golden glow. It is genial, affable, warmhearted. It is beautifully finished, too, for let nobody think that the art of "our dramatic critic" of the *Times* or of Mr. Lynd of the *Daily News* is an easy one. It is no despicable feat to start a million brains running at nine o'clock in the morning, to give two million eyes something bright and brisk and amusing to look at. But the night comes and these flowers fade. So little bits of glass lose their lustre if you take them out of the sea; great prima donnas howl like hyenas if you shut them up in telephone boxes; and the most brilliant of articles when removed from its element is dust and sand and the husks of straw. Journalism embalmed in a book is unreadable.

The patron we want, then, is one who will help us to preserve our flowers from decay. But as his qualities change from age to age, and it needs considerable integrity and conviction not to be dazzled by the pretensions or bamboozled by the persuasions of the competing crowd, this business of patron-finding is one of the tests and trials of authorship. To know whom to write for is to know how to write. Some of the modern patron's qualities are, however, fairly plain. The writer will require at this moment, it is obvious, a patron with the book-reading habit rather than the play-going habit. Nowadays, too, he must be instructed in the literature of other times and races. But there are other qualities which our special weaknesses and tendencies demand in him. There is the question of indecency, for instance, which plagues us and puzzles us much more than it did the Elizabethans. The twentieth-century patron must be immune from shock. He must distinguish infallibly between the little clod of manure which sticks to the crocus of necessity, and that which is plastered to it out of bravado. He must be a judge, too, of those social influences which inevitably play so large a part in modern literature, and able to say which matures and fortifies, which inhibits and makes sterile. Further, there is emotion for him to pronounce on, and in no department can he do more useful work than in bracing a writer against sentimentality on the one hand and a craven fear of expressing his feeling on the other. It is worse, he will say, and perhaps more common, to be afraid of feeling than to feel too much. He will add, perhaps, something about language, and point out how many words Shakespeare used and how much grammar Shakespeare violated, while we, though we keep our fingers so demurely to the black notes on the piano, have not appreciably improved upon *Antony and Cleopatra*. And if you can forget your sex altogether, he will say, so much the better; a writer has none. But all this is by the way—elementary and disputable. The patron's prime quality is something different, only to be expressed perhaps by the use of that convenient word which cloaks so much—atmosphere. It is necessary that the patron should shed and envelop the crocus in an atmosphere which makes it appear a plant of the very highest importance, so that to misrepresent it is the one outrage not to be forgiven this side of the grave. He must make us feel that a single crocus, if it be a real crocus, is enough for him; that he does not want to be lectured, elevated, instructed, or improved; that he is sorry that he bullied Carlyle into vociferation, Tennyson into idyllics, and Ruskin into insanity; that he is now ready to efface himself or assert himself as his writers require; that he is bound to them by a more than maternal tie; that they are twins indeed, one dying if the other dies, one flourishing if the other flourishes; that the fate of literature depends upon their happy alliance—all of which proves, as we began by saying, that the choice of a patron is of the highest importance. But how to choose rightly? How to write well? Those are the questions.

*

The Modern Essay

*

As Mr. Rhys truly says, it is unnecessary to go profoundly into the history and origin of the essay—whether it derives from Socrates or Siranney the Persian—since, like all living things, its present is more important than its past. Moreover, the family is widely spread; and while some of its representatives have risen in the world and wear their coronets with the best, others pick up a precarious living in the gutter near Fleet Street. The form, too, admits variety. The essay can be short or long, serious or trifling, about God and Spinoza, or about turtles and Cheapside. But as we turn over the pages of these five little volumes,* containing essays written between 1870 and 1920, certain principles appear to control the chaos, and we detect in the short period under review something like the progress of history.

Of all forms of literature, however, the essay is the one which least calls for the use of long words. The principle which controls it is simply that it should give pleasure; the desire which impels us when we take it from the shelf is simply to receive pleasure. Everything in an essay must be subdued to that end. It should lay us under a spell with its first word, and we should only wake, refreshed, with its last. In the interval we may pass through the most various experiences of amusement, sur-

* *Modern English Essays*, edited by Ernest Rhys, five volumes (Dent).

prise, interest, indignation; we may soar to the heights
of fantasy with Lamb or plunge to the depths of wisdom
with Bacon, but we must never be roused. The essay
must lap us about and draw its curtain across the world.

So great a feat is seldom accomplished, though the fault
may well be as much on the reader's side as on the
writer's. Habit and lethargy have dulled his palate. A
novel has a story, a poem rhyme; but what art can the
essayist use in these short lengths of prose to sting us
wide awake and fix us in a trance which is not sleep but
rather an intensification of life—a basking, with every
faculty alert, in the sun of pleasure? He must know—
that is the first essential—how to write. His learning may
be as profound as Mark Pattison's, but in an essay it must
be so fused by the magic of writing that not a fact juts
out, not a dogma tears the surface of the texture. Macaulay in one way, Froude in another, did this superbly over
and over again. They have blown more knowledge into
us in the course of one essay than the innumerable chapters of a hundred text-books. But when Mark Pattison
has to tell us, in the space of thirty-five little pages,
about Montaigne, we feel that he had not previously as-
similated M. Grün. M. Grün was a gentleman who once
wrote a bad book. M. Grün and his book should have
been embalmed for our perpetual delight in amber. But
the process is fatiguing; it requires more time and perhaps more temper than Pattison had at his command. He
served M. Grün up raw, and he remains a crude berry
among the cook meats, upon which our teeth must grate
for ever. Something of the sort applies to Matthew
Arnold and a certain translator of Spinoza. Literal truth-
telling and finding fault with a culprit for his good are
out of place in an essay, where everything should be for
our good and rather for eternity than for the March
number of the *Fortnightly Review*. But if the voice of
the scold should never be heard in this narrow plot,
there is another voice which is as a plague of locusts—
the voice of a man stumbling drowsily among loose

words, clutching aimlessly at vague ideas, the voice, for example, of Mr. Hutton in the following passage:

Add to this that his married life was very brief, only seven years and a half, being unexpectedly cut short, and that his passionate reverence for his wife's memory and genius—in his own words, "a religion"—was one which, as he must have been perfectly sensible, he could not make to appear otherwise than extravagant, not to say an hallucination, in the eyes of the rest of mankind, and yet that he was possessed by an irresistible yearning to attempt to embody it in all the tender and enthusiastic hyperbole of which it is so pathetic to find a man who gained his fame by his "dry-light" a master, and it is impossible not to feel that the human incidents in Mr. Mill's career are very sad.

A book could take that blow, but it sinks an essay. A biography in two volumes is indeed the proper depositary; for there, where the licence is so much wider, and hints and glimpses of outside things make part of the feast (we refer to the old type of Victorian volume), these yawns and stretches hardly matter, and have indeed some positive value of their own. But that value, which is contributed by the reader, perhaps illicitly, in his desire to get as much into the book from all possible sources as he can, must be ruled out here.

There is no room for the impurities of literature in an essay. Somehow or other, by dint of labour or bounty of nature, or both combined, the essay must be pure—pure like water or pure like wine, but pure from dullness, deadness, and deposits of extraneous matter. Of all writers in the first volume, Walter Pater best achieves this arduous task, because before setting out to write his essay ("Notes on Leonardo da Vinci") he has somehow contrived to get his material fused. He is a learned man, but it is not knowledge of Leonardo that remains with us, but a vision, such as we get in a good novel where everything contributes to bring the writer's conception as a whole before us. Only here, in the essay, where the bounds are so strict and facts have to be used in their nakedness, the true writer like Walter Pater makes these limitations yield their own quality. Truth will give it authority; from its narrow limits he will get shape and intensity; and then there is no more fitting place for some of those ornaments which the old writers loved and we, by calling them ornaments, presumably despise. Nowadays nobody would have the courage to embark on the once famous description of Leonardo's lady who has

learned the secrets of the grave; and has been a diver in deep seas and keeps their fallen day about her; and trafficked for strange webs with Eastern merchants; and, as Leda, was the mother of Helen of Troy, and, as Saint Anne, the mother of Mary . . .

The passage is too thumb-marked to slip naturally into the context. But when we come unexpectedly upon "the smiling of women and the motion of great waters," or upon "full of the refinement of the dead, in sad, earth-coloured raiment, set with pale stones," we suddenly remember that we have ears and we have eyes, and that the English language fills a long array of stout volumes with innumerable words, many of which are of more than one syllable. The only living Englishman who ever looks into these volumes is, of course, a gentleman of Polish extraction. But doubtless our abstention saves us much gush, much rhetoric, much high-stepping and cloud-prancing, and for the sake of the prevailing sobriety and hard-headedness we should be willing to barter the splendour of Sir Thomas Browne and the vigour of Swift.

Yet, if the essay admits more properly than biography or fiction of sudden boldness and metaphor, and can be polished till every atom of its surface shines, there are dangers in that too. We are soon in sight of ornament. Soon the current, which is the life-blood of literature, runs slow; and instead of sparkling and flashing or moving with a quieter impulse which has a deeper excitement, words coagulate together in frozen sprays which, like the grapes on a Christmas-tree, glitter for a single night, but

are dusty and garish the day after. The temptation to
decorate is great where the theme may be of the slightest. What is there to interest another in the fact that one
has enjoyed a walking tour, or has amused oneself by
rambling down Cheapside and looking at the turtles in
Mr. Sweeting's shop window? Stevenson and Samuel
Butler chose very different methods of exciting our
interest in these domestic themes. Stevenson, of course,
trimmed and polished and set out his matter in the tra-
ditional eighteenth-century form. It is admirably done,
but we cannot help feeling anxious, as the essay proceeds,
lest the material may give out under the craftsman's fingers. The ingot is so small, the manipulation so incessant.
And perhaps that is why the peroration—

To sit still and contemplate—to remember the faces of
women without desire, to be pleased by the great deeds of men
without envy, to be everything and everywhere in sympathy
and yet content to remain where and what you are—

has the sort of insubstantiality which suggests that by
the time he got to the end he had left himself nothing solid to work with. Butler adopted the very opposite
method. Think your own thoughts, he seems to say, and
speak them as plainly as you can. These turtles in the
shop window which appear to leak out of their shells
through heads and feet suggest a fatal faithfulness to a
fixed idea. And so, striding unconcernedly from one idea
to the next, we traverse a large stretch of ground; observe that a wound in the solicitor is a very serious thing;
that Mary Queen of Scots wears surgical boots and is
subject to fits near the Horse Shoe in Tottenham Court
Road; take it for granted that no one really cares about
Aeschylus; and so, with many amusing anecdotes and
some profound reflections, reach the peroration, which
is that, as he had been told not to see more in Cheapside
than he could get into twelve pages of the *Universal
Review*, he had better stop. And yet obviously Butler is
at least as careful of our pleasure as Stevenson; and to

write like oneself and call it not writing is a much harder exercise in style than to write like Addison and call it writing well.

But, however much they differ individually, the Victorian essayists yet had something in common. They wrote at greater length than is now usual, and they wrote for a public which had not only time to sit down to its magazine seriously, but a high, if peculiarly Victorian, standard of culture by which to judge it. It was worth while to speak out upon serious matters in an essay; and there was nothing absurd in writing as well as one possibly could when, in a month or two, the same public which had welcomed the essay in a magazine would carefully read it once more in a book. But a change came from a small audience of cultivated people to a larger audience of people who were not quite so cultivated. The change was not altogether for the worse. In volume III we find Mr. Birrell and Mr. Beerbohm. It might even be said that there was a reversion to the classic type, and that the essay by losing its size and something of its sonority was approaching more nearly the essay of Addison and Lamb. At any rate, there is a great gulf between Mr. Birrell on Carlyle and the essay which one may suppose that Carlyle would have written upon Mr. Birrell. There is little similarity between *A Cloud of Pinafores*, by Max Beerbohm, and *A Cynic's Apology*, by Leslie Stephen. But the essay is alive; there is no reason to despair. As the conditions change so the essayist, most sensitive of all plants to public opinion, adapts himself, and if he is good makes the best of the change, and if he is bad the worst. Mr. Birrell is certainly good; and so we find that, though he has dropped a considerable amount of weight, his attack is much more direct and his movement more supple. But what did Mr. Beerbohm give to the essay and what did he take from it? That is a much more complicated question, for here we have an essayist who has concentrated on the work and is without doubt the prince of his profession.

What Mr. Beerbohm gave was, of course, himself. This presence, which has haunted the essay fitfully from the time of Montaigne, had been in exile since the death of Charles Lamb. Matthew Arnold was never to his readers Matt, nor Walter Pater affectionately abbreviated in a thousand homes to Wat. They gave us much, but that they did not give. Thus, some time in the 'nineties, it must have surprised readers accustomed to exhortation, information, and denunciation to find themselves familiarly addressed by a voice which seemed to belong to a man no larger than themselves. He was affected by private joys and sorrows, and had no gospel to preach and no learning to impart. He was himself, simply and directly, and himself he has remained. Once again we have an essayist capable of using the essayist's most proper but most dangerous and delicate tool. He has brought personality into literature, not unconsciously and impurely, but so consciously and purely that we do not know whether there is any relation between Max the essayist and Mr. Beerbohm the man. We only know that the spirit of personality permeates every word that he writes. The triumph is the triumph of style. For it is only by knowing how to write that you can make use in literature of your self; that self which, while it is essential to literature, is also its most dangerous antagonist. Never to be yourself and yet always—that is the problem. Some of the essayists in Mr. Rhys' collection, to be frank, have not altogether succeeded in solving it. We are nauseated by the sight of trivial personalities decomposing in the eternity of print. As talk, no doubt, it was charming, and certainly the writer is a good fellow to meet over a bottle of beer. But literature is stern; it is no use being charming, virtuous, or even learned and brilliant into the bargain, unless, she seems to reiterate, you fulfil her first condition—to know how to write.

This art is possessed to perfection by Mr. Beerbohm. But he has not searched the dictionary for polysyllables. He has not moulded firm periods or seduced our ears

with intricate cadences and strange melodies. Some of
his companions—Henley and Stevenson, for example—
are momentarily more impressive. But *A Cloud of Pinafores* had in it that indescribable inequality, stir, and
final expressiveness which belong to life and to life
alone. You have not finished with it because you have
read it, any more than friendship is ended because it is
time to part. Life wells up and alters and adds. Even
things in a book-case change if they are alive; we find
ourselves wanting to meet them again; we find them altered. So we look back upon essay after essay by Mr.
Beerbohm, knowing that, come September or May, we
shall sit down with them and talk. Yet it is true that the
essayist is the most sensitive of all writers to public opinion. The drawing-room is the place where a great deal
of reading is done nowadays, and the essays of Mr. Beerbohm lie, with an exquisite appreciation of all that the
position exacts, upon the drawing-room table. There is
no gin about; no strong tobacco; no puns, drunkenness,
or insanity. Ladies and gentlemen talk together, and
some things, of course, are not said.

But if it would be foolish to attempt to confine Mr.
Beerbohm to one room, it would be still more foolish,
unhappily, to make him, the artist, the man who gives us
only his best, the representative of our age. There are
no essays by Mr. Beerbohm in the fourth or fifth volumes of the present collection. His age seems already a
little distant, and the drawing-room table, as it recedes,
begins to look rather like an altar where, once upon a
time, people deposited offerings—fruit from their own
orchards, gifts carved with their own hands. Now once
more the conditions have changed. The public needs
essays as much as ever, and perhaps even more. The demand for the light middle not exceeding fifteen hundred
words, or in special cases seventeen hundred and fifty,
much exceeds the supply. Where Lamb wrote one essay
and Max perhaps writes two, Mr. Belloc at a rough com-
putation produces three hundred and sixty-five. They

are very short, it is true. Yet with what dexterity the practised essayist will utilise his space—beginning as close to the top of the sheet as possible, judging precisely how far to go, when to turn, and how, without sacrificing a hair's-breadth of paper, to wheel about and alight accurately upon the last word his editor allows! As a feat of skill it is well worth watching. But the personality upon which Mr. Belloc, like Mr. Beerbohm, depends suffers in the process. It comes to us not with the natural richness of the speaking voice, but strained and thin and full of mannerisms and affectations, like the voice of a man shouting through a megaphone to a crowd on a windy day. "Little friends, my readers," he says in the essay called "An Unknown Country," and he goes on to tell us how—

There was a shepherd the other day at Findon Fair who had come from the east by Lewes with sheep, and who had in his eyes that reminiscence of horizons which makes the eyes of shepherds and of mountaineers different from the eyes of other men. . . . I went with him to hear what he had to say, for shepherds talk quite differently from other men.

Happily this shepherd had little to say, even under the stimulus of the inevitable mug of beer, about the Unknown Country, for the only remark that he did make proves him either a minor poet, unfit for the care of sheep, or Mr. Belloc himself masquerading with a fountain pen. That is the penalty which the habitual essayist must now be prepared to face. He must masquerade. He cannot afford the time either to be himself or to be other people. He must skim the surface of thought and dilute the strength of personality. He must give us a worn weekly halfpenny instead of a solid sovereign once a year.

But it is not Mr. Belloc only who has suffered from the prevailing conditions. The essays which bring the collection to the year 1920 may not be the best of their authors' work, but, if we except writers like Mr. Conrad and Mr.

Hudson, who have strayed into essay writing accidentally, and concentrate upon those who write essays habitually, we shall find them a good deal affected by the change in their circumstances. To write weekly, to write daily, to write shortly, to write for busy people catching trains in the morning or for tired people coming home in the evening, is a heartbreaking task for men who know good writing from bad. They do it, but instinctively draw out of harm's way anything precious that might be damaged by contact with the public, or anything sharp that might irritate its skin. And so, if one reads Mr. Lucas, Mr. Lynd, or Mr. Squire in the bulk, one feels that a common greyness silvers everything. They are as far removed from the extravagant beauty of Walter Pater as they are from the intemperate candour of Leslie Stephen. Beauty and courage are dangerous spirits to battle in a column and a half; and thought, like a brown paper parcel in a waistcoat pocket, has a way of spoiling the symmetry of an article. It is a kind, tired, apathetic world for which they write, and the marvel is that they never cease to attempt, at least, to write well.

But there is no need to pity Mr. Clutton Brock for this change in the essayist's conditions. He has clearly made the best of his circumstances and not the worst. One hesitates even to say that he has had to make any conscious effort in the matter, so naturally has he effected the transition from the private essayist to the public, from the drawing-room to the Albert Hall. Paradoxically enough, the shrinkage in size has brought about a corresponding expansion of individuality. We have no longer the "I" of Max and of Lamb, but the "we" of public bodies and other sublime personages. It is "we" who go to hear the *Magic Flute;* "we" who ought to profit by it; "we," in some mysterious way, who, in our corporate capacity, once upon a time actually wrote it. For music and literature and art must submit to the same generalisation or they will not carry to the farthest recesses of the Albert Hall. That the voice of Mr. Clutton

Brock, so sincere and so disinterested, carries such a distance and reaches so many without pandering to the
weakness of the mass or its passions must be a matter of
legitimate satisfaction to us all. But while "we" are gratified, "I," that unruly partner in the human fellowship, is
reduced to despair. "I" must always think things for himself, and feel things for himself. To share them in a
diluted form with the majority of well-educated and
well-intentioned men and women is for him sheer agony;
and while the rest of us listen intently and profit profoundly, "I" slips off to the woods and the fields and re-
joices in a single blade of grass or a solitary potato.

In the fifth volume of modern essays, it seems, we have
got some way from pleasure and the art of writing. But
in justice to the essayists of 1920 we must be sure that
we are not praising the famous because they have been
praised already and the dead because we shall never meet
them wearing spats in Piccadilly. We must know what
we mean when we say that they can write and give us
pleasure. We must compare them; we must bring out the
quality. We must point to this and say it is good because
it is exact, truthful, and imaginative:

> Nay, retire men cannot when they would; neither will they,
> when it were Reason; but are impatient of Privateness, even
> in age and sickness, which require the shadow: like old Towns-
> men: that will still be sitting at their street door, though
> thereby they offer Age to Scorn . . .

and to this, and say it is bad because it is loose, plausible,
and commonplace:

> With courteous and precise cynicism on his lips, he thought
> of quiet virginal chambers, of waters singing under the moon,
> of terraces where taintless music sobbed into the open night, of
> pure maternal mistresses with protecting arms and vigilant
> eyes, of fields slumbering in the sunlight, of leagues of ocean
> heaving under warm tremulous heavens, of hot ports, gorgeous
> and perfumed. . . .

It goes on, but already we are bemused with sound and neither feel nor hear. The comparison makes us suspect that the art of writing has for backbone some fierce attachment to an idea. It is on the back of an idea, something believed in with conviction or seen with precision and thus compelling words to its shape, that the diverse company which included Lamb and Bacon, and Mr. Beerbohm and Hudson, and Vernon Lee and Mr. Conrad, and Leslie Stephen and Butler and Walter Pater reaches the farther shore. Very various talents have helped or hindered the passage of the idea into words. Some scrape through painfully; others fly with every wind favouring. But Mr. Belloc and Mr. Lucas and Mr. Lynd and Mr. Squire are not fiercely attached to anything in itself. They share the contemporary dilemma—that lack of an obstinate conviction which lifts ephemeral sounds through the misty sphere of anybody's language to the land where there is a perpetual marriage, a perpetual union. Vague as all definitions are, a good essay must have this permanent quality about it; it must draw its curtain round us, but it must be a curtain that shuts us in, not out.

*

Joseph Conrad†

*

Suddenly, without giving us time to arrange our thoughts or prepare our phrases, our guest has left us; and his withdrawal without farewell or ceremony is in keeping with his mysterious arrival, long years ago, to take up his lodging in this country. For there was always an air of mystery about him. It was partly his Polish birth, partly his memorable appearance, partly his preference for living in the depths of the country, out of ear-shot of gossips, beyond reach of hostesses, so that for news of him one had to depend upon the evidence of simple visitors with a habit of ringing doorbells who reported of their unknown host that he had the most perfect manners, the brightest eyes, and spoke English with a strong foreign accent.

Still, though it is the habit of death to quicken and focus our memories, there clings to the genius of Conrad something essentially, and not accidentally, difficult of approach. His reputation of later years was, with one obvious exception, undoubtedly the highest in England; yet he was not popular. He was read with passionate delight by some; others he left cold and lustreless. Among his readers were people of the most opposite ages and sympathies. Schoolboys of fourteen, driving their way through Marryat, Scott, Henty, and Dickens, swallowed him down with the rest; while the seasoned and the fas-

† August, 1924.

tidious, who in process of time have eaten their way to
the heart of literature and there turn over and over a
few precious crumbs, set Conrad scrupulously upon
their banqueting table. One source of difficulty and disagreement is, of course, to be found, where men have at
all times found it, in his beauty. One opens his pages and
feels as Helen must have felt when she looked in her
glass and realised that, do what she would, she could
never in any circumstances pass for a plain woman. So
Conrad had been gifted, so he had schooled himself, and
such was his obligation to a strange language wooed
characteristically for its Latin qualities rather than its
Saxon that it seemed impossible for him to make an ugly
or insignificant movement of the pen. His mistress, his
style, is a little somnolent sometimes in repose. But let
somebody speak to her, and then how magnificently she
bears down upon us, with what colour, triumph, and
majesty! Yet it is arguable that Conrad would have
gained both in credit and in popularity if he had written
what he had to write without this incessant care for
appearances. They block and impede and distract, his
critics say, pointing to those famous passages which it is
becoming the habit to lift from their context and exhibit
among other cut flowers of English prose. He was self-
conscious and stiff and ornate, they complain, and the
sound of his own voice was dearer to him than the voice
of humanity in its anguish. The criticism is familiar, and
as difficult to refute as the remarks of deaf people when
Figaro is played. They see the orchestra; far off they hear
a dismal scrape of sound; their own remarks are inter-
rupted, and, very naturally, they conclude that the ends
of life would be better served if instead of scraping
Mozart those fifty fiddlers broke stones upon the road.
That beauty teaches, that beauty is a disciplinarian, how
are we to convince them, since her teaching is inseparable
from the sound of her voice and to that they are deaf?
But read Conrad, not in birthday books but in the bulk,
and he must be lost indeed to the meaning of words who

does not hear in that rather stiff and sombre music, with
its reserve, its pride, its vast and implacable integrity,
how it is better to be good than bad, how loyalty is good
and honesty and courage, though ostensibly Conrad is
concerned merely to show us the beauty of a night at sea.
But it is ill work dragging such intimations from their
element. Dried in our little saucers, without the magic
and mystery of language, they lose their power to excite
and goad; they lose the drastic power which is a constant
quality of Conrad's prose.

For it was by virtue of something drastic in him, the
qualities of a leader and captain, that Conrad kept his
hold over boys and young people. Until *Nostromo* was
written his characters, as the young were quick to perceive, were fundamentally simple and heroic, however
subtle the mind and indirect the method of their creator. They were seafarers, used to solitude and silence.
They were in conflict with Nature, but at peace with
man. Nature was their antagonist; she it was who drew
forth honour, magnanimity, loyalty, the qualities proper
to man; she who in sheltered bays reared to womanhood beautiful girls unfathomable and austere. Above
all, it was Nature who turned out such gnarled and
tested characters as Captain Whalley and old Singleton,
obscure but glorious in their obscurity, who were to
Conrad the pick of our race, the men whose praises he
was never tired of celebrating:

They had been strong as those are strong who know neither
doubts nor hopes. They had been impatient and enduring,
turbulent and devoted, unruly and faithful. Well-meaning
people had tried to represent these men as whining over every
mouthful of their food, as going about their work in fear of
their lives. But in truth they had been men who knew toil,
privation, violence, debauchery—but knew not fear, and had
no desire of spite in their hearts. Men hard to manage, but
easy to inspire; voiceless men—but men enough to scorn in
their hearts the sentimental voices that bewailed the hardness
of their fate. It was a fate unique and their own; the capacity

to bear it appeared to them the privilege of the chosen! Their generation lived inarticulate and indispensable, without knowing the sweetness of affections or the refuge of a home—and died free from the dark menace of a narrow grave. They were the everlasting children of the mysterious sea.

Such were the characters of the early books—*Lord Jim, Typhoon, The Nigger of the "Narcissus," Youth;* and these books, in spite of the changes and fashions, are surely secure of their place among our classics. But they reach this height by means of qualities which the simple story of adventure, as Marryat told it, or Fenimore Cooper, has no claim to possess. For it is clear that to admire and celebrate such men and such deeds, romantically, whole-heartedly and with the fervour of a lover, one must be posesssed of the double vision; one must be at once inside and out. To praise their silence one must possess a voice. To appreciate their endurance one must be sensitive to fatigue. One must be able to live on equal terms with the Whalleys and the Singletons and yet hide from their suspicious eyes the very qualities which enable one to understand them. Conrad alone was able to live that double life, for Conrad was compound of two men; together with the sea captain dwelt that subtle, refined, and fastidious analyst whom he called Marlow. "A most discreet, understanding man," he said of Marlow.

Marlow was one of those born observers who are happiest in retirement. Marlow liked nothing better than to sit on deck, in some obscure creek of the Thames, smoking and recollecting; smoking and speculating; sending after his smoke beautiful rings of words until all the summer's night became a little clouded with tobacco smoke. Marlow, too, had a profound respect for the men with whom he had sailed; but he saw the humour of them. He nosed out and described in masterly fashion those livid creatures who prey successfully upon the clumsy veterans. He had a flair for human deformity; his humour was sardonic. Nor did Marlow live

entirely wreathed in the smoke of his own cigars. He
had a habit of opening his eyes suddenly and looking—
at a rubbish heap, at a port, at a shop counter—and then
complete in its burning ring of light that thing is flashed
bright upon the mysterious background. Introspective
and analytical, Marlow was aware of this peculiarity.
He said the power came to him suddenly. He might, for
instance, overhear a French officer murmur "Mon Dieu,
how the time passes!"

Nothing [he comments] could have been more commonplace
than this remark; but its utterance coincided for me with a
moment of vision. It's extraordinary how we go through life
with eyes half shut, with dull ears, with dormant thoughts.
. . . Nevertheless, there can be but few of us who had never
known one of these rare moments of awakening, when we see,
hear, understand, ever so much—everything—in a flash, before
we fall back again into our agreeable somnolence. I raised my
eyes when he spoke, and I saw him as though I had never seen
him before.

Picture after picture he painted thus upon that dark
background; ships first and foremost, ships at anchor,
ships flying before the storm, ships in harbour; he
painted sunsets and dawns; he painted the night; he
painted the sea in every aspect; he painted the gaudy
brilliancy of Eastern ports, and men and women, their
houses and their attitudes. He was an accurate and un-
flinching observer, schooled to that "absolute loyalty
towards his feelings and sensations," which, Conrad
wrote, "an author should keep hold of in his most exalted moments of creation." And very quietly and com-
passionately Marlow sometimes lets fall a few words of
epitaph which remind us, with all that beauty and brilliancy before our eyes, of the darkness of the background.
Thus a rough-and-ready distinction would make us
say that it is Marlow who comments, Conrad who creates. It would lead us, aware that we are on dangerous
ground, to account for that change which, Conrad tells

us, took place when he had finished the last story in the *Typhoon* volume—"a subtle change in the nature of the inspiration"—by some alteration in the relationship of the two old friends. ". . . it seemed somehow that there was nothing more in the world to write about." It was Conrad, let us suppose, Conrad the creator, who said that, looking back with sorrowful satisfaction upon the stories he had told; feeling as he well might that he could never better the storm in *The Nigger of the "Narcissus,"* or render more faithful tribute to the qualities of British seamen than he had done already in *Youth* and *Lord Jim.* It was then that Marlow, the commentator, reminded him how, in the course of nature, one must grow old, sit smoking on deck, and give up seafaring. But, he reminded him, those strenuous years had deposited their memories; and he even went so far perhaps as to hint that, though the last word might have been said about Captain Whalley and his relation to the universe, there remained on shore a number of men and women whose relationships, though of a more personal kind, might be worth looking into. If we further suppose that there was a volume of Henry James on board and that Marlow gave his friend the book to take to bed with him, we may seek support in the fact that it was in 1905 that Conrad wrote a very fine essay upon that master.

For some years, then, it was Marlow who was the dominant partner. *Nostromo, Chance, The Arrow of Gold* represent that stage of the alliance which some will continue to find the richest of all. The human heart is more intricate than the forest, they will say; it has its storms; it has its creatures of the night; and if as novelist you wish to test man in all his relationships, the proper antagonist is man; his ordeal is in society, not solitude. For them there will always be a peculiar fascination in the books where the light of those brilliant eyes falls not only upon the waste of waters but upon the heart in its perplexity. But it must be admitted that, if Marlow thus advised Conrad to shift his angle of vision, the advice was bold. For the vision of a novelist is both complex and specialised; complex, because behind his characters and apart from them must stand something stable to which he relates them; specialised because since he is a single person with one sensibility the aspects of life in which he can believe with conviction are strictly limited. So delicate a balance is easily disturbed. After the middle period Conrad never again was able to bring his figures into perfect relation with their background. He never believed in his later and more highly sophisticated characters as he had believed in his early seamen. When he had to indicate their relation to that other unseen world of novelists, the world of values and convictions, he was far less sure what those values were. Then, over and over again, a single phrase, "He steered with care," coming at the end of a storm, carried in it a whole morality. But in this more crowded and complicated world such terse phrases became less and less appropriate. Complex men and women of many interests and relations would not submit to so summary a judgement; or, if they did, much that was important in them escaped the verdict. And yet it was very necessary to Conrad's genius, with its luxuriant and romantic power, to have some law by which its creations could be tried. Essentially—such remained his creed—this world of civilised and self-conscious people is based upon "a few very simple ideas"; but where, in the world of thoughts and personal relations, are we to find them? There are no masts in drawing-rooms; the typhoon does not test the worth of politicians and business men. Seeking and not finding such supports, the world of Conrad's later period has about it an involuntary obscurity, an inconclusiveness, almost a disillusionment which baffles and fatigues. We lay hold in the dusk only of the old nobilities and sonorities: fidelity, compassion, honour, service —beautiful always, but now a little wearily reiterated, as if times had changed. Perhaps it was Marlow who was at fault. His habit of mind was a trifle sedentary. He had sat upon deck too long; splendid in soliloquy, he was less apt in the give and take of conversation; and those "moments of vision" flashing and fading, do not serve as well as steady lamplight to illumine the ripple of life and its long, gradual years. Above all, perhaps, he did not take into account how, if Conrad was to create, it was essential first that he should believe.

Therefore, though we shall make expeditions into the later books and bring back wonderful trophies, large tracts of them will remain by most of us untrodden. It is the earlier books—*Youth, Lord Jim, Typhoon, The Nigger of the "Narcissus"*—that we shall read in their entirety. For when the question is asked, what of Conrad will survive and where in the ranks of novelists we are to place him, these books, with their air of telling us something very old and perfectly true, which had lain hidden but is now revealed, will come to mind and make such questions and comparisons seem a little futile. Complete and still, very chaste and very beautiful, they rise in the memory as, on these hot summer nights, in their slow and stately way first one star comes out and then another.

*

How It Strikes a Contemporary

*

In the first place a contemporary can scarcely fail to be struck by the fact that two critics at the same table at the same moment will pronounce completely different opinions about the same book. Here, on the right, it is declared a masterpiece of English prose; on the left, simultaneously, a mere mass of wastepaper which, if the fire could survive it, should be thrown upon the flames. Yet both critics are in agreement about Milton and about Keats. They display an exquisite sensibility and have undoubtedly a genuine enthusiasm. It is only when they discuss the work of contemporary writers that they inevitably come to blows. The book in question, which is at once a lasting contribution to English literature and a mere farrago of pretentious mediocrity, was published about two months ago. That is the explanation; that is why they differ.

The explanation is a strange one. It is equally disconcerting to the reader who wishes to take his bearings in the chaos of contemporary literature and to the writer who had a natural desire to know whether his own work, produced with infinite pains and in almost utter darkness, is likely to burn for ever among the fixed luminaries of English letters or, on the contrary, to put out the fire. But if we identify ourselves with the reader and explore his dilemma first, our bewilderment is short-lived enough. The same thing has happened so often before.

We have heard the doctors disagreeing about the new and agreeing about the old twice a year on the average, in spring and autumn, ever since Robert Elsmere, or was it Stephen Phillips, somehow pervaded the atmosphere, and there was the same disagreement among grown-up people about them. It would be much more marvellous, and indeed much more upsetting, if, for a wonder, both gentlemen agreed, pronounced Blank's book an undoubted masterpiece, and thus faced us with the necessity of deciding whether we should back their judgement to the extent of ten and sixpence. Both are critics of reputation; the opinions tumbled out so spontaneously here will be starched and stiffened into columns of sober prose which will uphold the dignity of letters in England and America.

It must be some innate cynicism, then, some ungenerous distrust of contemporary genius, which determines us automatically as the talk goes on that, were they to agree—which they show no signs of doing—half a guinea is altogether too large a sum to squander upon contemporary enthusiasms, and the case will be met quite adequately by a card to the library. Still the question remains, and let us put it boldly to the critics themselves. Is there no guidance nowadays for a reader who yields to none in reverence for the dead, but is tormented by the suspicion that reverence for the dead is vitally connected with understanding of the living? After a rapid survey both critics are agreed that there is unfortunately no such person. For what is their own judgement worth where new books are concerned? Certainly not ten and sixpence. And from the stores of their experience they proceed to bring forth terrible examples of past blunders; crimes of criticism which, if they had been committed against the dead and not against the living, would have lost them their jobs and imperilled their reputations. The only advice they can offer is to respect one's own instincts, to follow them fearlessly and, rather than submit them to the control of any critic or reviewer alive, to check them by reading and reading again the masterpieces of the past.

Thanking them humbly, we cannot help reflecting that it was not always so. Once upon a time, we must believe, there was a rule, a discipline, which controlled the great republic of readers in a way which is now unknown. That is not to say that the great critic—the Dryden, the Johnson, the Coleridge, the Arnold—was an impeccable judge of contemporary work, whose verdicts stamped the book indelibly and saved the reader the trouble of reckoning the value for himself. The mistakes of these great men about their own contemporaries are too notorious to be worth recording. But the mere fact of their existence had a centralising influence. That alone, it is not fantastic to suppose, would have controlled the disagreements of the dinner-table and given to random chatter about some book just out an authority now entirely to seek. The diverse schools would have debated as hotly as ever, but at the back of every reader's mind would have been the consciousness that there was at least one man who kept the main principles of literature closely in view; who, if you had taken to him some eccentricity of the moment, would have brought it into touch with permanence and tethered it by his own authority in the contrary blasts of praise and blame.* But when it comes to the making of a critic, nature must be generous and society ripe. The scattered dinner-tables of the modern world, the chase and eddy of the various

---

* How violent these are two quotations will show. "It [*Told by an Idiot*] should be read as the *Tempest* should be read, and as *Gulliver's Travels* should be read, for if Miss Macaulay's poetic gift happens to be less sublime than those of the author of the *Tempest*, and if her irony happens to be less tremendous than that of the author of *Gulliver's Travels*, her justice and wisdom are no less noble than theirs."—*The Daily News*.

The next day we read: "For the rest one can only say that if Mr. Eliot had been pleased to write in demotic English *The Waste Land* might not have been, as it just is to all but anthropologists, and literati, so much waste-paper."—*The Manchester Guardian*.

currents which compose the society of our time, could only be dominated by a giant of fabulous dimensions. And where is even the very tall man whom we have the right to expect? Reviewers we have but no critic; a million competent and incorruptible policemen but no judge. Men of taste and learning and ability are for ever lecturing the young and celebrating the dead. But the too frequent result of their able and industrious pens is a desiccation of the living tissues of literature into a network of little bones. Nowhere shall we find the downright vigour of a Dryden, or Keats with his fine and natural bearing, his profound insight and sanity, or Flaubert and the tremendous power of his fanaticism, or Coleridge, above all, brewing in his head the whole of poetry and letting issue now and then one of those profound general statements which are caught up by the mind when hot with the friction of reading as if they were of the soul of the book itself.

And to all this, too, the critics generously agree. A great critic, they say, is the rarest of beings. But should one miraculously appear, how should we maintain him, on what should we feed him? Great critics, if they are not themselves great poets, are bred from the profusion of the age. There is some great man to be vindicated, some school to be founded or destroyed. But our age is meagre to the verge of destitution. There is no name which dominates the rest. There is no master in whose workshop the young are proud to serve apprenticeship. Mr. Hardy has long since withdrawn from the arena, and there is something exotic about the genius of Mr. Conrad which makes him not so much an influence as an idol, honoured and admired, but aloof and apart. As for the rest, though they are many and vigorous and in the full flood of creative activity, there is none whose influence can seriously affect his contemporaries, or penetrate beyond our day to that not very distant future which it pleases us to call immortality. If we make a century our test, and ask how much of the work produced in these days in England will be in existence then, we shall have to answer not merely that we cannot agree upon the same book, but that we are more than doubtful whether such a book there is. It is an age of fragments. A few stanzas, a few pages, a chapter here and there, the beginning of this novel, the end of that, are equal to the best of any age or author. But can we go to posterity with a sheaf of loose pages, or ask the readers of those days, with the whole of literature before them, to sift our enormous rubbish heaps for our tiny pearls? Such are the questions which the critics might lawfully put to their companions at table, the novelists and poets.

At first the weight of pessimism seems sufficient to bear down all opposition. Yes, it is a lean age, we repeat, with much to justify its poverty; but, frankly, if we pit one century against another the comparison seems overwhelmingly against us. *Waverley, The Excursion, Kubla Khan, Don Juan, Hazlitt's Essays, Pride and Prejudice, Hyperion,* and *Prometheus Unbound* were all published between 1800 and 1821. Our century has not lacked industry; but if we ask for masterpieces it appears on the face of it that the pessimists are right. It seems as if an age of genius must be succeeded by an age of endeavour; riot and extravagance by cleanliness and hard work. All honour, of course, to those who have sacrificed their immortality to set the house in order. But if we ask for masterpieces, where are we to look? A little poetry, we may feel sure, will survive; a few poems by Mr. Yeats, by Mr. Davies, by Mr. De la Mare. Mr. Lawrence, of course, has moments of greatness, but hours of something very different. Mr. Beerbohm, in his way, is perfect, but it is not a big way. Passages in *Far Away and Long Ago* will undoubtedly go to posterity entire. *Ulysses* was a memorable catastrophe—immense in daring, terrific in disaster. And so, picking and choosing, we select now this, now that, hold it up for display, hear it defended or derided, and finally have to meet the objection that even so we are only agreeing with the critics that it is an age incapable of sustained effort, littered with fragments, and not seriously to be compared with the age that went before.

But it is just when opinions universally prevail and we have added lip service to their authority that we become sometimes most keenly conscious that we do not believe a word that we are saying. It is a barren and exhausted age, we repeat; we must look back with envy to the past. Meanwhile it is one of the first fine days of spring. Life is not altogether lacking in colour. The telephone, which interrupts the most serious conversations and cuts short the most weighty observations, has a romance of its own. And the random talk of people who have no chance of immortality and thus can speak their minds out has a setting, often, of lights, streets, houses, human beings, beautiful or grotesque, which will weave itself into the moment for ever. But this is life; the talk is about literature. We must try to disentangle the two, and justify the rash revolt of optimism against the superior plausibility, the finer distinction, of pessimism.

Our optimism, then, is largely instinctive. It springs from the fine day and the wine and the talk; it springs from the fact that when life throws up such treasures daily, daily suggests more than the most voluble can express, much though we admire the dead, we prefer life as it is. There is something about the present which we would not exchange, though we were offered a choice of all past ages to live in. And modern literature, with all its imperfections, has the same hold on us and the same fascination. It is like a relation whom we snub and scarify daily, but, after all, cannot do without. It has the same endearing quality of being that which we are, that which we have made, that in which we live, instead of being something, however august, alien to ourselves and beheld from the outside. Nor has any generation more need than ours to cherish its contemporaries. We are sharply cut off from our predecessors. A shift in the

scale—the war, the sudden slip of masses held in position for ages—has shaken the fabric from top to bottom,
alienated us from the past and made us perhaps too vividly conscious of the present. Every day we find ourselves doing, saying, or thinking things that would have
been impossible to our fathers. And we feel the differences which have not been noted far more keenly than
the resemblances which have been very perfectly expressed. New books lure us to read them partly in the
hope that they will reflect this re-arrangement of our
attitude—these scenes, thoughts, and apparently fortui-
tous groupings of incongruous things which impinge
upon us with so keen a sense of novelty—and, as literature does, give it back into our keeping, whole and
comprehended. Here indeed there is every reason for
optimism. No age can have been more rich than ours
in writers determined to give expression to the differences which separate them from the past and not to the
resemblances which connect them with it. It would be
invidious to mention names, but the most casual reader
dipping into poetry, into fiction, into biography can
hardly fail to be impressed by the courage, the sincerity,
in a word, by the widespread originality of our time.
But our exhilaration is strangely curtailed. Book after
book leaves us with the same sense of promise un-
achieved, of intellectual poverty, of brilliance which has
been snatched from life but not transmuted into literature. Much of what is best in contemporary work has
the appearance of being noted under pressure, taken
down in a bleak shorthand which preserves with astonishing brilliance the movements and expressions of the
figures as they pass across the screen. But the flash is
soon over, and there remains with us a profound dissat-
isfaction. The irritation is as acute as the pleasure was
intense.

After all, then, we are back at the beginning, vacil-
lating from extreme to extreme, at one moment enthusiastic, at the next pessimistic, unable to come to any

conclusion about our contemporaries. We have asked the critics to help us, but they have deprecated the task. Now, then, is the time to accept their advice and correct these extremes by consulting the masterpieces of the past. We feel ourselves indeed driven to them, impelled not by calm judgement but by some imperious need to anchor our instability upon their security. But, honestly, the shock of the comparison between past and present is at first disconcerting. Undoubtedly there is a dullness in great books. There is an unabashed tranquillity in page after page of Wordsworth and Scott and Miss Austen which is sedative to the verge of somnolence. Opportunities occur and they neglect them. Shades and subtleties accumulate and they ignore them. They seem deliberately to refuse to gratify those senses which are stimulated so briskly by the moderns; the senses of sight, of sound, of touch—above all, the sense of the human being, his depth and the variety of his perceptions, his complexity, his confusion, his self, in short. There is little of all this in the works of Wordsworth and Scott and Jane Austen. From what, then, arises that sense of security which gradually, delightfully, and completely overcomes us? It is the power of their belief—their conviction, that imposes itself upon us. In Wordsworth, the philosophic poet, this is obvious enough. But it is equally true of the careless Scott, who scribbled masterpieces to build castles before breakfast, and of the modest maiden lady who wrote furtively and quietly simply to give pleasure. In both there is the same natural conviction that life is of a certain quality. They have their judgement of conduct. They know the relations of human beings towards each other and towards the universe. Neither of them probably has a word to say about the matter outright, but everything depends on it. Only believe, we find ourselves saying, and all the rest will come of itself. Only believe, to take a very simple instance which the recent publication of *The Watsons* brings to mind, that a nice girl will instinctively try to soothe the feelings of a boy who has been snubbed at a dance, and then, if you believe it implicitly and unquestioningly, you will not only make people a hundred years later feel the same thing, but you will make them feel it as literature. For certainty of that kind is the condition which makes it possible to write. To believe that your impressions hold good for others is to be released from the cramp and confinement of personality. It is to be free, as Scott was free, to explore with a vigour which still holds us spell-bound the whole world of adventure and romance. It is also the first step in that mysterious process in which Jane Austen was so great an adept. The little grain of experience once selected, believed in, and set outside herself, could be put precisely in its place, and she was then free to make of it, by a process which never yields its secrets to the analyst, into that complete statement which is literature.

So then our contemporaries afflict us because they have ceased to believe. The most sincere of them will only tell us what it is that happens to himself. They cannot make a world, because they are not free of other human beings. They cannot tell stories because they do not believe the stories are true. They cannot generalise. They depend on their sense and emotions, whose testimony is trustworthy, rather than on their intellects whose message is obscure. And they have perforce to deny themselves the use of some of the most powerful and some of the most exquisite of the weapons of their craft. With the whole wealth of the English language at the back of them, they timidly pass about from hand to hand and book to book only the meanest copper coins. Set down at a fresh angle of the eternal prospect they can only whip out their notebooks and record with agonised intensity the flying gleams, which light on what? and the transitory splendours, which may, perhaps, compose nothing whatever. But here the critics interpose, and with some show of justice.

If this description holds good, they say, and is not, as

it may well be, entirely dependent upon our position at the table and certain purely personal relationships to mustard pots and flower vases, then the risks of judging contemporary work are greater than ever before. There is every excuse for them if they are wide of the mark; and no doubt it would be better to retreat, as Matthew Arnold advised, from the burning ground of the present to the safe tranquillity of the past. "We enter on burning ground," wrote Matthew Arnold, "as we approach the poetry of times so near to us, poetry like that of Byron, Shelley, and Wordsworth, of which the estimates are so often not only personal, but personal with passion," and this, they remind us, was written in the year 1880. Beware, they say, of putting under the microscope one inch of a ribbon which runs many miles; things sort themselves out if you wait; moderation and a study of the classics are to be recommended. Moreover, life is short; the Byron centenary is at hand; and the burning question of the moment is, did he, or did he not, marry his sister? To sum up, then—if indeed any conclusion is possible when everybody is talking at once and it is time to be going—it seems that it would be wise for the writers of the present to renounce for themselves the hope of creating masterpieces. Their poems, plays, biographies, novels are not books but notebooks, and Time, like a good schoolmaster, will take them in his hands, point to their blots and erasions, and tear them across; but he will not throw them into the waste-paper basket. He will keep them because other students will find them very useful. It is from notebooks of the present that the masterpieces of the future are made. Literature, as the critics were saying just now, has lasted long, has undergone many changes, and it is only a short sight and a parochial mind that will exaggerate the importance of these squalls, however they may agitate the little boats now tossing out at sea. The storm and the drenching are on the surface; and continuity and calm are in the depths.

As for the critics whose task it is to pass judgement upon the books of the moment, whose work, let us admit, is difficult, dangerous, and often distasteful, let us ask them to be generous of encouragement, but sparing of those wreaths and coronets which are so apt to get awry, and fade, and make the wearers, in six months time, look a little ridiculous. Let them take a wider, a less personal view of modern literature, and look indeed upon the writers as if they were engaged upon some vast building, which being built by common effort, the separate workmen may well remain anonymous. Let them slam the door upon the cosy company where sugar is cheap and butter plentiful, give over, for a time at least, the discussion of that fascinating topic—whether Byron married his sister—and, withdrawing, perhaps, a hands-breadth from the table where we sit chattering, say something interesting about literature. Let us button-hole them as they leave, and recall to their memory that gaunt aristocrat, Lady Hester Stanhope, who kept a milk-white horse in her stable in readiness for the Messiah and was for ever scanning the mountain tops, impatiently but with confidence, for signs of his approach, and ask them to follow her example; scan the horizon; see the past in relation to the future; and so prepare the way for masterpieces to come.